Mobile Wife

Living the Dream in the House in the Postcard

by

Shena Matchett

**Grosvenor House
Publishing Limited**

This book is published by
Grosvenor House Publishing Ltd
28-30 High Street, Guildford, Surrey, GU1 3HY.
www.grosvenorhousepublishing.co.uk

A CIP record for this book
is available from the British Library

ISBN 978-1-907211-41-6

For Alex

Best wishes to Helga:
'Heureux qui, comme Ulysse, a
fait un bon voyage'

Shena Matchett

' . . . would I were
In Grantchester, in Grantchester!
. . .oh! yet
Stands the Church clock at ten to three?
And is there honey still for tea?'

The Old Vicarage, Grantchester
Rupert Brooke

Contents:

Preface: Mobile Wife

For most of my adult life, I've been a 'mobile' wife, a trailing wife some would call it, an expat moving from country to country as my husband's job in the oil industry dictated. Don't get me wrong; I've chosen to accompany him to far-flung parts and enjoyed almost every minute of it. Expatriate wives can feel either madly frustrated or joyously liberated by living overseas in unfamiliar places.

After an initial honeymoon period of excitement and anticipation, you can begin to experience negative feelings of uneasiness, homesickness, and perhaps acute unhappiness. You have lost your identity and are defined by what your husband does, his position within the company. You have lost the familiar signs and cues. The endless differences in the unfamiliar, alien culture make you feel like an outsider. Culture shock is legendary when you step into another world and face its challenges.

On the other hand, you can see it as a fascinating, enriching step into another world full of great moments and opportunities to learn about yourself, the country you are visiting and your fellow expats. On your voyage of discovery, you acquire a broader outlook on life, develop inner resources and make lifelong friends.

I've experienced all of these feelings, but on the whole being a mobile wife has been a positive experience. After more than twenty years of living as expats in Iran, Indonesia, Australia, Singapore, the US and Europe, we bought a second home, *une maison secondaire,* in a small village in Provence where we spend several months each year. There, we meet up with the lifelong friends that we have made on our travels and reminisce about happy times.

La Ruine, rue Ventabren sous l'église: The Ruin, Ventabren Street under the church

We didn't set out to buy a house in Provence. Especially not in Gigondas – we'd never even heard of the village. But, as darkness fell, we found ourselves many miles from our intended destination in Languedoc. "Let's head for the nearest village with a mention in our ancient guidebook and call it a day," I suggested. That decision was to change our lives

Fortunately, at that moment we were in Haut-Vaucluse, at the foot of the spectacular Dentelles de Montmirail Mountains, and about twenty five minutes from Avignon. We spotted a signpost pointing clearly up the mountain road to a hotel and restaurant, Les Florets. And that's how we ended up visiting Gigondas, falling in love with the village, and wanting to stay for ever.

At first, we began looking at houses as a bit of fun, something to do on the occasional wet day. It's not always sunny in sunny Provence, although it does boast around three hundred and twenty five days of sunshine. We were not in the market for the large farmhouses, *mas,* featured every month in the glossy, addictive magazines *Maisons et Decors* and *Côte Sud.* Lovely to look at, to admire the tastefully created interiors furnished with local antiques and bric-a-brac. However, this was an idyll we couldn't afford. In fact, could we afford anything? Prices were rising. True, it wasn't Peter Mayle country, but many of his readers, inspired by his depiction of wonderful food and wine, of eternally blue skies and balmy breezes, of fields stippled with sunflowers and lavender, had begun to look further afield. The Lubéron villages might be full up with second home owners, but less fashionable Vaucluse was beckoning.

Why not take a look at a few houses, just out of interest? We would gain a greater insight into how the French really lived. What started as a whimsy soon became a serious mission. We had fallen in love with voluptuous Provence and wanted a part of it. We began to realise that a small, traditional village house might just be within our means.

Over the next two years, we made many trips to Provence. Friends joked, "Aren't you tired of spending every holiday in the same place?" No, we weren't. We always felt drawn to the area and increasingly we felt drawn to scan avidly the windows of likely looking *agences immobilières.* Anxious for business, more than once the estate agent would spot us hesitating outside and entice us inside with, "It doesn't cost anything to look!", or words to that effect. My French is rusty, despite six years of learning the language at school and one year of study at university. I know quite a bit about French history and culture; I can read a tabloid French newspaper with relative ease; and understand most of what is said to me (although I struggle with the soupy southern twang where any word with a nasal *in* or *en* becomes something like *aing*, and *vin* becomes *vaing*). However, I lack confidence actually to speak the language. Unlike today where schools emphasise the spoken word, we spent most of our schooldays labouring over verb tenses and agreement. I know how to use the subjunctive (not very useful this as I don't mix in social circles where it is used much), but talking to estate agents and architects about the finer points of building was outside my experience.

Once inside the estate agent's, my husband, lost for words but not lacking in confidence, managed by mime, Pidgin English and the odd French word dragged up 'om long-gone schooldays to communicate what we h d decided we wanted: a simple, traditional house in *un vii 'ge perché,* a perched village rising steeply from a plai or clinging perilously to a cliff or rocky outcrop. Prove 'e is full to bursting with these perched villages, each on more stunning than the last

We got 'he particulars of and viewed amazing houses, amazing in the sense of unbelievable. "What hovels people live in!" frequently crossed our minds. Yet, these were traditional stone dwellings and people in Britain had lived in a similar fashion, in the same buildings as their animals, as recently as the nineteenth century

Slowly, with each visit to Provence, we moved further and further afield. We rented *gîtes* or stayed in small hotels in unexplored areas. At October half-term, we stayed in an ancient almshouse in Bonnieux, made famous by Peter Mayle's descriptions of the yearly goat race event and the quirky inhabitants. We were very taken by the village, but alas its fame and popularity had put even the smallest property out of our price range.

We always gravitated back to that first village, Gigondas, where fate had stopped us in our travels. Gigondas is a famous wine-producing village, perched on a rocky cliff, rising up from a patchwork of vineyards, surrounded by partially restored medieval defensive walls, and as the tourist information brochure states: 'dominated by its church and the ramparts of the castle of the Princes of Orange, accessible by the picturesque lanes'. Apart from looking stunning, however, it's difficult to understand why the village attracts so many visitors. True, the strong, full-bodied wines are considered by many to be one of the best Côtes-du-Rhône in France. Around the main square there are at least half a dozen *caves* within weaving distance of each other, which stock wine from around forty different *domaines*. The wine is rather famous, widely regarded as second in quality to Châteauneuf-du-Pape. Tourists flock to sample *une dégustation*, a tasting, of the full-bodied, spicy red wine, with its fruity bouquet of plums and kirsch (or, depending on your taste buds, blackberries and cherries), debating loudly the merits of different *vignerons* (wine producers), vintages and *cuvées*.

After completing the tasting and wine purchases, what to do next? The village square is pretty with its bunting, fountain and protective plane trees, although it is a little lacking in shops: an *épicerie*, literally a grocer's but more like an American 711 plus bakery, a café, a *salon de thé*, a restaurant, a one-computer Internet café, the modern post office and the mayor's office, *la mairie*. All that can be seen in about ten minutes, then visitors discover the signs to the oldest part of the village and the sixteenth century church of Saint Catherine. They huff and puff their way to the top of the steep hill. The pretty, winding, uneven lanes are very picturesque, but tricky to navigate in holiday high-heeled mules and flip-flops. They're relieved to find that the church really is worth the climb, with its gilded statues of Saint Cosme and Saint Damien, patrons of the parish, its rather primitive fresco and wooden statue of Notre-Dame de Pallières. But what's so amazing is the view from the church. There's an extraordinary panorama over the entire Rhône Valley; the extensive, terraced Gigondas vineyards; the partly-restored, medieval, honey-stoned village walls; the undulating, misty blue Cévennes hills and the Roman chapel of Saint Cosme, built on the site of a pagan temple. The Romans used to stop here on their way from Orange to Vaison-la-Romaine. They liked it so much that they named it *Jocunditas,* meaning 'joy', later to become Gigondas. According to Pliny, part of their delight was the wine. That wasn't what attracted us to the village, but we did come to love the intense, spicy, earthy wine.

We'd looked round the village many times, searching in vain for something for sale – anything. Obviously, many people viewed it as a perfect village. Then, one evening, cooler than most, we took a different route and climbed up rue Ventabren to the church. Nestling just beneath the church, barely discernible through the tangled undergrowth, we spotted the sign: *A Vendre*. At last! Only it wasn't a very attractive proposition. The house, more accurately the ruin, was reminiscent of the impenetrable vegetation hiding Sleeping Beauty. It didn't look as if anyone had occupied the building for a long, long time.

I can't say it was love at first sight, *un coup de foudre*, but it was in the right village, a village with which we'd fallen in love. Surely it had possibilities? We could barely discern the phone number of the agent handling the sale, but we did, and soon we were practising our rudimentary French on estate agent Monsieur C. He was aghast. But, of course, no one in his right mind would buy such a house! Surely we were interested in the two nearby *gîtes* also for sale, although no *A Vendre* sign hinted at this? We couldn't convince him, but agreed to meet the following evening to view the *gîtes*. Come the appointed time, he met us in the village outside his idea of a desirable property and proudly showed us round. See how modern the kitchens are? How the old fireplaces have been torn out to make way for progress? Not really what we were looking for. What we admired were traditional old buildings and interiors. We wanted something with a history, with character, a challenge. And the ruin was certainly that. *Monsieur* shook his head and exclaimed that you would have to be mad to take on such a property.

My Sleeping Beauty analogy wasn't so far-fetched. To get into the property, we literally had to beat our way through shoulder-high brambles. Not many viewers then! The studded wooden door creaked open to reveal – very little. Most of the building had collapsed in on itself. We could glimpse the sky through the roof; huge oak beams that had once held the ceiling in place now lay at odd angles among the piles of debris. Only the original kitchen was recognisable by its fireplace, a stone sink and a mysterious cupboard with two holes set into the stone base. We later learned that this was a cupboard used for cheese-making. Perhaps the whey drained through the muslin-lined holes into buckets below? Eventually Monsieur C was convinced of our seriousness: "It has character, *non*?" he enquired, now resigned to the quirky tastes of his foreign clients.

"Yes, it's perfect – we'll take it!"

What rash words. Gingerly we proceeded up the crumbly, winding staircase leading from the kitchen to a bedroom. This was almost habitable – a ceiling and a floor. But it was the view from the window which reassured me that we'd made the right decision. We could see very clearly as there was no glass left in the rotting window frames and the decaying shutters swung widely at every gust of wind. From this window, there was a magnificent, clear view for about fifty miles of the Rhône Valley, across red-tiled rooftops, green vineyards and toy-town villages, to the Cévennes hills, hazy in the distance.

Right there and then I decided that I wanted my bed positioned in the premier viewing spot. I imagined myself lying in bed looking out on this view every morning, watching the sunrises and sunsets, the changing seasons. And so it came to pass, but not as quickly as we'd hoped. We did indeed have to decide the position of the bed which would determine the position of the electrical sockets for the bedside lamps, but before this there was so much planning to do. We had to imagine the bigger picture. The process to buy the crumbling ruin commenced. Reconciled to our stubbornness, the estate agent gave us all sorts of useful advice, recommending an architect/ builder whom he had personally used to oversee some renovation work. Later, we would come to regret this kindly meant recommendation. But all this was in the distant future. "One word of advice, *madame*," he implored earnestly. "Do not pay the builder large sums of money. Pay him in stages, or he will down tools and go on the 'java'!" All this delivered with gyrating actions to describe the dancing and partying that would accompany such a folly. Was it the same in Britain, in America? We assured him that it was.

It was certainly a challenge to imagine how the house had once looked, how it could be made to look. An old postcard for sale in the Tourist Office shows the church and below it our house looking fairly whole, still with roofs intact. Much renovation was needed before it looked like that again. On a second visit, we discovered that by means of a rickety ladder we could climb into the hayloft. It had certainly had some connection with animals and farming – the wooden feeding boxes were still attached to the wall and the dirt floor was well-trodden. Later, much later, this was to become our forty foot long, airy, beamed *salon*, but it was difficult to imagine the possibilities then.

The house is tucked in right beneath the church, hence our picturesque address: *rue Ventabren sous l'église*. Like the clock in Rupert Brooke's poem *The Old Vicarage, Grantchester*, when we bought the house, the hands of the church clock never moved. They did not 'stand . . . at ten to three', however, they were stuck permanently on five to four, quite a good time to take tea. Over the years, the clock has been mended many times, but when a storm brews and the *mistral* is particularly strong, it gives up the fight and we miss its hourly repeater chime.

The hill slopes sharply and our house clings to the hill, meandering down it, not a straight wall in sight, with the hayloft nearest to the church and the kitchen at the bottom, on the gable end. It is probably one of the oldest houses in the village, as traditionally building started at the top of the hill. It's constructed inside the ramparts, vestiges of which still stand today. Had our house some connection with the church? It seems likely. On one of the fireplaces still intact we found a raised motif of three bishops' hats. Not grand enough for a bishop's residence, but perhaps a parish priest? The latest inhabitant, we learned, had died ten years previously. She had been the wife of the mayor, and it seemed likely that she had retreated gradually down the hill as rooms became uninhabitable. *Madame* had lived in the kitchen and bedroom above, which would have been warmed by the kitchen fire. Years later, we were sitting round the dining table at one end of the salon with friends Hugo and Francine, Dutch permanent residents of the village. We depend on them to keep us up-to-date with all the news and gossip from the village. Suddenly Francine said excitedly, "This was the exact spot where old Madame C kept her goats!" This was a revelation and tied in with the cheese-making cupboard in the original kitchen. Now, every time I eat at that table, especially if I'm tucking in to *fromage de chèvre*, I think of the goats.

Armed with the name of the architect/ builder highly recommended by Monsieur C: "He converted my new *immobilière* office and added a floor of living quarters. *Incroyable*! *Superbe*!" we arranged a meeting to discuss plans and dreams. A warning bell should have sounded when the meeting failed to take place – a small misunderstanding of time, of place – but at this stage we were still very tolerant and eager to believe that our limited French had led to the misunderstanding.

Two days later, we made another arrangement to meet up with Monsieur W, accompanied by his English speaking friend, Monsieur V. Monsieur W spoke no English! The French, and all Europeans, put us to shame with the ease in which they switch from one language to another. Mr W was of Polish extraction but seemed to have spent all his life in rural Provence, so why no English? Monsieur V arrived in pressed chinos, an immaculate beige linen jacket and tasselled, highly polished Italian loafers, worn fashionably with no socks. He stepped gingerly over rotten beams and pools of mud, wrinkling his elegant nose. But Mr W was more encouraging: "*Pas de problème. Ce sera un travail difficile, mais pas impossible!*" A difficult job, but not an impossible one.

Very encouraging words. We adjourned to the café in the village and over *cafés crèmes* and *croissants* jotted down rough plans for our dream house. Not easy to envisage what use could be made of all that space. So much just wasn't there. The kitchen, the most habitable room, was rather dark, low down on the hill, overlooking neighbours' properties. In the middle was what had probably been the original *salon*, but by today's standards it was rather small for a family sitting room. The hayloft, on the top storey, was very basic, yet through the one little window in the front wall that marvellous panoramic view stretched, the same view that I had admired from the bedroom.

Mr W had a stroke of genius: "Why don't we move the kitchen to the original *salon*?" It was certainly light and airy. I'd told him that I loved to cook, had always dreamed of owning a kitchen big enough for a long, wooden, farmhouse table, where people could sit and chat as I cooked. The room was small as a family sitting room, but ideal as a kitchen. It would be the hub of the house, with French doors opening on to a large terrace where we could eat in the warmer months.

At this point, we needed to use a lot of imagination. The 'terrace' was still covered in a tangle of brambles and an old woodshed lurched drunkenly where the outdoor dining table would finally come to rest. But it seemed possible. Where would the *salon* then go? The hayloft, of course. All it needed were a few re-sited stair-cases, new floors, roof, beams, windows – everything was possible.

We were very excited by the whole project and the plans looked impressive. Down to the finer details – I wanted small-paned windows, like those I'd drooled over in the glossy magazine *Maisons Sud*.

"*Mais, non, ce n'est pas possible! Ces fenêtres sont Parisiennes!*" protested Mr W. Horrors! I'd contemplated putting in Parisian windows!

I was easily persuaded. The planning department approved of our proposed traditional Provençal windows, but it was not so easily persuaded to accept our plans for 'fancy doors'. For years I'd perused the fashionable house magazines and had been particularly taken by Terence Conran's conversion of a large farm-house in Provence. Of course, our dwelling was a simple village house, once shared by animals and humans, but I did so admire his curved French doors. Eventually, the powers that be decided that as Gigondas was a conservation village, our curved doors were an aberration. They would allow us one set of curved doors, opening from the new kitchen on to the terrace, but the proposed doors in the *salon* had to be traditionally rectangular. Not very logical, but we were grateful for their decision. However, after the *salon* doors were in place we had another problem. We received an official letter from a neighbour's legal representative telling us that we must remove the doors as they overlooked the neighbour's land. Fortunately, in our first flush of enthusiasm we had taken numerous photos from every angle of the ruin pre-renovation, and we were able to provide evidence that a door had always existed in that spot. A few further half-hearted protests, then we heard no more.

But, I'm jumping ahead. It took a full year actually to buy the house. Under French property law, when some-one dies the house belongs to all members of the family. Our house belonged to ten different people, one of whom was in some kind of institution and incapable of making such a decision. A judge had to do that for her. Time after time a date was set for the hearing, but at the last minute more pressing business would surface and our plea to buy the ruin was shelved until the following month. We were patient. Finally, the sale was agreed and Mr W came up with a schedule of works.

"*La maison sera terminée pendant neuf mois.*"

Only nine months to completion! We began to imagine al fresco croissants, *apéritifs* on the terrace to admire the sunset and walks in the neighbouring *Dentelles* Mountains. Worryingly, Mr W had a heated exchange with his doubting friend: " . . . *tu es sûr*, Didier?"

We lost the rest – just as well really. This was to be the pattern all the way through our relationship with Mr W and Mr V. It reminded me of Don Quixote and Sancho Panza. Mr W was a fantasist, always tilting at windmills. He assured us that things were happening according to plan, that staircases were installed, the house about to be finished. In vain, we waited for the promised computer images which would confirm the progress made, but they came rarely.

During the next few months, we visited the site regularly. If we gave advance warning, there was a hive of activity, with builders scurrying up and down ladders, extremely noisy cement mixers churning. If we arrived unexpectedly, there was no activity – not even a roof on any part of the building now. We began to despair. Letter followed letter – all in French; thanks to the wonders of a computer translation program. We arranged meeting after meeting. On every occasion, Mr W would assure us earnestly that the work was on schedule; it would be finished in weeks. Mr V always adopted a worried expression at this pronouncement: "Are you sure, Didier? Is it within the realms of possibility?" Or words to that effect.

Three years later, we were assured that the house was finished – finally. By this time, we knew the area well. We'd stayed in almost every small hotel, eaten in almost every local restaurant; and we'd even met some of our neighbours. The fax was clear: we could arrange for our furniture to be delivered as the house was now complete. We were so excited.

For many years, we'd lived a nomadic existence, moving from country to country as my husband's job assignments dictated. On our travels we'd accumulated various pieces of excess furniture and lots of knick-knacks, mementos from our stays in Iran, Indonesia, Singapore, Australia, New Zealand and the US. At last we'd found a home for them! We arranged for a Trans-International removal company to pack up our worldly goods and we set out for Provence in the wake of the van.

I'd fallen in love with the hand-painted Provençal furniture, so we'd ordered some for our bedroom. It was to take three months for completion – you can't rush true craftsmen. I could hardly wait to lie in the Louis XVI style bed, drooling over the view. That furniture was also scheduled to arrive on the same day as our removal van from England.

As we stepped gingerly over the mud where the paving for the terrace should have been, we were able to enter straight into the kitchen – because there were no French doors, Conran-like or otherwise. There was no floor. Worse, there were no bathrooms. Sitting in the middle of the *salon* where someone was laying a floor were three lurching WC's and a bidet. The three shower rooms each had a shower but no WC's or washbasins and no tiling. How could this, by the wildest stroke of imagination, be termed 'finished' and ready for occupation?

Mr W definitely had told us that the house was finished. There had been no misunderstanding. Just then, my mobile rang – the removal men from England, asking for last minute directions. "Where are you?"

"Just entering the village."

What a mess! Our precious furniture with all its memories was carted with some difficulty from the van, down the hill to the house. The village has no vehicular access. The steep, twisting lanes are very picturesque and keep the inhabitants fit, but moving things in and out can be difficult. Even ferrying shopping can become a bit of a route exercise.

No point in unpacking anything. Everything, still in boxes, was placed in the one habitable room. My lovely cream American sofa, purchased while on assignment in Houston, was dumped in the one tiled patch of *salon* floor and draped in a sheet. Quickly, we phoned the workshop of the bed-maker and made another tentative date for delivery. So, no lying in my bed that night watching the stars and the marvellous view, not yet, anyway.

Bitterly disappointed, we exchanged heated words with Mr W and promised we'd be back in two weeks to view progress, and we wanted to see lots of it. We took off for Nice, still warm in October and as yet unvisited by us, and consoled ourselves with people-watching on the *Promenade des Anglais* and forays through the flea markets and fashionable shops. I longed to buy armfuls of the colourful blooms from the Saturday flower market, but the pathos was that I had no home for them.

Five months later, my husband returned to Gigondas, having received further assurances from Mr W that the house was now, indeed, finished. It was certainly habitable, although never completely finished by the builders. "It was a difficult job. The builders would only work two days at a time. Access impossible . . ." All the same excuses were trotted out. My husband decided to withhold the last payment until the *réception*, or snag-list, had been completed. This *réception* is a requirement under French law. Meanwhile, he began to finish things off himself. Recently he had taken early retirement and he enjoyed completing jobs: painting the interior walls – not a straight line in sight – and supervising the more skilled job of painting the shutters Provençal blue. Three years before, I had chosen this vibrant colour from a shade card, little envisaging how long it would be before the painting commenced. He settled into a routine: working on the house, dealing with the paperwork and socialising with the neighbours. At the top of this *village perché*, most of the houses are owned by expats: Danish,

Dutch, Belgian, German, Swiss and one Brit. Why? Our theory is that these houses are the oldest in the village and were gradually left to fall into ruin. Along came the expats who saw the possibilities in owning and restoring a piece of a Provençal village. It seems that the French prefer to live in new, lurid, pink cement villas, on the edges of villages, with no dampness, crumbling walls, constant repairs. When we first met our nearest French neighbour, Jean-Baptiste, a *vigneron*, he confided, "I knew that a foreigner must have bought the property. No-one else would have been mad enough to take it on!"

Many of the surrounding villages had fallen into disrepair and were only restored after the Second World War. In the post-war years, many of the younger generation deserted the old ways, lured away from the traditional lifestyle by the bright lights, and work, in the big cities. And I can understand this. I too grew up in a small, stultifying village, in Scotland, and longed for excitement.

Gigondas seems idyllic to us: six hundred and fifty inhabitants, around six hundred and thirty five of whom are involved in the wine business. The big draw for visitors is the renowned, full-bodied, earthy reds and the crisp, perfumed rosés. The largest concentration of vineyards in Provence is in the Vaucluse area and the stripes of vines stretch as far as the eye can see. But what is there for the young people?

In the surrounding area there are wine festivals, musical concerts, *soirées lyriques* and the *fêtes votives*. Local teenagers seem more interested in *Zakariah's*, a disco in the countryside a few miles from the village and from any habitation. Intentional? Difficult to tell, as the 'action' doesn't get going until midnight. I once passed the building at six thirty a.m., en-route to the TGV station at Avignon, and there were still revellers pouring out – and going in!

Further along the coast, post-war restoration has thrown up some architectural horrors that dog the south, suffocating the Côte in concrete, and heavy industry has done its share of environmental damage in the salt marshes west of Marseilles. However, since the 1980's – when President Mitterrand granted the region a limited form of autonomy – there has been an enthusiastic rediscovery of regional identity and dialects, with Occitan appearing as a dual language. The road signs around Gigondas are written in French and Occitan. Not that I think many people speak the Provençal language – I've only heard it a few times in a café while sitting over a *café crème*. But it's not like Paris where everyone seems to speak and understand English. For survival in Provence, a little French is essential. Locals appreciate your halting, stumbling attempts and are much friendlier towards you than if you made no effort at all. Sometimes my limited French has led to a misunderstanding; sometimes I think that I have misunderstood something, but, in fact, my understanding has been spot on.

So it was with our hand-painted Louis XVI style bed, the one whose delivery was postponed as the builders were so far behind with our restoration. Several months later, a new delivery date and time were set and eagerly we awaited the bed. Come the promised time and no sign of the delivery, we decided to go out and eat. Mealtimes are sacrosanct in France and nothing happens at mealtimes. Everything closes at 12 or 12:30 and shops re-open, if you're lucky, at 3:30. In some cases, it can be 5:30. Time for a **proper** meal, and no meal in France ever takes less than two hours. The same happens in the evening when shops and businesses close no later than 7 to allow time for the *apéritif* and evening meal. In Britain, we work the longest hours in Europe. Nearly 1.4 million Brits routinely work more than 60 hours a week. Only Ireland among EU countries has a higher proportion of people working long hours. Apparently, they are driven by a culture of so-called presenteeism, because they are expected by their bosses and co-workers to spend long hours at the workplace. I think the French have the right idea with their 35 hour work week. Of course, it's a bit confusing for the tourists when they arrive in the village and discover that the Tourist Information Office is now closed on Sundays as well as Mondays, and, of course, for the two hour lunch break. However, it looks like things are going to change. The French parliament has agreed that under certain conditions French workers can now work 48 hours a week

Next day, when I phoned the shop, the man on the end of the line seemed to be telling me that my bed had been stolen! Surely not? I must have misunderstood. Our children are fairly fluent in French and I asked my son to telephone and get the full story. It was totally our fault. The delivery men had turned up at 9 p.m. and nobody was at home! They'd humped the bed back up the hill, loaded it into the van and driven for one and a half hours to the workshop in St Rémy. As it was now so late, they had decided to unload the mattress and leave the rest of the carved bed in the van overnight. Unfortunately, by the morning the van and my bed had disappeared – stolen. An unlikely story, but you couldn't have made it up. I'd been very attracted by the display model in the showroom. It had initials lovingly entwined on the blue footboard. In a mad, romantic gesture, my husband requested my name, Shena, to be similarly carved. Now someone had **my** bed, with **my** name on it!

Back to the drawing board, or rather the *atelier*, the workshop. For some reason, the mattress had been unloaded and therefore had escaped the dastardly robbers, so that was delivered to our house, and we slept on the mattress laid on the floor for another two months while a new bed was carved and painted. This time, the carving merely contained my initials, but we were so glad finally to have the bed that we said little about this discrepancy.

But this was a small setback. We hadn't heard from the builder for a few weeks, when without warning an official appeared on our doorstep and served us with a legal document. Mr W was taking us to court for non-payment of the final sum owing. The case would be heard in the law-courts in nearby Carpentras in a week's time. What a blow! How could we pay him when the job wasn't finished? There had been no warning that he was about to do this. What should we do? We were foreigners in a country still practising Napoleonic law, and, of course, in French.

One of our kindly neighbours, a retired lawyer, came to the rescue. He put us in touch with a friend of his who agreed to look at the facts and determine if we had a case. Fortunately, he advised us that we had everything on our side. Next, the mayor recommended a local lawyer who had done work for his office – "Excellent!" – and we had ourselves a solicitor, *un avocat*.

The case was postponed several times, but at last was called. My husband attended the law court with an English speaking neighbour who translated what was going on. Against all the odds, we won the case. The decision went against Mr W and he was given a time-frame to complete the outstanding work before any additional payment was made. We have nothing but admiration for the French legal system.

On the last day of the week specified by the court, Mr W and his builders arrived and half-heartedly attempted to complete a few of the items identified at the *réception*. We never saw them again. Since then, we've employed someone to floor the cellar and my husband has honed his DIY skills. The case is not dead, but who knows if it will re-surface.

We've learned to live with little imperfections in our house with the blue shutters, under the church. Ironically, what *was* completed is wonderful. The house is bigger than we expected, full of character. Almost everyone who passes stops to look at the "*jolie maison*". Feedback suggests the locals respect that we've turned an eyesore into something so attractive, so Provençal, so in keeping with the rest of the village. Inside, the furnishings are a mixture of local pieces – more *brocante* than *antiquité* – and our furniture collected during our 'mobile' period of living overseas. My family made me promise that I wouldn't fill the house with twee Provençal fabric. I haven't, but the temptation was there – I love the myriad of prints that assail your eyes every time you visit a local market. The clashing but not jarring combinations of blues and yellows; reds and yellows. When we close the shutters at night, there is total darkness and unbelievable quiet.

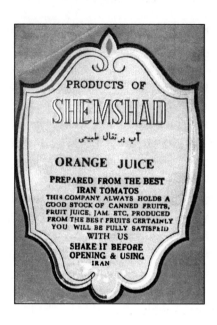

PRODUCTS OF

SHEMSHAD

آب پرتقال طبیعی

ORANGE JUICE

PREPARED FROM THE BEST
IRAN TOMATOS
THIS COMPANY ALWAYS HOLDS A
GOOD STOCK OF CANNED FRUITS,
FRUIT JUICE, JAM. ETC. PRODUCED
FROM THE BEST FRUITS CERTAINLY
YOU WILL BE FULLY SATISFIED
WITH US
SHAKE IT BEFORE
OPENING & USING
IRAN

A Persian Carpet: Isfahan is Half the World

Our first overseas assignment and our first experience of living as expats was in Ahwaz, southern Iran, from 1976 to the end of 1978. At that time, Iran was OPEC'S second largest oil producer and had the world's second largest natural gas reserves. My husband John, an electrical engineer, was going to work for OSCO, the Iranian oil company, as an instrument specialist, and as a family we would eventually move to Gachsaran, a remote mountain town about six hours from Ahwaz. We were young and innocent, with two children under five. I'd always wanted to travel the world. On my sole visit to the Careers Officer at university, I told her of my ambition. "How about teaching on a sheep station in New Zealand?" It wasn't quite what I had in mind. John also wanted to travel, to see something of the world other than the arduous daily commute to central London. We'd already taken the huge step four years earlier of moving from the suburbs of Glasgow to the south of England. At the time, there was a housing boom and we'd had difficulty in finding anything affordable to buy. Yet we'd survived, made friends and got used to not having relatives on the doorstep. But there was never anything over at the end of the month, despite me teaching part-time. The salary package offered by OSCO seemed huge. For the first time in our married life we might even be able to save some money. Plus, the Middle East seemed exotic.

As we planned, processed and packed we felt excited, anticipating a new and unfamiliar adventure. We had no conception how tough life could be. The house promised before we left the UK did not materialise and we lived for three months in the best hotel available, which was less than luxurious. It was tough.

After the VIP welcome and the initial euphoria felt as we explored the unfamiliar sights, sounds and smells of the bustling, colourful bazaar, we began to experience niggling, negative feelings. The hotel served dinner from 9 p.m. – much too late for a three and four year old – and the food was dire. The meat was stringy, tasteless and unrecognisable. The dessert trolley wheeled to the table with much pride and ceremony every evening contained four different coloured jellies, wobbling in unison. What to do? I followed the advice of the thirty or so expats ensconced in the *Astoria Hotel* and bought a two-ring electric hotplate to cook wholesome, familiar food for my children. Children's routines and security are largely family-based. What a fire risk! All these electric hotplates in bedrooms. In the washbasin, I cleaned lettuce and tomatoes, using baby-bottle sterilising fluid brought from home – and the children thrived. At teatime there was local canned orange juice – worryingly labelled as 'prepared from the best Iran tomatoes' – and familiar bread and honey, readily available to buy in the bazaar. In ancient Persia, newlyweds are said to have drunk honeyed water, hence the word 'honeymoon'.

We began to worry about the non-arrival of our shipment, packed with home comforts, familiar things and toys for the children. We began to notice unpleasant sights and smells on our daily forays, the life-threatening, choking traffic, the ever-present, suffocating heat, dirt and intrusive flies, to bemoan the lack of familiar things and friends from home. We became more critical, judgmental and comparative. I couldn't help noticing that the children were doing better than the grownups. They took better to the change of habitat. They missed their friends, but quickly made new ones. In England, they'd already attended two different nursery schools and thought nothing of starting at a third. They moved up to school with their friends from nursery, to an international school where everyone knows what it's like to be the new kid on the block.

But the week before Christmas things perked up. We found a small, slightly lop-sided fir tree in the bazaar and together we made simple paper decorations. I hand-sewed two red velvet stockings and outlined the children's names in sequins. My 'children' still use these stockings today. The hotel restaurant began to serve Christmas lunches a week before the event – turkey and all the trimmings. "No, we'll wait until Christmas Day before we have the turkey," insisted my husband. We both love the ritual of Christmas. Such expectation. The present problem was solved on Christmas Eve when a visiting salesman from Fischer Price arrived at the hotel with his three remaining toys. I bought two: a garage and a musical merry-go-round. What a relief as in the bazaar I'd never seen any toys for sale. Children at that age are easily satisfied – a few chocolate bars, some colouring pencils, a tangerine and a toy apiece. Just perfect. Except that when we went down to lunch that Christmas Day the Christmas menu was 'off' – replaced by rice, lamb stew and multi-coloured jelly, the standard daily fare. What a disappointment. We declined, feeling rather sorry for ourselves. Fortunately, a Dutch friend, already settled in a house, came to the rescue. She phoned to wish us a Merry Christmas and invited us over for afternoon tea. Egg mayonnaise on homemade brown bread – nothing ever tasted so good. The delectable sandwiches saved the day. Later, in the evening, we joined in a multi-national cricket game played with gusto in one of the long hotel corridors – surreal, but lots of fun. It was a Christmas that we'll never forget, and every year we reminisce.

In our house in Provence, we have a gallery of photographs meandering up both stairwells. The first pictures are black and white mementos of Iran: an old, toothless man sitting in the dust at the side of the road with a duck tied to his foot. Some days he sported a chicken, indicating the variety of eggs he had to sell that day. My husband's job assignment took him out in to the remote countryside and frequently he came across villagers sitting at the side of the road, or he was invited into the goatskin tents of nomadic tribes. In our area the Baktiari tribe predominated and they travelled around from place to place with their goats and sheep. They wove beautiful wool carpets in ancient traditional patterns, using natural plant dyes. Frequently, he would be invited to share the communal meal where the rice plate would be passed around the circle. You had to remember to use your right hand to scoop the rice into a ball as the left is considered by Moslems to be unclean.

The chador-clad lady in the adjoining photograph is holding up a warning finger as my husband snapped her. I'd only once worn a chador, hired especially to gain entry to Daniel's Tomb, in Susa. I'd gone there on a trip with a group of colleagues from the International School where I taught English to the children of British and American expats. The females had no problem with covering up to enter the Holy site. Unfortunately, someone saw a photo opportunity, and in securing the chadors (basically one long, slippery length of black material), we collapsed into giggles. This didn't go down well with the custodians and we were refused entry. We'd travelled for hours in a hot, rickety mini-bus to see the fabled site, but in the end only the male members of the party were admitted. We had to be content with second-hand accounts of the relics. Our children did manage to pick up some relics, shards of ancient pottery abandoned by French archaeologists who had excavated the site at the beginning of the twentieth century. Bizarrely, the site was dominated by a large, multi-towered château, constructed by the French to carry out their explorations and store the artefacts before shipping them to French museums. There were no warning signs to keep out; no guided tours or information booklets – not really set up to ensnare tourists. I'm ashamed to say that shards from an ancient civilisation are still in the toy box in our attic.

The next photograph is of a smiling young girl carrying all the family dishes on her head, on her way back from washing them at the well – no running water for the locals. Hardly surprising that from time to time someone took an axe to the pipeline running past the mud-hutted village which carried fresh, cool water to the expat 'mansions'. Then, the bent old man ploughing his fields with yoked oxen, exactly I suppose just as in Biblical times – great memories. Up until now, I'd travelled little: a school trip to Norway and Denmark; in the university vacation, a six-week hitch-hike round France and Spain. The Middle East was still an exotic destination. I'd never seen a bazaar, yet within a day of arriving I was pushing two small children round the crowded streets brimming over with exotic and unfamiliar shapes and smells. We were all very pale-skinned and very blonde and attracted much attention. Most of it was friendly, but I had to be constantly alert to the unsuitable sweetmeats pressed into the hands and mouths of my unsuspecting children.

Over time, I lost my negative feelings about Iran, my feelings of "What happened to paradise?" I lost my uncertainty about how to function, my irritability, my restlessness. Back home, I'd embraced ideas of feminism, however, now was a time to embrace compromise and accommodation, to shift my focus to what I **could** have in my life. I could have stayed all day in the cocooning refuge of our air-conditioned home, living in an expat bubble, only venturing out to join the other trailing wives who passed their days lounging by the swimming pool, comparing tans, counting the days until the first trip home. But I chose to broaden my life, to explore our new surroundings, and eventually, when the children started at nursery and infant school, to obtain a job at the international Passargad School. I became used to the adventure of shopping for paper in Paper Street; vegetables in Vegetable Street; pots in Tin Street – very logical if you think about it. Much easier to compare prices and quality when all the holes-in-the-wall display the same wares.

Meat Street was the biggest challenge, a huge culture shock. Until now, I'd bought my meat neatly packaged in polystyrene and Clingfilm from Sainsbury's, or from the village butcher's pristine, refrigerated and neatly labelled display. I had to brace myself to brush past the myriad of buzzing flies and address the swinging carcass hanging by hooks from the mouldy ceiling. The smiling Iranian butcher was very eager to serve me, but which bit of the sheep provides lamb mince? Gingerly, I pointed at what I hoped was an appropriate section of the animal; it was duly hacked off, wrapped in newspaper and carried home by me to mince. A lot easier than killing your own sheep. One day, my three year old daughter rushed home excitedly to tell me of the new pet that her little Iranian friend next door had been given. The two children had played all morning with the lamb, until it was time for their nap. While my daughter was sleeping, I glanced out of the window just in time to witness the 'pet' being given a drink of water, strung up to the car-port, slaughtered by cutting its throat, and carried into the house ready jointed for the cooking pot or freezer. She was inconsolable when she discovered that the pet lamb mysteriously had disappeared. The meat we bought in the bazaar under such doubtful circumstances always tasted delicious, and we never got sick from eating it. I grew bolder and more confident in my choice of cuts, however, it was a whole lot easier to go to the shop next door and buy frozen, pre-packaged pork, sold by non-Moslem Armenians. We ate a lot of rice, and excellent it was too. I still cook a Persian rice dish, flavoured with turmeric, cinnamon sticks, cloves, almonds and sultanas; a family favourite.

I relished the local produce, adapted local recipes, but occasionally I longed for something from home. The local commissary where we bought our staples received a shipment about twice a year. Such excitement! Eagerly I viewed the recently arrived international products and stocked up with childhood essentials such as tins of Heinz baked beans. Later that summer, while on home leave and staying with relatives, our children went on a shopping trip with their grandparents. They were very young and had rarely been inside a supermarket. Suddenly, our son darted to a brimming shelf and exclaimed: "Look, grandma, baked beans!" He then began excitedly to shovel tin after tin of beans into the shopping trolley. Laughingly, his grandparents explained that there would be plenty of baked beans on the shelf the next day, and the day after that.

There was great excitement when a pizza restaurant opened nearby. Restaurants were thin on the ground; certainly nothing even vaguely Italian. And that's what the new restaurant was: vaguely Italian. The pizzas looked suspiciously like the indigenous flatbread. The toppings included such well-known Italian favourites as walnut, tamarind and pomegranate; and stewed lamb with spinach, pistachios and prunes. Actually, the pizzas were tastier than I've made them sound, made even tastier by the liberal application of the standard jar of *sumac* and bottle of chilli sauce thoughtfully provided on each table. Even more bizarrely, the restaurant also served Mexican food, better food than subsequently I was ever to eat in Mexico. Had the chef learned his trade in Mexico? Been given a Mexican cookbook by a grateful diner? Who knows? At the height of the revolution, just before we left Iran, hoping to take our minds off the worsening political situation, we paid a final visit to the pizza restaurant. We received the usual warm and enthusiastic welcome. Somehow, the restaurant looked different. It seemed very dark. Eventually, we realised why: the windows had all been bricked up. "Some fanatic threw a petrol bomb through our window last week. Not a good bomb. Good for us because little damage. No problem. All safe now!" The manager had tried to reassure us, but his words reinforced our feeling that it was about time to give up eating pizza.

On Sundays, we went regularly to the Golf Club where, for some unexplained reason, curry was served as the dish of the day. It came in generous quantities, complete with naan-type bread, poppadoms and excellent *Shirin Pollo*, sweet pilau-like rice. It was the highlight of the week for many expat families, perhaps missing their local takeaway back home, and also seeking some emotional support in an alien environment. I've come to realise that when people are living overseas they greet people warmly from their own country when back home they possibly wouldn't give them the time of day. And it was a place where our children could meet up with their friends. The curry feast was followed inevitably by fragrant rose-water ice-cream, an acquired taste with a very peculiar texture. At home, I'd empty bowls full of the rejected local ice-cream into the kitchen sink, but in the morning it was still sitting there intact! Goodness knows what it was made from. The golf course was also very popular. It was beautifully green, perfectly maintained, kept that way by a constant supply of cool, arching water delivered by sprinklers. Behind the perfect, lush, green expanse sat a traditional village of mud-walled houses with no running water. When the revolution came, towards the end of 1978, the golf clubhouse was the first building to be torched.

As our second Christmas approached, feeling homesick, I created a little bit of familiar culture. I baked a traditional fruit cake and made shortbread, a staple of my Scottish childhood. I got a bit carried away with quantities and froze a batch for later. In March, Iranian New Year, *Now Ruz*, meaning New Day, came around. This is an ancient celebration, dating back about three thousand years and is deeply rooted in the rituals and traditions of the Zoroastrian belief system. I had thought that Persia had always been Moslem, but in fact I learned that it had only been so since the seventh century. *Now Ruz* is still the biggest celebration in Iran and the people celebrate for thirteen days, from 21 March.

I watched as my Iranian neighbour's extended family descended on the house for the extensive celebrations. Soon, the bedrolls spilled on to the covered verandah and there were sounds of partying at all hours. Traditionally, presents are exchanged and sweets and special meals are consumed. I wanted to contribute something to the festivities, so I delivered my frozen batch of Christmas shortbread to the maid next door. The next day my neighbour appeared on my doorstep to compliment me on the gift: "Lovely and crunchy and cold!" I suspect that they ate the shortbread while still frozen, but they seemed to have enjoyed it.

She also brought with her a Betty Crocker packet cake mix: "I would like so much to make this cake, but I do not understand English very good and I do not know what I must do." Well, I could help with this, although I'd never actually used a cake-mix. She joined me in the kitchen and watched mesmerised as I added the required egg and the measured water to the brown ingredients from the box, and beat everything in my Kenwood Chef for the required fifty strokes. Magic! Next, she handed me a metal jelly mould which she had been clutching all this time and mimed that she would like the cake mixture poured into this (in my opinion) totally unsuitable vessel. We set off next door to place the cake in the oven, but I received another surprise. She opened the doors below the hob to reveal – no oven. She wanted to cook the cake on the outdoor barbecue. It may have worked – who knows – but I wasn't taking any chances, so I carried the mixture back to bake in my own oven. I didn't want the stress of trying to turn the finished cake out of the jelly mould, so I presented it intact. My neighbour was thrilled. The first cake she'd ever baked. The following year, when we left Iran in rather a hurry, she bought my cooker, baking tins and the food mixer, so perhaps her cake baking really took off.

I also made my own wholemeal bread. The indigenous flatbread is delicious but has to be eaten very fresh, preferably hot. We would arrive at the brazier in the next street, where a man was cooking the dough in a kind of makeshift pizza oven. He would feed the dough on a long, long shovel into that blazing hole and hungry customers would catch the discs of aromatic bread, charred at the edges, as they emerged from the flames. Hastily, we threw the bread into a plastic carrier to keep it pliable and rushed home to enjoy it, dipped in to thick yoghurt, wrapped around chunks of succulent, grilled lamb. The lamb was delicious. The sheep were called by the locals something that equated to 'fat-tailed sheep', and they did indeed have very fat tails. "All the fat is in their tails. No fat on the meat. Very lean." True or not, the lamb we bought in the fly-infested shop in the bazaar was always lean and very tasty. In restaurants, the *chelo kebab* would arrive with steaming basmati-like rice and a raw egg which was broken over the rice at the table and then mixed in – an acquired taste, but similar to the Italian *carbonara*. Another acquired taste was the burnt crust from the bottom of the rice pot. A cotton dish towel was stretched over the boiled rice to steam it and a large wodge of butter placed on the bottom of the cooking pot to build up the two inch crust. When the rice was turned out on to the serving plate, this 'delicacy', the *tah dig*, was first offered to an honoured guest. I dreaded having to force it down while trying not to break my teeth and keeping a smile in place.

For everyday breakfast and lunchtime sandwiches, I baked the bread, wholemeal, coarsely ground, definitely no additives. I made huge batches and froze the excess for my husband to use during our long absences. In summer, temperatures reached 140 degrees Fahrenheit, much too hot for me and the children, so we decamped to cooler climes. This usually meant Scotland, to stay with relatives as our Richmond house had tenants. It was lovely to catch up with parents, aunts and cousins, to go for long walks in the hills where swarms of midges and the grey skies were the only annoyance, to shop in stores piled high with consumer goods – and toys. However, living at close quarters for an extended period puts a strain on any relationship, and after the tearful farewells we always looked forward to returning 'home' to Iran.

On our return from such a vacation, my husband related how he'd invited a visiting bachelor to share the vast house in our absence. They rubbed along amicably until the poor chap inadvertently left out a whole home-baked loaf of bread on the kitchen work-surface. By the evening, it was rock hard and inedible. My husband had ranted at the poor chap, explaining how precious bread was. He must have thought us very strange indeed.

Our first *Now Ruz* also saw the acquisition of our first, and only, pet. A dog was out of the question. A few expats had brought their dogs with them, however, the only dogs available in Ahwaz were packs of mangy, wild, marauding dogs which terrorised the neighbourhood and trashed the garbage. A friend's child was bitten which resulted in ten excruciating anti-rabies injections in her stomach. No cats or hamsters available either. The solution came when we visited the bazaar one day during the holiday period. The house always had several small, speckled lizards, geckos, running across walls, falling from door jams and surprising you, but they could never be regarded as pets. Our plentiful supply of cockroaches didn't count either. We couldn't believe it – almost every stall was crammed with bowls of live goldfish, which were disappearing fast. Very strange. An Iranian friend enlightened us: "We must set our *Now Ruz* table with seven specific things beginning with the letter 's'. In addition, the table must have a copy of the Holy Koran, a mirror and a bowl of water containing a goldfish, *mahi ghermez*, to bring luck. In ancient times, each thing corresponded to one of the seven creations and the seven holy immortals protecting them."

We weren't much the wiser; however, the children were thrilled to have a pet at last. In fact, we now had three pets, three goldfish, rapidly named by our son Suki, Sara and Abadan. Rather strange names, but children have their reasons: 'Suki' was the name of a seal in a favourite book he was reading at that moment; 'Sara' the name of his sister; and 'Abadan', Iran's City of Oil on the Persian Gulf which we visited from time to time, once for my first and only experience of delicious Caspian Sea caviar, mostly to fly back to the UK. For a few weeks, the pets thrived, despite their cramped conditions and the suspected over-feeding from generous owners. The children skipped home eagerly from Nursery School and the first thing they did was to rush over to the goldfish bowl.

Soon, it was time to go home for the summer, leaving my husband to join us later. Tearful farewells were made to the pets. Little did we know what fate lay in store for them. As my husband had to be away on business for a few days, he transferred the goldfish to the cavernous bath, thinking they would be happier there and have more chance of survival. Unfortunately, the weather became even hotter than usual and the surge in the use of air-conditioning caused a power cut. Poor fish! Their bath must have become hotter and hotter until eventually they expired. My husband returned to find them floating on their backs, very dead.

What to do? In Britain when a beloved pet dies, you run out to the pet store and buy another one, preferably one which looks just like the original. However, *Now Ruz* was now over and goldfish were nowhere to be seen. When I returned with the children, we had to break the sad news to them. Their first experience of death. They accepted it very stoically, prepared a shoebox with cotton wool, into which the goldfish were gently laid, and dug a hole in the garden. At their father's suggestion, a small wooden cross marked the spot. Asked if he wanted to say anything, our son said very solemnly, "Abadan is dead." Why no words for Suki and Sara, I do not know. It's one of his earliest memories.

We never did move to Gachsaran, up in the mountains, where my husband was to be the instrument specialist advisor for the oil wells there. By the time that our house and my husband's job were ready, we were comfortably settled in Ahwaz. The children were happy in the local international school where I had a job teaching English. In every overseas assignment it's been important for me to find something meaningful to occupy my time. We'd grown used to local ways. The town could never be termed attractive, but most things were available if you looked long enough. I got used to the teeming bazaar, the heated bargaining for the 'best price', even the unwanted attention that our blonde hair attracted. Our established routine was supportive and fulfilling. The highlight of my week was a trip to the downtown bookstore to stock up for the coming week. We had a lively social life – clubs, various sporting facilities, frequent parties, but no television. We saw this as a plus of living overseas. The children watched (and enjoyed) reels of extracts from *Bambi*, *Jungle Book* and *Born Free*. By the time we left, we all knew them off by heart, which didn't stop us going to see the full-length version of *Jungle Book* five times.

However, good friends did move to Gachsaran and we visited for a few days. The journey up into the rugged, arid mountains was torturous, but this soon gave way to forests, pomegranate trees, lush pastures and much cooler temperatures. Obviously plenty of water here. Our self-sufficient friends were very happy living in this isolated spot, where there was only one other expat family. In the market, we collected food-stuffs for a picnic, including freshly picked, jewelled pomegranates. On our way home to England for our summer break, I was stopped and searched at the airport by a suspicious British customs officer who failed to recognise the pomegranate syrup (an essential ingredient of the spectacular Iranian chicken and walnut stew, *Koresht-e-Fesenjan*) in my hand baggage. Today, pomegranate produce seems commonplace; you can even buy pomegranate green tea in oriental-look bottles, claiming to protect you against heart disease, cancers and the effect of aging – a magic elixir; a superfood.

Walking round the market, we admired the brightly coloured, embroidered, beaded and mirrored costumes of the local nomadic tribesmen, the Qashquai. From a stall next to the one selling vegetables, I bought the exquisite black lace, gold-spangled tribal headdress which I still wear today as a shawl. Later that day, at the picnic site among the lush, undulating hills, we came across a young, barefooted Qashquai girl washing her elaborate headdress in a stream before herding her sheep further up into the mountains. We have a photograph of her in our 'gallery' in Provence, in her beautiful mirrored, embroidered tribal dress and multiple, multi-coloured petticoats, adjusting the newly-washed headdress.

On the drive back to Ahwaz, our son complained of being hot, feeling unwell. On his face, spots began to sprout, diagnosed later that day as chickenpox. At the picnic in Gachsaran, he'd played with local children who had never been exposed to the virus. Later, I learned that several of them had been really ill. Beware of foreigners bearing gifts.

We have such fond memories of our time in Iran. Ahwaz is an oil boom town, not very pretty, but we made a memorable trip to Isfahan, a beautiful city full of wonderful buildings, hidden gardens and an ancient bazaar. The city is full of outstanding Islamic architecture and is one of the great monumental cities of the world. We stayed in the luxurious old but faded Shah Abbas Hotel (now re-named, of course – the Abbasi), an oasis of wonderful, exotic perfumed gardens and a traditional, outdoor tea-house. That's one of the advantages of working abroad as an expat: almost always you earn a lot more than you would do at home, to make up for the 'hardship' of the posting. In fact, when I started work, we could live comfortably on my salary and save my husband's. For the first time in our lives, we had money to spare.

The hotel is built on the spot where one of the famous royal *caravanserais* was situated. Every afternoon, we took tea in the gardens, sipping from tiny, jewel-coloured, embellished glasses, lolling on huge, overstuffed, embroidered cushions and Persian rugs, languorously watching men enjoy the painted glass 'hubble-bubble' pipes. We have a photograph in our gallery in Provence of our daughter, framed by the multiple white arches of the hotel, smelling the highly perfumed roses which reminded us so much of England.

Great excitement in the hotel lobby one morning when we spied the actor Anthony Quinn, in full make-up and tribal dress, off to shoot the film *Caravans*, an adaptation of James Michener's best-selling novel. He was playing Zulffiquar, an aging tribal chief. I expect he needed the luxury of the five-star hotel after a hard day spent charging around on horseback and lolling in a goatskin tent. The film was a co-production between America and Iran but had the misfortune of being released just as relations between the two nations began to sour. It's worth seeing for the genuine nomadic Quashquai extras used and the wonderful photography of Iran which stood in for Afghanistan.

We set off to spend hours in the four hundred year old, vaulted-roof bazaar which winds for miles through the heart of the city. It was built by the great Shah Abbas who made Isfahan the capital of the land, truly worthy of the title 'half the world'. Caravans of camels came from China and India, laden with silks, spices, ivory and gold. We spent our time sipping sweet tea from tiny glasses, nibbling politely the proffered pistachios and brightly coloured sweetmeats, and haggling over extremely fine, intricately patterned, Persian rugs; exquisite miniature paintings on ivory; and traditional filigree gold and turquoise jewellery. Beware carpet sellers bearing cups of tea. One of these rugs, a red, tribal Baktiari, now takes pride of place on the dining room floor in Provence. A long way from Iran, but there are similarities in the two cultures. After all, French is the official second language of Iran after Farsi.

Isfahan is such a beautiful, cosmopolitan city, renowned for its outstanding mosques, gardens and bridges, and the following year when the opportunity to re-visit presented itself, I jumped at it. On this occasion, my husband babysat and I flew off with a party of work colleagues. We had only vague plans: "Don't worry," reassured Richard, kindergarten teacher and the self-elected group leader, "there won't be any difficulty in finding somewhere to stay." However, it was the Shah's birthday, hence a public holiday when all the schools and workplaces were closed. On landing, people were milling everywhere, a worrying sign. We started off optimistically at the top, presenting ourselves in the lobby of the luxurious Shah Abbas Hotel which had been half-empty on my previous visit. "Sorry, full up. Everything is full." Surely not? But it was true. We trekked dispiritedly from one small hotel to another. Even the park benches were full. What to do? Fortunately, Richard remembered that a friend he'd met the previous year at a Christian conference ran a refuge in the city. As he spoke fluent Farsi, we were quickly given directions and turned up unannounced on the doorstep of the refuge which was hidden behind a high wall with guards on the gate. We were made very welcome and eighteen mattresses were thrown on the floors of two adjoining rooms – one for the males and one for the females. So much for the romantic weekend some of our party had envisaged! Still, we had a bed for the night. The only downside was that there was a nine-o'clock curfew, why I didn't really understand. We set off gaily for dinner at a nearby French restaurant. Earlier in the day, we'd sought it out and elbowed our way through the crowds of people outside trying to get a reservation. I'd impressed my colleagues by catching the head waiter's eye and, in my best French, booking a table for seven thirty for eighteen people. "Yeah, sure, the table will be waiting for us!" But in fact it was, neatly laid for the required number, the best table in the house. Service was very slow but the rich food and wine delicious and we had a wonderful time. Suddenly, we realised that it was five minutes to nine.

Hurriedly, the bill was paid and a few of the men hurried off to the refuge compound, with us trailing behind. They kept the guards on the gate chatting while we scuttled in about ten minutes past the curfew. It would have been too much if we'd been locked out. That night we laughed and laughed. So much for a wild weekend. Still, we had a bed and good company, and there would always be other trips to sample the night-life.

My souvenirs from this trip were rather bizarre: two silver coloured toy cowboy guns in red leather holsters, one for each of our children. A few weeks before, the American school guidance counsellor had tested all the kindergarten pupils. One of the tests involved an observation of which toys a child chose when presented with a wide choice. "You've got to buy your son a gun!" the counsellor implored me. "He picked out all the aggressive toys: a model tank, GI Joe and a plastic water pistol!" Hardly a Natural Born Killer then. I considered myself a Pacifist; I was over-protective of my children. Despite being brought up on a diet of cowboy movies and avidly playing Cowboys and Indians as a child, I was strongly against any depiction of war or violence. I'd been able to 'protect' our children as one of the advantages of our expat existence was that we had no television, no cinema. I took her advice and reluctantly purchased the replica guns in Isfahan. Great excitement when I handed over the gifts. The guns were played with for two days and then relegated to the bottom of the toy box. Lots of more interesting things to do. My philosophy had been wrong; my fears had been unfounded. Our children were not about to turn into American Wild West monsters, despite the comments by a welcoming American lady greeter, employed by the company to orientate us to Ahwaz. When we met up with her, the children were wearing matching denim dungarees and brightly coloured t-shirts. "Why, hi there. Welcome to Ahwaz! Gee, your children look charming. They look just like American kids!" In her eyes, probably the best compliment ever.

The guns were joined by leather 'cowboy' hats bought in Corfu against the scorching sun. Selfishly, we decided during the second year to spend our month's vacation on a white-sanded beach in Greece rather than go home to see family. It was idyllic, completely undeveloped, and for the first time in our lives we agreed that life **can** be a beach. It was a very simple, stress-free existence. Our three and four year old loved the unfamiliar – digging in the sand, building castles, swimming in the unpolluted sea, and floating around in their little blow-up dinghy. We ate every day at a rather basic *taverna* on the beach: char-grilled, herb-infused fish caught that morning, rubber-band squid, salty feta salad, plump, purple figs and oozing combs of honey. There was almost nothing to buy in the cove, no ice-creams to whine for. We did purchase eggs from the apron of the old lady who lived a few yards from our beachside villa. We made a few excursions on the local rickety bus, sharing space with old ladies in black and their goats and chickens, careering round the mountains to Corfu town and 'civilisation'. It was one of the best holidays ever.

But soon we experienced some real life violence and suddenly being an expat in Iran was very scary. Politically, changes were afoot. Towards the end of 1978, we were caught up in a civil war and we lived under martial law for three months. No more parties; gatherings of more than three people were forbidden; you were not allowed to be out on the streets later than nine in the evening. Soldiers wielding serious guns guarded the petrol pumps. On one occasion, I had trouble getting the petrol pump to work and the soldier kindly did it for me, first of all handing me his gun to free up both hands! And what seemed like half an army battalion, complete with tanks moved into our school compound. I had a heavy-duty machine gun mounted just outside my classroom window. Rather than reassure me, I found it extremely unsettling. The pupils too found it difficult to concen-trate on preparing for the Common Entrance exam for entry into British boarding schools. Every morning, I took the register and drew a line through the names of pupils who had withdrawn. Daily, companies were pulling out and evacuating their staff and families. Daily, school management and representatives from the oil companies met to discuss the situation and how to proceed. Ours was the only school remaining open in the area and it seemed that we were being kept open as a symbol that the Shah was still in control. We were reas-sured that there was nothing to fear, but it was difficult to believe and we felt very afraid. At home, we'd moved the children's mattresses into our bedroom. The house was enormous – the children could ride their small, two-wheeled bikes round and round the living room – and their bedrooms were too far away from ours. As usual, we had company guards protecting our house twenty four hours a day, however, at night, all around us, we could hear the sounds of looting as locals took advan-tage of the recently vacated homes. In the streets there were daily demonstrations and violent protests. There was a strike at the local oil company where my husband worked. He went to work every day, however, protected by armed soldiers, he had no work to do. A cinema and a mini-bus in the capital city of Abadan were bombed. Food was difficult to come by. Travel was prohibited. Bottled gas was in short supply and we depended on this for cooking. And we had a serious problem when someone stole our gas bottles. How they got past the guard on duty, driving a truck required to transport the huge, heavy bottles, was a mystery. Our four twenty-four hour guards had always proved very trustworthy. Perhaps the *baksheesh* we paid them every month helped just a little. It was too much of a coincidence that our Iranian neighbour, who refused to pay up, had his house burgled twice while away on vacation, while our identical house remained intact. You couldn't beat the system. During our first few weeks in the house, we'd had an ongoing problem with burst garbage bags, debris scattered all the way down the path, and itinerant cows coming into the garden by the open gate to munch their way through the tastier morsels – plastic bags were a particular favourite. Only when finally we gave in and paid the garbage collector who arrived every day with his wheel-barrow his requested small stipend did the problem mysteriously disappear.

Feeling somehow responsible for our loss, the trusty guard who had been on duty offered to pay for our missing gas bottles. A few weeks before, I had placed the children's hardly worn but outgrown sandals and shoes, bought on a serious shopping trip in the UK, on the high wall in front of our house. We went out and on our return the guard and his stout stick were fiercely protecting from marauders the undisturbed row of shoes. I explained that they were surplus to requirement but still in good condition and he was welcome to take them for his young family. I hope they got some further use. Shortly before we left the country, imitating our American friends, we held a yard sale, and the same guard bought at rock-bottom price my husband's twice-worn dinner suit. He insisted on putting it on immediately, *sans* shirt and complemented by his black and white, chequered head-cloth and sturdy cudgel. The last we saw of him, he was roaring down the street on the back of a friend's motorbike. The friend was more conventionally dressed.

It wasn't an easy time. Iranian friends who had invited us to their parties and given our children presents at Christmas now studiously avoided us. A teaching colleague's Iranian husband was spirited away during the night to the local prison. Ironically, he was on the 'right' side, an opponent of the Shah. Our immediate, affluent Iranian neighbours disappeared; it was rumoured, to stay with relatives in Isfahan, to avoid confrontation with those now in control. Our daughter was too young to register what was going on, but for months afterwards all our son's drawings were of tiny figures shouldering guns. Eventually, we'd had enough. We decided that we couldn't wait for official evacuation. We began to sell off the contents of our house at bargain prices, to arrange a shipment home of some books and tools, the children's toys and our few souvenirs.

I was relieved to be going home. The exciting, exotic environment had never seemed more threatening, more alien. On my last day in Ahwaz, I went down town to the bank to cash my final pay cheque. I was accompanied by two tall, burly men who helped me to elbow my way to the first floor cash desk and make the withdrawal. It was chaos as people jostled and screamed, desperate to withdraw their savings before the collapse of the régime. When we came back downstairs, the huge plate glass window of the bank had been blown out and the street was full of glass and mayhem. We'd had a close shave.

My husband resigned and the children and I left on the first available plane. There had been no regular air service for several weeks. At the last minute, the Principal of the school asked me if his young children could accompany me. They were going to stay in safety with their grandparents in the US. So much for his repeated reassurances that there was nothing whatsoever to worry about! The plane was packed with anxious travellers loaded down with possessions and beloved pets in baskets. We didn't have much, but I did pack my treasured Baktiari rug. We'd sold our second rug back to the vendor. What a wonderful system. You can enjoy your rug for two years, then return it and receive what you had originally paid for it.

Nothing on board the plane to eat or drink during the seven hour flight, but we were all so relieved to be going home. A few weeks later, my husband joined us. His American boss, who lived in the next street, had been assassinated at seven in the morning as he set out for work. This was the catalyst. That evening we watched the BBC news and saw many of our friends disembarking in Athens. All remaining expatriates had been evacuated to this 'half-way house'. A makeshift school was set up, but when it became clear that the situation in Iran was only going to get worse, families drifted back to their points of origin. On January 16, the Shah of Iran, Reza Pahlavi, was deposed and the new régime took over, headed by Ayatollah Khomeini. He had been exiled from Iraq to France in 1978 and had orchestrated the unrest. In February 1979, he left France and returned to Iran. On 1 April, 1979, the Islamic Republic of Iran was proclaimed. This is more or less the same regime that we have today in Iran. The latest leader is traditional and fundamentalist.

Our middle-class Iranian friends had worn the latest Paris fashions to the numerous cocktail parties and dinners; now the all-enveloping, black chador with not a scrap of hair showing was *de rigueur*. Several of our American friends were married to Iranians. Two of their husbands were put in jail as supporters of the Shah. One husband, a tall, moustached, seemingly very western Iranian who only a few weeks before had danced the night away to the latest hits, disappeared, abandoning his American wife and four young children. He was a tribal Kurdish chief and had gone to lead his people. His wife was distraught. As far as I know, she never heard from him again. One American wife was cast off by her Iranian husband who no longer had any need of a blonde, foreign wife, and she lost custody of her children. The last three months in Iran had been a tense time for us, but we could return to England and re-group as a family.

Gradually, we settled back into the British way of life. We moved back into our home in February of 1979, a bitterly cold winter with deep drifts of snow, even in the 'soft' south. Our five year old daughter hated the cold, the coat, hat, scarf and gloves that had to be donned before venturing outside. In Iran, she'd been used to getting herself dressed for school, slipping into shorts, t-shirt and sandals. Now, she squirmed as I helped her into the thermal vest, shirt with tiny pearl buttons, tie, grey, pinafore dress, cardigan – more buttons – thick woollen tights and stiff, buckled shoes. She cried every morning as we left her in the school playground. Heartbreaking for us. Her teacher called me in: "Is your daughter shy about getting undressed? She refuses to change for PE." In fact, we discovered that our uninhibited daughter was only afraid that even if she managed to somehow struggle out of the multiple, bewildering items of school uniform, she'd never manage to get them all on again! We rose earlier, she learned to dress herself, made new friends, got used to the more formal style of schooling, and even the weather.

We too gradually re-adjusted, re-established links with local friends and a few of the expats we'd known in Iran and got over our culture shock. I had a small panic attack in the supermarket on my first big shop – so many people, so many things to buy, no friendly eye contact or exchange of greetings. I'd forgotten how congested our roads are, how inconsiderate other drivers can be. Things are never quite the same when you return after a period of absence. I was a different person. It's a bit of a Rip van Winkle syndrome. I was excited and full of anticipation, yet somehow things were not quite as I remembered. Close family and old friends sometimes see your time abroad as an extended holiday. The idea that life overseas is a full-time job is an alien one. I had been involved with new places and people and the past at home seemed a long time ago. For the people who stay at home, the past was only yesterday. We'd been away for two and a half years, yet the greengrocer greeted me with: "Oh, hello. You haven't been in for a while. Been away on holiday, have you?" It takes time to re-assimilate yourself back into the community, and by that time you may have been given another assignment and be on the move again.

Ten months later, we received a call from international shippers to say that our overseas shipment had arrived and was sitting on the quay at Tilbury Docks. The wooden container had sat in an Arab village for nine months during the rainy season, so there was little to salvage. The union had forbidden the dock workers to deal with the debris until it had been treated by Rentokil. When we arrived, a small heap of belongings was all that had survived. We extracted the toolbox, largely unscathed, some metal souvenirs, and I rescued a few books for sentimental reasons, among them my favourite *Don Quixote* (in Spanish; why I thought that I was going to dredge up my rusty Spanish to re-read this in Iran, I do not know). The books are readable, but every time I pick up my Iranian cookery book, rather than invoking the smell of spices from the mysterious East, a smell of decay and damp wafts from the page. We still have a string of brass camel bells lurking somewhere in our attic.

During our two years as expats in Iran, we'd made many friends. Sadly, we've lost contact with the Iranians who befriended us, but we work hard at maintaining our international friendships. Lacking siblings, cousins, grandparents, expat friends pick up and assume these roles and support each other. In this and subsequent postings overseas, we have made lasting, life-enhancing friendships which we maintain with regular correspondence: postcards, letters, telephone calls, increasingly e-mails. We exchange visits, tell anecdotes, laugh a lot, and reminisce fondly about our common experiences.

Tales from the Jungle: Sumatran Safaris

Next to the Iranian photographs in our house in Provence we have our Indonesian shots, where everyone looks happy and smiling. Indonesians smile a lot. From 1985, we lived for three and a half years on the edge of the rainforest, in the Moslem province of Aceh, Northern Sumatra, a very remote area. Since 1979, we had enjoyed six years of life in Richmond as my husband worked for the large American oil company Mobil (now Exxon-Mobil). He was based at the Head Office in London, only going abroad on short business trips, so our children could attend local schools and I could resume my teaching career. There was a rather unsettling eighteen months when he worked offshore in the North Sea. Unsettling because he worked two weeks on and two weeks off. Sounds idyllic, doesn't it? However, we all missed him when he was away and I took on the role of single parent and disciplinarian. When daddy returned, there was a party atmosphere, then two weeks later life would revert to 'plain clothes and porridge'.

All that changed in the spring of 1985 when he was assigned as an instrument specialist to Sumatra, Indonesia. I must admit that initially I had to look up Sumatra in an atlas. We were excited about living overseas again. The job seemed challenging, but we were looking forward to living the expat life once more; to exploring the as yet unvisited Far East. I'd learned a great deal from living in Iran and being older and wiser felt that I could make a go of it. The only downsides were that I would give up my teaching job and the children, now 12 and 13, would go to boarding school. There was no suitable expat school. We felt that a British boarding school would provide stability. Our thirteen year old son settled well, however, our daughter took longer to adjust. It was heartbreaking leaving them at school. It never got any easier. They visited us three or four times a year and I made regular trips to the UK to visit them, but as the end of the holidays loomed, we all dreaded the parting. We had chosen a school in Scotland, close to my parents' home, so at least they had someone to stay with during exeats, someone to watch them playing in the school orchestra. Many children don't have the opportunity to really get to know their grandparents. I have regrets, but on the whole I think that boarding school was the right decision, and they did see a lot of the world, were exposed to different cultures and developed a broader outlook as a result, and they become very independent and self-sufficient. By this time, I'd accepted that I was never going to have a conventional career. Although I loved my job in Richmond teaching English, I was ready to give it up and join my husband in remotest Indonesia.

During our time in Aceh, we didn't just sit in our luxurious expat houses on the hill, totally insulated from local life. When we were told about a new assignment, the first reaction was usually of excitement and we planned, packed and said farewells. On arrival, we were treated as VIPs, the new kids on the block, and we were curious about the nationals, their country and their customs. I would seek out language classes, eager to attempt to interact with the locals and avoid many of the problems and frustrations that arise when you cannot communicate. However, this feeling of euphoria can wear off quickly and you begin thinking: "What happened to Paradise?" You begin to notice the heat (or cold, in the case of Boston); you feel drained of energy and begin to suffer stomach upsets or minor illnesses. When we arrived in Aceh, I couldn't understand why people were always complaining of being ill, of suffering from vague illnesses, why the doctor's surgery was always full, why people made frequent trips to Singapore to see specialists. Of course, people did suffer from the usual colds, headaches and diarrhoea, but perhaps there was also an element of finding yourself in a hostile environment, with a lot of time on your hands. Oh, and of course we all had private medical insurance.

Sometimes in an expat living situation, everything felt alien and I longed for the familiar. Rather than give up and go home, the best solution was to adopt a positive attitude, settle down to an established routine, and find something fulfilling to do. This approach can get you over the feelings of culture shock. However, at times it seemed as though I'd lost my identity and was defined by what my husband did, his position within the company. The opportunity for work for 'dependent' wives in Sumatra was extremely limited. Here, society values women who spend their time in cultural pursuits, learning about Indonesia, and giving up time to charities and welfare organisations. I had to seek and find personally satisfying and meaningful activities. However, sometimes I kept myself so busy that I felt as if I was on an ever-circling roundabout and I couldn't get off.

I did keep very busy. I became Vice President of the local branch of the Women's International Group (WIC) with a membership of 150 and I travelled to conferences in other parts of the Far East, exchanging ideas with women of all nationalities. Yet again, this experience would probably not have presented itself if I had not been a mobile wife. And I carried the experiences with me when I returned home. And I was a different person.

Indonesia was and still is a very poor country and Northern Aceh one of the poorest areas. I was heavily involved in a local social welfare programme, raising money through donations from oil companies and the proceeds from a highly organised Christmas bazaar. We provided practical help and funds to a retirement centre, a centre for the handicapped, a clinic with an immunisation programme, two orphanages, various villages and a leper colony. This colony is on the coast near Lhoksukon, approachable only by walking precariously across fish farms for twenty minutes. At first glance it seemed idyllic: very clean and shaded by coconut palms, right on the beach. The lepers' medication was supplied free, but they had to walk miles to collect it as the locals' fear of contamination meant that the colony was far away from civilisation. We worked with a local doctor to train volunteers how to provide medication and dressings, and as the lepers had no fresh water we organised a water drop and improved collection of rain water by installing basic guttering on the roofs of the houses. Rice and needed supplies were brought in at regular intervals. We also oversaw the building of a two-family house. Some of the materials were re-cycled; others purchased with funds and manpower donated by local companies. Within the day, the large longhouse was complete and ready to move into – quite a contrast to building experiences back home. Actually, when I first got involved, we were supporting two leper colonies and had built a wooden longhouse for the neediest villagers. However, when we returned a few weeks later to see how they were getting on, we discovered that the lepers had sold the longhouse which was now filled with several families we'd never met. Perhaps they needed the money more than the shelter. However, the WIC committee decided that the community would be dropped from our social welfare programme.

Helping the villages took many different forms. Some of the expat wives, including Kathi, our close friend, had been nurses in their home countries and worked with the local doctors to set up an immunisation programme and a harelip project. For some reason, there was a high incidence of harelips and cleft palates, and WIC helped with a system of pre and post-operative care through a group of foster aunts. Most of the mothers and children spoke Achenese, an oral language, rather than the official language, Bahasa Indonesian, so frequently communication was difficult. We gave one village a sewing machine, fabric and scissors, followed up by weekly sewing lessons over three months. The idea was that the villagers would learn to make their own clothes and perhaps establish a small cottage industry. This worked well, but when I returned to the village to see how things were going, the Headman asked for a television set. Not a totally unrealistic request, except that the village had no source of electricity.

My friend Isabel was in charge of the orphanage project and I went with her to the orphanages, where we provided food, toys, books, bedding, and on one occasion two much-needed goats – practical gifts which were greatly appreciated. We donated kitchen equipment: a *kompor* (kerosene cooking stove), woks, large saucepans, ladles and rice bowls. The children there always seemed very happy, despite their lack of western comforts, or even basic cooking equipment and sleeping mats, and they gave us a warm welcome. We enjoyed the visits as much as the children and it was good to travel with Indonesian friends out into the villages through the lush Sumatran countryside. Every shade of green imaginable: lime green ferns, pastel fan-palms, deep green mango trees, luminous green rice paddies. The Dutch engineered a road system to take advantage of Sumatra's plantation wealth of rubber, tobacco and spices, thus the roads, though narrow, are in pretty good shape.

As an expat wife I had plenty of time to give and soon I was also co-editing and writing for a local newspaper. Thus I was able to give our projects a great deal of publicity. This engendered very generous donations from the numerous big foreign companies working in the area. On one occasion, when I visited a remote village with my friend from Dallas, I was used as a 'propaganda piece' by the local midwife: "Look, you too can be fat and rich like this lady with only two children, if only you will take the contraceptive pill!" I didn't know whether to be flattered or not, but it seemed to help a few volunteers to come forward. Over-population is the main cause of poverty, and increased Family Planning is a must. Girls frequently marry at twelve and have four children by the age of sixteen. Life expectancy has risen to around 50, however, over 60% of children die before the age of five and only 12% of people have access to clean water. In our home, it was the maid's first job every morning: to boil water for twenty minutes to render it safe for drinking. All our vegetables, fertilised by human excrement, had to be sterilised using either Clorox bleach, or Milton, a baby-bottle sterilising solution.

I often worried what would happen to these people when our financial help was withdrawn. I wonder how much was actually going on beneath the veneer while we were living the life of rich, benevolent expats?

The language barrier made it difficult sometimes to gauge what was going on. I received a phone call early one morning – around 6 a.m.; the heat means everything has to be accomplished as early as possible. It was one of my Indonesian fellow committee members. After the usual pleasantries came: "You are the most senior wife in town at the moment (there was an exodus of wives in the summer months as the heat built up) and today you must plant a tree." Not something I'd ever been asked to do before, but I wasn't scheduled to do anything else that day, so I donned my best frock and waited for the transport to pick me up. You would think that in an expat community, on the edge of the jungle, the dress code would have been very casual and relaxed? Not a bit of it. Seven a.m. meetings were common and all the ladies would appear fully made-up and coiffed, wearing dresses, stockings, high heels, jewellery – the lot. Looking back, it seems mad, but I accepted it at the time. As Aceh is a heavily Moslem area, dresses were always modest with high necks, longish hemlines and sleeves. Yes, you could swim or play tennis, but you wore an enveloping cover-up to travel to your destination. People did not stroll around in short shorts and bikinis. I didn't feel resentful; it's important to respect the customs of the country you are visiting. You cannot adopt the attitude, "My way is the only way! This would never happen in my country!" However, I have heard disgruntled expats, suffering from culture shock, express these sentiments.

Anyway, we set out, very late as usual as the transport hadn't arrived on time. In my experience, Indonesians are not good timekeepers; they believe in 'rubber time'. I gave weekly English lessons to two groups of ladies, Japanese and Indonesian. The Japanese always arrived en-masse, on time. If they were going to be five minutes late, someone phoned in advance to apologise. They were all very keen to improve their English and did their homework religiously. My Indonesian students, on the other hand, viewed the session more as a social experience. On more than one occasion, someone arrived on my doorstep the day after the scheduled class and expected me to drop everything and get involved in some English conversation: "I am here for the English class – is all right?" And of course I would try to make the time for a short lesson. After all, teaching English is my first love. I made some great friends among both communities and we all have some annoying habits. It's a running joke in my family that our daughter appears to have inherited my gene for punctuality. It's so bad that we're both always early for appointments. It can be a bit disconcerting for the dinner party hostess.

When we arrived finally at the remote village, the eating and drinking were finished – much to my relief as food sitting out for hours in the sun always filled me with dread, especially if it was something like *gulai otak* (beef brain curry) – and speeches were in full flow. I was ushered through the hundreds of people gathered and a few unlucky guests were ejected from the front row of seats to make room for me and my entourage. I felt very embarrassed, but nobody seemed resentful. Within minutes, I was called on to shovel a few spades of soil into a pre-formed hole, round the base of a very spindly tree. I felt like the Queen! Next, I was handed a large stone to place next to the tree. I smiled a great deal and when beckoned sat down on the heavily festooned, brightly glittering wedding bed erected next to the tree, and surreally had my photograph taken with the wife of the Governor of Aceh dressed in her best silk batik. Then we bundled into the minibus for the long journey home. Batik is still worn as everyday clothing, but for important or formal occasions, men don long-sleeved batik shirts with patch pockets, usually worn loose, outside the trousers or sarong. Ladies have more choice, but batik dresses, some made from fine silk, can look very elegant, not just attire for the beach. As part of the WIC educational programme, I took a class in batik-making. This involved much uncomfortable crouching in front of a sweltering charcoal fire, heating wax in a wok and creating vegetable dyes. I found it excruciatingly difficult. I did create two batik pictures, but they're so poor that they reside in the shed at the bottom of the garden.

I speak a little Bahasa Indonesian, a little more then, but I wish that I'd made more effort to learn the language. There aren't that many places that you can use Bahasa Indonesian, but that's not a good excuse. I'm less lazy now about trying to learn the language of the countries I visit. It helps you to settle in more quickly and avoid some of the frustrations of daily life. Weeks later, I saw my picture in the local paper, of me standing next to the tree and the stone. Seems I'd laid the foundation stone of a new secondary school. I wish I'd understood that at the time.

Life in Aceh wasn't all do-gooding. There was a mad social whirl. Imagine living in an area with no shops, apart from holes-in-the-wall, no cinema and no television. Under such circumstances, expats invariably re-create their own culture. They seek out each other for emotional support and create a mini national enclave: club houses, sports clubs, enthusiastic celebration of national holidays, and shared information about the availability of national foods in speciality shops. On the plus side, we had huge, grand houses. We once held a party for a hundred guests and there was room in one of our living rooms for them all to dance at the same time. The gardens were full of what to us were exotic plants: trumpets of red hibiscus, wild fringes of fuchsia-coloured bougainvillea, waving and rustling in the monsoon storms, intoxicating gardenia and frangipani, lime trees, banana palms and coconut palms – rampant tropical greenery. Every week I bought fat bunches of purple orchids at my door from the 'flower lady', and mangoes, mangosteen, pineapples and papaya. Mangoes for breakfast – what luxury! My children complained when they visited that we ate homemade soup followed

by fresh pineapple every day for lunch. What deprivation! The soup may seem a strange choice, but it was
light, nutritious and reminded us of home. When we
were growing up in Scotland, there was a lot of soup,
probably to keep us warm. My maid chastised me
for eating pineapple every day. Why? I never could
fathom it, but it seemed to be tied up with some superstitious belief in loss of fertility if females ate too many
pineapples.

We busied ourselves with new activities. Every
weekend, my husband and a group of friends would go
out 'hunting' for elephants. There was Ray, a Canadian
from Alberta, an accountant and business manager;
Ted, originally from Pocatello, Idaho, the headmaster
of the school who had boundless energy and was into
everything; and Russ from somewhere near Calgary –
not sure what his job was but he was an outstanding
mechanic and always got our jeep going after one of
its frequent breakdowns; and now and again various
hangers'-on who fancied a change of scene. What they
all had in common was an assignment with Mobil. No
guns involved in the hunting; just cameras.

For months there would be no sightings, then a local
they'd befriended, Anwar, would send out word that the
herd had destroyed virtually a whole village by uproot-
ing banana palms, pineapple plants, leaning on stilted
bamboo homes so that they collapsed. The locals weren't
as enamoured of the elephants as the expats. However,
Anwar always seemed to enjoy his role as guide, track-
ing the movements of the herd. When my husband first
met him, he and his family were living in a one-room
shack provided as part of a re-settlement programme.
Java, the main island in Indonesia, is very overcrowded,

and the government had re-distributed the population somewhat by moving a few families to the North Sumatran jungle. By the time we left, he had earned enough from his guiding activities to extend his living quarters considerably and purchase a few animals, plant a few crops. In Provence, we have a photograph of him in our gallery, clad in his usual garb of shorts and trusty black Wellingtons.

On our doorstep was the beach, a long cove of white sand, with sailing in company-owned Hobby Cats (catamarans) readily available every weekend. Even the sailing was easy – the boat-master rigged all the boats, ready to be pushed off from shore as soon as you arrived. A sailing regatta added a little more excitement. The idea was to sail down the coast for about twenty land miles, then sail back to Pioneer Camp Beach. On the trial run, with the sun shining and perfect conditions, it had taken about two hours. My husband and his co-crew, Doug, a six foot four Texan, set off confidently. The sea was relatively calm and the overcast sky meant less chance of sunstroke. However, a few miles into the race, storm clouds gathered. Soon, the sea was raging, huge waves lashing the fragile craft. The Hobby Cat turned over, the mast pointing straight down to the sea-bed, and despite their valiant efforts, they were unable to right the craft. They struggled for hours. They despaired of ever finishing the race, of even making it to safety. Luckily, they were blown in to shore, although not 'our' friendly shore, and they landed close to a small village. Doug was left to guard the expensive boat, while my husband walked to the road, hitched two lifts, on a motorbike and a bus, and returned to the rescue in his jeep. Unfortunately, his attached boat trailer couldn't navigate the fish farms which separated the boat from the village and road. Undaunted, they persuaded some villagers to lift the heavy vessel over the obstacles and hitch it to the trailer.

Meanwhile, I was far away on a trip to Singapore, and I would have been oblivious of the drama unfolding if well-meaning 'sailing widows' hadn't kept me up to date with hourly bulletins on the lost at sea saga. Some of the sailors had been rescued by other craft; some had made it safely to the finishing line, although about five hours late. Amazingly, no lives were lost, but it was a very worrying time for everyone. For several hours, I feared I might become a real sailing widow. After this harrowing event, my husband lost a little of his enthusiasm for sailing.

People vied with each other to provide the best dinner parties. What was difficult was pinning people down to a date, getting them to commit. Sometimes it seemed as if people were holding back, waiting to see if a better offer materialised. And the agonising over why you hadn't been invited to a certain party . . . It certainly took a lot of effort to source the ingredients, especially if serving meat, but the fisherman arrived on our doorstep twice a week with his latest catch of swordfish, red and white snapper, giant prawns and lobster. At least, he did before he discovered that building mosquito-proof, open porches on to our new houses was a lot more lucrative than fishing. I learned how to clean lobster and cook it – a terrifying experience as I plunged the live lobsters into the pot of boiling water and watched the pot lid move as they struggled to escape their fate. I soon learned that placing them in the freezer for a short while before cooking stunned them and seemed kinder. Think of this next time you cook lobster! Actually, how often do you get the opportunity to cook lobster? It's so expensive in every other country that I've been to.

Kathi visited us recently in Provence and reminded me of the Indonesian tabletop we shared in Indonesia. "Do you remember that we used to get our gardeners and maids to carry the large wooden table extension between our two houses?" Of course I did. How else could I have held sit-down dinners for sixteen people! It was delicately balanced on top of the regular sized rattan dining table. Goodness knows what the locals must have thought of our antics. We didn't have shops, but you could have anything made up in the local bazaar, as long as you provided a drawing or a garment to copy. The ingénue actress in an amateur dramatics Noel Coward play wore a copy of a drop-waist Chanel dress belonging to my stylish, elegant good friend and next door neighbour, Yolanda. We've remained good friends, visiting each other in the US and the UK. When my husband went on assignment to Houston, Yolanda was living there and I saw her every few weeks. Like me, she didn't like Houston much, but she was making the most of it, and that's what most expat wives do. They support their husbands who are there to do a job and find something to do that interests them. Yolanda is always immaculately groomed and beautifully dressed – not like me at all. When I shared a room with her in a Singapore hotel after a spell in hospital, I watched in awe as she pressed every item of our clothing with a travel iron and polished all the shoes before we could venture outside. We share a love of movies and reading and e-mail each other with recommendations.

While living in Sumatra, we were always having parties, most of them based on a theme, necessitating fancy-dress. I hear you cringe – me too. Normally, I wouldn't be seen dead dressed up as a cowgirl for a Fourth of July party. Actually, I rarely go to a fancy dress party – not really my thing. In our picture gallery in Provence, we have a photograph of my daughter wearing a red bandana and an old straw cowboy hat purchased from somewhere visited in my husband's youth. You must understand – we celebrated **everything** in our community – the Royal Wedding (Prince Andrew and Sarah Ferguson), Chinese New Year, Valentine's Day, Canadian Trappers' Day, Cinco de Mayo, the Fourth of July, Oktoberfest, Canadian and American Thanksgiving, and of course Christmas and New Year. And these are only the ones I can remember. Expats depend on each other for emotional support and this enthusiastic celebration of national holidays is part of that. The Fourth of July should have been etched on our memories, however, years later, while working on another project, my husband phoned the States from the UK with an urgent query. The phone rang and rang and eventually was picked up. "Where is everyone?" my husband asked tetchily. "Is it a holiday or something?" "Sir, everyone's off celebrating the Fourth of July, Independence Day."

How can you celebrate a British Royal Wedding on the edge of an Indonesian jungle? Easy. All it needs is a bit of imagination and time, and we had plenty of that. Over the few days before the wedding appeared a mock-up of a London double-decker bus. Elaborate invitations were designed and distributed (by hand of course) and children were instructed to assemble at the snack bar at ten thirty a.m. wearing the specially commissioned tee-shirts. The sizing of these was rather on the generous side, so some ended up looking more like mini-dresses or nightshirts. The Royal Coach drew up, driven by a fully costumed Beefeater, and everyone was transported to the venue in great style. There was something for everyone that day: a Treasure Hunt, coconut shies, a Swap Shop where you could exchange your old rubbish for someone else's, and huge quantities of British food and drink, including a wedding cake. The 'bride', wearing traditional white, cut the cake and the main entertainments commenced.

Sounds mad, doesn't it? But it wasn't as mad as celebrating Canadian Trappers' Day in the boiling hot sun of June. Now, as you know, Canada is renowned for its snow. Maybe there isn't any snow in high summer, but these festivities included sledge races. Nancy, a retired teacher living in Sunriver, Oregon, who visited us in Provence during Easter 2003, was reminiscing after a few glasses of Gigondas wine: "Do you remember when I had to sit on the wooden sledge, dressed in my maple leaf T-shirt, and be pulled along in a race by two huge rugby players?" Of course we did! Not many people have such memories to keep them going in their old age. They must have been short of Canadians that day as Nancy is from California. At the same event, there was a log-chopping contest, and best of all, the chicken-catching contest. Whether these events are actually part of a genuine Canadian Trappers' Day celebration I've never been able to find out. Perhaps there isn't even such a celebration? The chickens were let loose and then grown men raced to catch the squawking and terrified birds and push them into a sack. As the young Americans and Canadians present were heard to say: "Gross!" I agreed with them – Horrific! How cruel! Unbelievable! I used my role as editor of the local newspaper to start up a Chicken Protection Society. We created cardboard badges and wrote spoof 'disgusted of Lhokseumawe' letters. These ran for weeks and the local headmaster, Nancy's husband, Ted, (I think the chicken-catching contest was his idea) took it all very seriously and eventually gave me a typed apology to be placed prominently in the newspaper the following week. Only eighteen years after the event did I pluck up the courage to tell him that I'd made all the letters up – there had been no indignant letters.

We miss Ted. Sadly, a few months before his wife Nancy visited us, Ted was killed in an ambush of a convoy of teachers (including his wife) headed for a picnic near the huge US owned Grasberg gold mine in Papua New Guinea. One other American was killed and six very badly injured. Ted and Nancy had only arrived three weeks earlier for Ted to take up a position of Principal at the international school. It was a sad loss for everyone as Ted had given so much of himself to any community in which he lived. My husband mourned losing one of his closest friends and fellow elephant hunter. Ted would have appreciated that he influenced American foreign policy. The incident became the biggest impediment to any further military aid between Indonesia and the US. It wasn't until November 2006, when the main separatist rebel perpetrator was given life imprisonment and his accomplices seven years, that the matter was finally resolved.

Recently, I was reminiscing with my co-editor of the Sumatran company newspaper, Laura, who was visiting us in London from Houston. "Do you think people guessed that on a slow news week we made up a lot of the 'news'?" I don't think they ever did. Only on visits to Singapore or Jakarta did people get a chance to read world-class newspapers and I think we provided a welcome service in this remote community. We produced the English section of the rag which was also read by many Indonesians. I suppose it gave them some sort of insight into expat life, given a rather positive slant. A critical Czech-Canadian reader, Hana, recently arrived, asked me, "Do you have to put such a positive slant on every little committee meeting? Every fund-raising party held?" I think I did. It kept up morale and attracted funds for our needy causes. We became friends and remain so, although when Hana visited us in London last summer we hadn't met up for thirteen years. Yet it seemed like we'd just talked yesterday. I've found that friends made during my years as a mobile wife usually remain friends. She now lives in St John's, Newfoundland, where they have serious snow.

Trappers' Day was followed by the Fourth of July celebrations. It made sense. The expat community was made up of many different nationalities, with Americans in the majority. What didn't make sense was that I, a Brit who had never been to such a celebration, was asked to organise it. No problem. I honed my strong delegation skills over the next few weeks which were to stand me in good stead when I returned to civilisation and the work-force. At any celebration there should be dancing and I quickly delegated the light of feet to teach groups of ladies, including Indonesians, the Cotton-Eyed Joe and the Texas Two-Step. Someone must have given me these names, but I'd never seen them performed. Food was to be catered: the usual hamburgers, hotdogs, sweet corn, gumbo, and barbecued beans – things people missed from back home. Someone else suggested that we have a Casino Evening, so the Wet Bar was transformed into Las Vegas for the evening. The invitations requested Black Tie (remember, this is the tropics) and the directive was interpreted in a variety of interesting ways. No-one escaped. The Hostess (me – coerced) equipped those who arrived minus a tie with a fetching piece of black ribbon, to be worn round the neck *bola* style. All the usual games such as Black Jack and Roulette were there and the croupiers, looking very patriotic in their outfits of red, white and blue, dealt the cards and spun the wheel as though they'd been born to it. Actually, only two of them could claim to be American, and there had been some frantic, last minute tuition in shuffling the cards, but the results were very impressive. Lots of money – Monopoly money fortunately – was lost and won, there were prizes for the most original costumes, and everyone received a commemorative Fourth of July tee shirt. I've still got mine – it brings back happy memories.

I've also got great memories of weekend forays into the jungle. Actually, I went out only a handful of times, desperate to see wild elephants. This required rising literally at dawn. My interest in wildlife had been stimulated but never completely satisfied by a steady diet of quality BBC television programmes. The opportunity of a first-hand experience seemed too good to pass up. Months before, my husband and a few friends had taken to going out exploring every Saturday in the old American jeep that I drove during the week. It was like a tank; when I saw a corner looming up fifty metres ahead, I would begin frantically to turn the wheel. However, I relished the independence it gave me. Every day, I had eager 'drivers' knocking at my door: "Missus want a driver? I'm very good. Very experienced. No accidents." Even though our company would have paid for a driver, I didn't want one. Many of these men had been driving for a very short time. They were more used to riding on oxen or donkeys or bicycles. The roads were almost traffic-free, but driving could be hazardous, owing, I suppose, to the inexperience of the drivers. How had they ever passed a driving test? Probably the way I'd passed mine.

When I first arrived, I had made friends quickly with Thelma, a South American as determined and independently minded as myself. We decided to apply for our driving permit. "It is very unusual. Never before. Ladies don't drive," we were told firmly. Nothing daunted, we proceeded to pursue the licence. Someone reluctantly drove us to the nearby town where our fingerprints were taken – a very messy business this as each finger was rolled in black ink, with nothing provided to clean away the mess. Then, we were taken upstairs to a waiting room and handed about twenty pages of illustrated road signs. "Will be back in ten minutes, said our examiner cheerfully." Well, we hadn't expected this. Our knowledge of Bahasa Indonesian was basic, and our knowledge of most of these road signs was almost non-existent. So surely it would be hazardous for us to drive? Not at all. In our area, I only ever saw three of these signs. Perhaps the others existed in sophisticated Jakarta? At first, we were horrified, then the humour of the situation asserted itself and we laughed and laughed. As promised, the examiner returned and said: "You understand all signs? Good. Please write signature at bottom of every page to show this, please." With a sense of relief, this we duly did. We never did receive our driving permits; however, as we'd passed the test, we drove confidently from that day onwards. In all honesty, there weren't many places to drive to, and the company would have provided a driver for any expeditions, however, we relished our new-found independence.

The four-wheel drive jeep was ideal for hunting elephants, with dreams of shooting the perfect picture, or maybe even spotting one of the rare, endangered Sumatran tigers. Locals are tempted to ensnare the precious tigers as rich foreigners are eager to pay up to £5,500 for a tiger skin rug. Tiger teeth alone can be sold for a healthy sum to expats as souvenirs. Even the penis, prized in Chinese medicine, can find a buyer. Game spotting wasn't easy; you could travel for miles, months without spotting anything more significant than a monkey or a wild pig. However, on my first trip out we got lucky. From the start we had a growing awareness that elephants were in the vicinity. As our eyes became more focused and practised in the dark jungle, we were able to spot their trails, see where they had spent the night, their droppings, where they had fed. We could gauge their numbers and size from footprints and where they had rubbed themselves against trees, and their awesome strength from broken trees and *kampong* huts nonchalantly pushed over as they sauntered past. As you can imagine, the villagers living in the *kampongs* were not too keen on the elephants that frequently destroyed everything in their path.

A successful sighting did not come easy and my husband had been searching for the elusive elephants for five months. Even after enlisting the help of a local guide,

Anwar, he was having little success. But his luck changed. Anwar got word to us that a herd of females had been spotted in a patch of primary jungle off the Pipeline Road, in the general direction of the village of Mbang.

By this time we had become well-known for our interest in the elephant, or *gajah*, but this first sighting would have been impossible without local knowledge and expertise. We learned from locals that elephants form a matriarchal society, with the males either solitary or in pairs following the female group. In this area, the female group consisted of about thirty elephants. Viewings were made difficult as they never seemed to move in a consistent direction. One theory is that they move into the wind and change direction with the wind. Also, they seem drawn by memories of good, easy feeding and return to wreak more damage on once-visited villages.

Big though they are, elephants are difficult to see and photograph clearly in dense, virgin rainforest. Sometimes, we have been so close that we could see the trees shake and hear the elephants' stomachs rumbling, yet we never caught a glimpse. Perseverance paid off and I got lucky. After a gruelling hike as we followed tracks through the jungle, we spotted the two males from the herd standing quietly on their own, munching on one of their favourite snacks, bamboo. The guide motioned us to silence and we crouched for about ten minutes watching them. It really was a most amazing experience and the ensuing photograph takes pride of place in our gallery in the house in Provence. This photograph also won first prize in the Lhokseumawe photographic competition and I had the honour of presenting the prize to the winner, my husband.

One of the most interesting sightings – I wasn't present but have heard the story so many times that sometimes I believe that I was – was of three female elephants lying on their sides, sleeping. If they sleep, elephants usually do it standing up, so this was a rare viewing. Unfortunately, they sensed the watchers and woke up. My husband lived to tell the tale, but he was lucky. He survived by throwing himself under a huge, hollowed, fallen log, and admits that he trembled there as the disturbed elephants trumpeted over the log and crashed into the jungle.

It didn't put him off the jungle expeditions, but the intrepid hunters almost got more than they'd bargained for when a huge King Cobra – estimates ranged from 10 – 20 feet depending on the eyesight/ petrifaction of the onlooker – reared up in front of them. It showed that it meant business by spreading its fan-like hood. True to form, the trio took time to focus their lenses and 'shoot' the snake in the act. This is fairly typical behaviour. When I spotted what I took to be a small black snake marooned on our living room floor, my husband told me not to move or make a sound. He then proceeded to fetch his tripod, set it up, attach the camera and appropriate lens and shoot away. Only after he had exhausted all photographic possibilities did he examine the 'snake' at close range. In fact, it was a harmless salamander-type creature, but it **might** have been a dangerous snake. In the case of the cobra, amazed by the performance of its foes, it lost its nerve and fled.

Another less scary encounter with a snake happened a few months later. In a jungle clearing, we came across a group of villagers with a large python in a rattan basket. On enquiring, we were informed that they had captured the snake and were taking it to Medan, a ten-hour car journey away, where they had a Chinese buyer. Apparently, it was considered by the Chinese to be a delicacy and they expected to get a good price. We matched the price and rescued the snake. It ended up in the Science laboratory for a short time where it was fed on live mice bred for the purpose. More outrage, more 'disgusted' letters in the local newspaper, and as far as I know it is still enjoying old age in the Sumatran jungle to which it was returned.

Our experience with snakes came in handy in the summer of 2004, in Provence. My husband was just about to place some recently purchased wine in the wine rack, situated in the laundry (not the best place, we know). Out of the corner of his eye he caught sight of a smallish grey-green snake with vivid markings, coiled nonchalantly round the metal rack. Typically, he took the time to come upstairs to tell me about it, and to fetch the camera. More sensibly, he also picked up his trusty gardening gauntlets, long-nosed pliers, and a serious Bowie-type knife. Two photos duly taken, he grasped the snake behind the head with the pliers, lunged at it with the knife, and stood well back from the flickering, forked tongue, the hissing and spluttering. In slow motion, the snake unfurled itself and dropped to the floor. Just two days earlier, I had drawn his attention to an illustrated article in *The Daily Telegraph* about a Brit in France who had been bitten by a viper and had almost died of analytic shock. We'd paid particular attention to the markings of this viper, and the snake in the laundry looked exactly like it! Gingerly, the comatose serpent, dripping blood from its pale underbelly, was carried outside to a waste piece of ground. When he went back later to check on the snake, it was nowhere to be found.

Neighbours in the village pooh-poohed our story. "No vipers in this area. Maybe on the slopes of Mont Ventoux . . . "However, we were convinced. Next day, I described the snake in detail to the local *pharmaciste* when I went to purchase an anti-venom snake kit. "*Oui, c'est une vipère*," she confirmed. She had piles of these kits displayed prominently at the front of the counter, with a clear picture of *une vipère*. Identical to our snake! If there are no vipers in the area, why such precautions . . . ? "I'll take one of those, please."

We surmised that the snake must have slithered in through a recently made hole in the wall of the laundry, so this was speedily plastered over. From time to time, it's good to look at the photos of the viper, but we'd rather not have any more hissing snakes in the house. Not all snakes can be charmed. The only memento is a few, miniscule drops of blood on the floor, beside the wine rack. Most people would assume that they are drops of spilled red wine.

Our dream while in Indonesia was to see a Sumatran tiger, a much endangered species; there are probably only about four hundred which have survived in the gradually disappearing rainforest. When we arrived in Sumatra, we could drive for ten minutes and be in virgin rainforest. When we left, as a result of over-enthusiastic logging, the journey took forty-five minutes. We had heard stories from Alex, one of the old-timers, about seeing a tiger draped over the oil pipeline at the side of the road, nonchalantly sun-bathing. No photos, but sensible men swore to it. While we were living in Sumatra, a professional photographer working in the area to obtain material for a book had set up cameras all over the jungle and enlisted the help of villagers. Eventually, he got his picture, of a startled, open-mouthed tiger. The Sumatran tiger is much smaller than its relatives, but I wouldn't like to encounter one face to face. On our walks, we smelled the spoor of tiger on many occasions and spotted telltale tracks. However, the nearest we got to a tiger was taking a plaster cast of a paw print, surprisingly large. Oh, and we've seen one in Regent's Park Zoo – smaller than I had imagined.

Yes, life was never dull in Sumatra, and if you fancied a change of scene, travel was relatively easy and the time was available. At the beginning of 1986, my attempts to visit Kashmir thwarted by a harsh winter and a frozen lake, I made a short trip to Nepal. I vaguely remembered that this was the country where thousands of Tibetans had fled after the takeover of Tibet by the Chinese. As a child, I had been enthralled by the vision portrayed in *Seven Years in Tibet*, and it was years later before someone thought to tell me that things were very different now and the Dalai Lama was in fact living in exile in India. I had been brought down further to earth in recent times by reading *Return to Tibet* where the author bemoaned the vast changes that had taken place in his adopted country. Of the original 3,800 monasteries in Lhasa, only 13 remain. It seemed likely that I would find my 'traditional' Tibetans in Nepal rather than Tibet itself.

Kathmandu is a fascinating place – I could have sat in Durbar Square all day just watching life go on around me. The hippies had been moved on or smartened up, but the place was alive with a kaleidoscope of colour and sound. On every corner were men carrying trees of flutes, playing such well-known local favourites as *Frère Jacques* and *London Bridge is Falling Down*. I don't suppose they would have been there at all but for the tourists, however, they seemed to belong. Every so often, I was pestered by touts trying to sell me the usual 'genuine antiques' of erotic sculptures, clearly made very recently if not that very morning. Others were anxious to change money for me (foreign currency is highly regarded) or supply me with 'stick'. Nepal may have been cleaned up, but drugs of every kind were very readily available. The government discourages with harsh penalties, however, it is difficult to discover crops of hashish and opium growing in the steep, remote terrain.

Tibetans were everywhere, selling their brightly coloured woollens of yak hair, paintings, bells, scarves and vivid carpets, or just sitting in groups, smoking huge, fat cigarettes and passing the time of day. They looked contented. The Nepalese Government, I was told, had tried to help them by establishing refugee villages, setting up schools and health centres, allowing them to become citizens after twelve years. Will they ever return to Tibet? Well, as far as I know, they haven't as yet. Probably their life in Nepal is a more comfortable existence and here they are allowed to worship freely at an abundance of temples. I read an article very recently which said that even the conquering Chinese were unhappy living in the fairly basic conditions in Tibet. And China's rise as a global power has made Tibet's fight for independence less appealing to the western world. British Prime Minister Tony Blair has not met the Dalai Lama since 1999, however, Prince Charles made the effort on a recent visit here; French President Jacques Chirac has not met the Dalai Lama since 1998; and in

Germany, Chancellor Gerhard Schroder has never met him. Even Nepal seems to be changing its policy of tolerance and now hands over escapees to the custody of the Chinese embassy in Kathmandu.

The Buddhist temples were a surprise. The previous summer I had holidayed in Thailand and thought I'd seen every variation of temple, *wat* and Buddha – but these were different. Each *stupa* is painted with all-seeing eyes that seem to follow you wherever you go. Floating out from the top of the tower are Tibetan prayer-flags of all shapes and colours, carrying supplications upwards. Round the base of the *stupa* are prayer wheels, constantly in motion as people turn them; each one contains prayers for the rotator's salvation. Tibetan women, dressed warmly in padded jackets and bright woollen skirts, their long braids interwoven with red wool and beads, walk round and round the temple, whirling the prayer wheels, counting off their 'rounds' on something similar to a rosary. They endeavour to circle the *stupa* 107 times, an auspicious number. Inside, an elderly Tibetan man was prostrating himself on the cold, marble floor in front of the revered Buddha. He too seemed to be striving for the magic number and I admired his vitality and obvious faith. Later that day, I bought a minutely detailed *Tangka,* depicting the path to Enlightenment. A *Tangka* is a scroll painting of scared images, used for meditation and it often takes years to complete. I feel at peace when I look at it. I'd felt the same after the flight I took over Everest; a touristy thing to do, but very special. It made me feel as though I could reach out and touch the snowy peak. Everyone on board was silent as we drifted past, overawed by the beauty, the majesty, the stillness.

People of different religions seem to live tolerantly here, a Buddhist temple juxtaposing with a Hindu one. They seem to accept that not everyone is the same: the Nepalese themselves come from fourteen different tribes.

I returned again and again to Durbar Square, the hub of activity. I watched the brightly painted, two-sided 'devil' puppets bobbing up and down. They looked rather like condemned men waiting for a reprieve and I rescued two of them. Then I visited the palace of the Kumaris, the Living Goddess, a rather dark, eerie building in the Square where the re-incarnation of a goddess is kept incarcerated, appearing at an upstairs window when summoned. A very young girl is chosen after numerous rigorous initiation tests and she reigns until she first lets blood. The goddess's feet are not allowed to touch the ground; so on the rare occasion when she leaves the palace, she is carried. The small, heavily kohled face which appeared at the window looked very sad – it didn't seem much of a life for any four year old.

On my last day, I sampled what most people come to Nepal for – a trek. Mine was a very gentle mini-trek over a very small mountain and down the other side. The clear, unpolluted air and the views were magnificent. Nepal certainly is an awe-inspiring, magical place. I only really got a taste of it during my short stay there, but one day I'll go back to sample more of life at the top of the world.

Pearl of the Orient: Not Quite *Raffles*

We always seemed to be planning the next holiday.
Sumatra was considered a hardship posting, difficult to
believe sometimes surrounded by the lush, tropical vegetation. At other times, it felt very remote from anywhere. Singapore looks very close on the map, however,
it required two road journeys and two plane rides, in total at least seven hours of travelling in very hot, humid
temperatures to reach civilisation. So, breaks for R &
R, rest and recuperation, were frequent. Travel within
Sumatra was difficult – no longer any trains; very few
roads; and even fewer internal airports. We'd visited
Singapore so many times, sometimes just for the weekend, to pick up our children arriving from Boarding
School, so we decided as a change to have a break in

Penang, off the north-west coast of Malaysia. Again, very close indeed on the map, but forty minutes by plane from Singapore. Penang, the first British settlement on the Malay peninsula, is a popular holiday destinations; only ten miles wide and twenty miles long, a perfect size to explore on a short break. It's in the north of the peninsula and strangely consists of one part island and one part mainland, connected by an eight-mile bridge which is the longest in the world.

We were attracted to Penang by its British colonial heritage. In 1786, a settlement was established to provide Britain with a trading and military base east of India. It helped to protect the Straits of Malacca. We'd loved what we'd seen of India, and we'd read that Penang is the British Raj in miniature. You have the imposing Fort Cornwallis for defence never put to the test; nearby, the handsome colonial architecture of banks, trading firms and government buildings. Add to that an Anglican church, a cathedral, and a *padang* which boasted two cricket clubs and you have the basic pattern of the Empire, created in grand form in Delhi, Calcutta, Bombay, Hong Kong and Singapore.

On our trips to Singapore, we never tired of visiting *Raffles*, so we were tempted to stay in the sister hotel, the *E & O* (*Eastern and Oriental*). Like *Raffles*, it had been built and managed by the Armenian Sarkie brothers, along with the *Strand Hotel* in Rangoon, Burma, or Myanmar as it is now known. The previous year, we'd tried to visit Burma, but at that time visas were in short supply and we didn't luck out and get allocated one of the few hundred on offer.

Friends decided to come along. Except, they were hesitant about committing to the *E & O*. We'd been able to obtain very little information about the hotel. All we knew was that it had been grand in its heyday, the 1930's, and the room rate was very attractive. Not convinced, our friends plumped for a modern hotel on *Batu Ferringhi Beach*, several miles from our base in the capital, Georgetown.

At the airport, we separated, arranging to meet up in two days' time. They would link up with us in Georgetown and we would join them for a day at the beach. The colonial past was evident as soon as we unloaded at the hotel: the doorman, and the porter standing behind him, were dressed in pith helmet, knee-high socks, uniform complete with gold epaulettes, white gloves, and a welcoming smile. True, the exterior of the *E & O* was a trifle shabby, the brown paint peeling, the walls a little pitted. The interior was even shabbier, however, it was easy to imagine how grand it had once been when you glanced up at the domed lobby and sweeping staircase. Reception was warm; occupancy rate was low at the moment, so we could have an upgraded sea-view suite for the price of the standard room we'd paid for.

The suite was huge, cavernous, more like a ballroom. In addition to the substantial bed draped in muslin mosquito netting, we had two cavernous, red velvet covered sofas, two matching armchairs and several coffee tables. The *pièce de resistance* was the enormous, cast-iron, claw-footed bath standing in the middle of the bathroom which was bigger than most people's bedrooms. What splendour! To take advantage of the sea-views and palm- fringed terrace and promenade, we re-configured the furniture, moving it to face the French windows which opened on to a wrought iron balcony and a cooling sea breeze. I'd been a bit worried about the apparent lack of air-conditioning, but the open windows and ceiling fans would be fine.

Gradually, we learned some of the hotel's history. It had been the premier hotel of its time, boasting more than a hundred rooms, baths with hot and cold water and individual telephone lines, unheard of luxuries. The hotel was the social playground for scores of rich people. The creaking lift with metal gates pulled across by the porter who'd carried the bags is the oldest Otis lift in Malaysia – easy to believe. The ballroom once had been very grand. Now, the mirrors were mottled and hazy, the beautiful ornate cornicing dusty and incomplete. The ballroom was being used as a storage room for excess furniture and cardboard boxes of supplies. However, it wasn't difficult to imagine people in their evening finery waltzing around the polished floor, the mirrors and chandeliers gleaming. Years later, we saw the movie, *The King and I*, starring Jodie Foster as Anna, the governess. Ostensibly set in Siam (Thailand), it was actually shot in Penang, some of the scenes in this ballroom and on the vast terrace outside our bedroom window. The dark, wooden-panelled hotel bar also had a story to tell. The walls were covered in framed sepia photographs of proud colonials holding aloft prize fish, or standing erect with rifle, one foot proudly resting on a dead tiger. They transported you to another world, where conservation of endangered species was yet unheard of.

We explored Georgetown by trishaw, pedalled by a very fit young Malay who was extremely knowledgeable about the history of his birthplace. Penang, the oldest settlement in Malaysia, was founded by Sir Francis Light, who also founded Adelaide, in Australia, where he lived for two years. We visited the cemetery where he is buried. Perhaps a morbid thing to do while on holiday, but something we're fond of doing in each country we visit. You can learn a lot by reading tombstones: 'Mary Agnes McKenzie, died aged 22 on the voyage out from England'; 'George James Smith, died aged 3 months of dysentery'. It was a whole social history and very poignant. Life was hard for the settlers and many did not survive the journey out, the harsh climate and malaria. A high, stone wall separated one section of the cemetery from the other. We soon realised that the largest section was where the Protestants were buried, separated from the Catholics, even in death.

We cycled past beautiful colonial mansions, ornate with carvings and tiles, which once housed prominent European families or wealthy Chinese traders. Most of the buildings in the town remained unchanged; the red post-boxes inscribed 'VR' were still in daily use. Penang is a real melting pot of diverse cultures: Chinese temples where among the clouds of incense worshippers juggled fortune sticks to foretell their future; Sikh temples; Hindu temples; Buddhist wats; mosques; a large Anglican church; and the Catholic cathedral still used mostly by the large Eurasian population descended from the colonialists. The streets along which we rode reflected the British past: Jalan Farquhar, Jalan Macalister, Jalan Logan and Jalan Dunn. We felt quite at home.

Later, we took the thirty minute ride on the funicular railway to the top of Penang Hill to admire the town laid out below, the lush vegetation. During colonial times, we were told, British people were carried up and down the 2730 foot hill in sedan chairs mounted on bamboo poles. Fine for passengers; exhausting for the carriers. It was cooler up here. Good to get away from the steaming temperatures in town.

Another highlight was the temple of the Azure Clouds where, according to local mythology, venomous vipers had suddenly appeared on its completion in 1850. The snakes have remained ever since, hundreds of them, coiled in writhing heaps, draped sinuously over fountains, statues and shrines. The air was full of incense which drugs the snakes and renders them harmless – allegedly.

We found Georgetown, and the *E & O*, charming. So too did our friends when they paid us a visit, drank planters' punch in the bar and ate the excellent buffet in the faded splendour of the hotel dining room, of sinus-clearing Malay curries, chicken *satay* with thick peanut sauce and freshly caught seafood. The next evening, we dined in their beach hotel, on *Batu Ferringhi*. The bar boasted 'Tudor charm and tradition'. We had a choice of eating in the Japanese restaurant or the European Fine Dining Room. We plumped for the latter – sufficiently bizarre. The restaurant was over air-conditioned, formal ("Gentlemen must wear jackets in the dining rooms"), the central table decorated with a dripping ice-sculpture in the shape of a swan. The succulent, imported steak **was** delicious, however, our friends rated our authentic experience of the previous evening the better meal. They were quite envious of our colonial hotel, the faded splendour.

We brought home an old, traditional, tiered wedding basket, modelled on a *tiffin* carrier (a metal or bamboo tiered food transporter), where a bride would once have stored her wedding trousseau. It makes an excellent sewing basket. In the foyer of the hotel,

I bought a logoed key-ring, used for our front door key in Provence, and some old dinner plates, some chipped, decorated with the faded maroon livery of the E & O, a lovely memento. I like to think of the myriads of colonials who would have dined off these plates in the hotel's heyday.

Browsing the Internet recently, I came across an advertisement for our charming hotel. Headed '*The Eastern and Oriental Hotel*: a return to elegance', it showed a gleaming white edifice framed by waving palm trees and described the major restoration and refurbishment which had cost RM 75 million (Malaysian *ringgits*). The hotel looked magnificent, a match for Singapore's *Raffles*, but we preferred the old, nostalgic E & O.

Thailand: The Golden Triangle

In between living in Indonesia and Australia, we had a holiday in Thailand. Today, it sometimes seems as if everyone and his dog have visited Thailand. It is a favourite destination for young people on their gap year. They backpack round the crossroads of South East Asia and meet up with all their old school friends, thus missing some of the foreignness of the country.

Twenty years ago, we didn't know anyone who'd travelled to Thailand. We spent a few days in smoggy, trafficclogged Bangkok, overdosing on temples. Years later, on the way home from working non-stop for six months straight in Singapore, we enjoyed an idyllic two week holiday on the Thai island of Phuket: sun, sea, beach, canoeing, Hemingway deep-sea fishing – and no visits to temples. In Bangkok, it was easier to travel on the river, teeming with life, and death. It was just as the travel guides promised: people were washing themselves and their clothes in the murky waters; brown children were brushing their teeth and smiled and waved as we passed; vendors hawked their fruits and vegetables; and coffin makers hammered at planks of wood. In 1993, on a teaching conference jolly, I saw a seamier side to Bangkok on a pilgrimage to Patpong Road, full of massage parlours, sex shows, escort agencies, pickup coffee shops and brothels. We ended the evening in a restaurant called *Cabbages and Condoms*, run by ex-prostitutes. On closer inspection, the 'flowers' on the table turned out to be brightly coloured condoms. The menu offered such delights as 'Spicy Condom Salad, guaranteed not to cause pregnancy'. No-one was brave enough to try it. In place of an after-dinner mint, we each received a condom flower. Our sole male companion passed on the free vasectomy offered at the clinic next door.

On the visit with my family, what we really wanted to see was the North, the Golden Triangle where Thailand, Myanmar and Laos meet. The area is home to around twenty hill tribes who at that time lived a fairly unspoilt life. We set out for Chiang Rai, about one hundred and fifty kilometres from Bangkok. Doesn't sound much, however, roads were poor and transport even poorer. We went by bus to Fang, on the Burmese border, which has some of the elements of a Wild West frontier town mixed in with the mysteries of the East. Our overriding memory is of lunching in the restaurant next to the landing stage on stringy, grey, tasteless water buffalo. Not an experience I would ever wish to repeat. Any Thai food I've eaten since has been delicious, but on this trip the food was memorably awful, practically inedible. I think that the locals were wary of using too many spices and chillies in the foreigners' dishes. Each dish was blander than the one which had preceded it, and there was an over-abundance of offal, never on our list of favourite foods. Anyway, we hadn't come to Thailand for a gourmet culinary experience.

The Yao tribes live in the mountains around Fang, the women particularly distinctive in their black hats decorated with red woollen pom-poms, their babies strapped to their backs. We visited one of their villages where the people had been encouraged by the government to grow crops of potatoes, corn, coffee, tea and garlic and to keep chickens and pigs. Otherwise, the tribes people survived by growing and selling opium. The village seemed very poor and dirty; people were scratching a living. I'm very anti-drugs, yet I could understand the people's resistance to relinquishing their lucrative poppy crops. Obviously, there was still plenty of opium around. Some of the older members of the community, perhaps hardened addicts, were openly smoking pipes of opium. We were offered a pipe, still warm, for a few *baht*.

Many of the tribes were prospering, aided by government subsidies and a sizeable tribal development programme. When we visited the Red Karen tribe, somewhere between Chiang Mai and Chiang Rai, the village seemed much more prosperous. The Karens are of Tibetan-Burmese origin and many of them are Christian. For a long time, the main contact between the hill tribes and the outside world was the missionaries, mostly Americans. They elected to go and work among them, learning their languages, and often living as much as five days' walk from the nearest civilisation. Here too, the women wore the more colourful dress: elaborate striped head cloths; patterned red woven skirts; strings of black beads; and novel bracelets made of shirt buttons. Their distinctive weavings and handicrafts have become popular in Bangkok and are exported abroad, providing them with another income. To further educate the tribes people about the dangers of opium, the Border patrol police have helped to build schools in the villages.

To get to Chiang Rai, the easiest route seemed to be by river, so we hired a boat for the five hour journey down the Mekong River. This journey proved to be one of our most memorable. The craft looked very fragile, a narrow longboat with a basic motor, steered by the boatman. Gingerly, we stepped in. I was next to the boatman who didn't exactly reassure me by constantly bailing water from the bottom of the boat. Most of this seemed to end up being poured over my leg, so I was wet for the whole trip. In Provence, we have a photograph on the wall of my daughter, aged twelve, looking absolutely miserable, peeping from a hooded waterproof cape solicitously provided by the boatman. He seemed to run out of capes before reaching me.

A few minutes into the journey, we stopped at a checkpoint and picked up a bare-breasted soldier, complete with huge machine-gun. He was a scary sight, dressed in combats, beret, bandolier and vivid tattoos. The boatman reassured us: "He is from the Border Patrol. These soldiers are descendants of Chiang Kai-shek's Kuomintang Army who fled China in the 1940's."

He had the explanation so off-pat that he must have been asked about him many times before. But why was he there? Later, we learned that the border is a hive of opium smuggling and the troops are a valiant attempt to seal a porous border. But why was he on our boat? Apparently, the previous week, a party of three Dutch tourists had been attacked on the river by pirates. After being robbed, they were thrown into the river and drowned. We were glad that we didn't know this until after the journey!

My biggest worry was the fast flowing river, teeming with rapids. The boatman was very skilled, scaling each rapid with apparent ease, but it was still pretty scary. I'm not a strong swimmer and I kept eyeing the shore, speculating if I could make it to the bank in case of upset. Later, when I shared my fears with my husband, he said that in his opinion no-one would have survived. On reflection, we were mad to undertake such a dangerous journey, with not a lifejacket or lifebelt anywhere to be seen.

We were all relieved to step out of the boat at Chiang Mai and be whisked by rickshaw to our hotel, the *Wiang Inn*. The rickshaw drivers vied with each other to carry our waif-like daughter, wishing to avoid transporting the hefty adults. The hotel was delightful, built in a traditional style, and the bedrooms were well-equipped. The only rather strange thing was a card in each room, outlining, in both Thai and English, the cost of each item: bedspread 1000 baht; pillowcases 50 baht, bed sheet 300 baht, big handcrafted basket 90 baht, shower curtain 200 baht, water grass (sic) 10 baht – all had a price against them and a dire warning to 'souvenir-minded guests' against removing said items from the room.

Childishly, I removed the card and it now hangs framed in our downstairs loo in London. It always raises a smile.

The town of Chiang Mai is charming and when we visited it seemed to have escaped the blights of modern development and commercialism. We went to the Night Market where we mixed with tribes people identified to us as Lahu, Lisu, Skaw, Blue and White Meo, Red and White Karen. Each group was colourfully and distinctively dressed; each group speaks its own language. Although members of some tribes have embraced Islam, Buddhism or Christianity, most retain strong animist convictions, like the Bataks in Sumatra. They protect their homes and villages with altars, fertility symbols, totems and magic objects to ward off evil spirits. In the evening, we attended a cultural event and watched the various tribes dance their traditional dances and sing to the accompaniment of traditional instruments. It didn't seem in the least touristy. We brought home a set of Thai bagpipes which no-one can figure out how to play.

Our next stop, Chiang Rai, was much larger, more bustling, more developed. We stayed in a very western style hotel and we had great hopes for the food. It was my daughter's birthday. Her brother had been fortunate to celebrate his in Bangkok with a made-to-order birthday cake. It didn't look as though the hotel could manage that, but surely a slice of cake? "You know what I'd really like?" said my daughter plaintively. "Hamburger and chips!" Our children have never favoured junk food, but the restricted, tasteless diet of the past week had obviously got to her. The order was duly made, and the kitchen rustled up a hamburger with onion rings. Not quite chips, but delicious all the same. "It's the best meal I've ever eaten!" was the verdict.

That night, we took the unprecedented step of ordering the 'Western Option' from the extensive menu. We'd all had enough of tasteless, grisly, unidentifiable meat and the ubiquitous sticky rice. I had a Marcel Proust moment as I tucked into the delicious chicken (free range?), carrots and potatoes. Many years later, my daughter amazed us by confiding just how much she had disliked this trip to Northern Thailand. She had been at an age when she didn't appreciate the rather primitive conditions, the appalling food, the cockroaches, and the truly horrendous, life-threatening river trip. Really, what she would have liked was a trip to Disneyland. However, she did choose to major in South Eastern Asia for her Master's Degree at the LSE and her first job was at the Thai Embassy in London. She returned to Bangkok on a harrowing business trip, to interview police about child prostitution and to visit British prisoners, including Sandra Gregory, in the jail affectionately known as the Bangkok Hilton.

Fatchett's Fantasy: Indian Odyssey

Our appetite whetted, a few months later we visited India, with American expat friends Ray and Kathi and their daughter Brenna. This, through a number of misunderstandings, became known as *Fatchett's Fantasy*. I'd travelled to India on my own in 1979, but it was the first trip for everyone else. Living in Sumatra as expats allowed us plenty of time for dreaming and planning. The plan was, on the face of it, not particularly adventurous. We intended to travel round what is popularly called the Golden Triangle route in twelve days, fitting in as much as possible and hopefully gaining an introduction to mystical India. Yes, we wanted to see the Taj Mahal and the

Amber Fort in Jaipur, but my husband also wanted to go on safari at an old maharajah's hunting lodge at Sariska (and perhaps see a tiger at last), and visit the Krishna Temple of the Nimbarkachan sect at Salembah. We were prepared to rough it a bit – no desire to view India from temperature-controlled cocoons – but to avoid too much of an adventure, we took a soft option for our first night in Delhi and asked an Indian friend to book accommodation at a four-star hotel. All appeared to be going well. We'd arrived more or less on schedule and, after a fair bit of haggling, picked up a hired minibus and driver at the airport. They would smooth our way through the bureaucratic layer which everything in India seems to require.

The owner overcame our initial reluctance by offering a trial run; we could have the vehicle and driver for a free, one-day trial to see the sights of Delhi. Seemed like a good deal. Except that the term 'minibus' turned out to be a shade optimistic – more a Del-boy van. Our tallest member of the party – six foot three – clung on for dear life as we hurtled round corners; his feet dangled perilously close to the ground from the swinging rear doors of the vehicle. Definitely non-air-conditioned reality. Even worse, the driver spoke no English, quite unusual in India. He was very obliging and took us to some very off the tourist track places, great for photo opportunities, however, we could have benefited from someone to explain the local colour, relate the history of the faded colonial buildings. When he dropped us at our hotel that evening, we'd already negotiated with the boss for a bigger vehicle, one into which we'd all fit comfortably, and as a bonus he'd thrown in an English speaking guide, his son. This proved to be a shrewd move. Never had we seen such driving as we encountered on the long, arduous journey to Rajasthan. Impossibly crowded buses with passengers and their bundles clinging to the roof; bullocks pulling bulging carts; bicycles decorated with lurid streamers and bells, riders weaving unconcernedly as if protected by a magic cloak. I complain about the drivers in France and Italy who see it as their duty to overtake, regardless of the road conditions, but they're lambs compared to Indian drivers. The son really made our holiday. He was probably in his late thirties, looked like a hippie who'd dropped out and never dropped in again, and was amazingly knowledgeable about local history and customs.

The adventure began when we tried to check into our first hotel. The clerk scanned the hand-written register. "Very sorry, no booking in name of Matchett." How could that be? We'd received a fax in confirmation. The booking clerk was adamant: the hotel was full and we had no booking, therefore we had nowhere to stay. Eventually, losing patience, I turned the hotel register round towards me and ran my finger down the names. *Voila!* Two rooms booked, in the name of Fatchett! It could only be us. Smiles all round and sighs of relief.

On the way to Jaipur, we stayed at the Sariska Palace Hotel, on the edge of a wildlife reserve where my husband hoped that he might finally glimpse a tiger. The journey from Delhi had been a long and arduous scrummage as the driver swerved to avoid overturned cars and lorries, tuk-tuks belching out fumes, camel-drawn carts, totally unconcerned cows, a whole flock of sheep fatalities, and numerous potholes. Factor in the stultifying heat, the 97 per cent humidity, the choking dust, the flies, the overpowering reek of the roadside dung fires and the *bidis* (thin, cheap cigarettes bound together with cotton) smoked non-stop by the driver, the incessant, bellowing horn-blasts, and the grinding poverty of the rural villages we passed, and you can imagine how we were all feeling as we approached Sariska. "Tonight we'll all be staying in a maharajah's palace," promised my husband. "Sheer luxury!" Everyone had his doubts. I imagined that we would round a corner and come upon some semi-ruined hovel with minimal accommodation. But, as we crested a hill, the promised blindingly-white palace floated in to view. It had certainly seen better days, but it rose majestically from the plain and promised a comfortable stay. A haven of tranquillity. Our room was huge, cooled by a punkah-wallah style fan. The only furniture was a giant four-poster bed with richly embellished hangings and a claw-footed bath sitting in the middle of the room. What more could you ask for? Dinner was taken in some style, in the baronial dining hall, where we were watched over by the only other two intrepid diners and a moth-eaten, stuffed tiger. It was the only bad meal we encountered in India: British colonial-style curried egg and cauliflower, followed by tinned fruit and very doubtful, very yellow custard. At dawn, huddled in sweaters and scarves against the freezing temperatures, we set out on a jeep safari with two rangers. We saw lots of wildlife: spotted deer, sambar, wild boar, and great excitement from the rangers when we spotted a rare, fox-like wild dog. However, the twenty two pairs of panthers and the twenty nine sets of tigers eluded us. We were destined again to see merely tracks of tigers at the waterhole. We were a little disappointed, but it was a magical place to stop and refresh ourselves. Recently, I read that poachers had wiped out the entire tiger population at Sariska, so that could explain the dearth of big cats.

We enjoyed scratching the surface of the unhurried pace of rural village life in Rajasthan, avoiding vetted, safe restaurants and recommended emporiums of exploitation, but we were ready for some comfort. You can overdo the non air-conditioned, sweaty reality. When we finally reached the pink city, Jaipur, after many adventures on the way, we tried to bluff our way into the very full, five-star *Jaipur Palace Hotel*. "Perhaps the booking was made in the wrong name – try Fatchett." All to no avail and we ended up spending two nights in a much less salubrious residence. It didn't really matter, as most of our time was spent outdoors, in the bustling, noisy, ginger and cardamom-spicy, astonishingly colourful bazaar where we were draped in garlands of pungent marigolds and persuaded to buy armfuls of coloured plastic bangles and a traditional green and red sari, still used today at Christmas to frame the decorations. Later, we visited the stunning, pink Amber Palace, reached by clinging to the howdah on the back of a garishly decorated elephant.

Sadly, we don't have a commemorative photograph, but in our gallery in Provence, there's a picture of the five of us, posed serenely before the heart-stopping Taj Mahal, just in front of the bench where years later Princess Diana was poignantly photographed alone. Viewers always remark, "Where are all the people? How did you manage to take a photo without getting hundreds of other people in the frame?" With difficulty, but a five a.m. rise and the baksheesh slipped to the custodian of the pulse-racing palace undoubtedly helped.

There's another puzzling photograph in our picture gallery of my family dressed in Indian clothes, my daughter and I sporting a red blessing mark and my husband

and son yellow and white stripes on their foreheads. The backdrop appears to be Christmas tinsel and a gaudy red and green sari. This was, of course, taken at our Indian party. I've mentioned how keen everyone was on dressing up in our expatriate community. As we travelled around India, inevitably the ladies found things to buy. Every time we spotted another must-have, one of the men would groan, "What do you want that for?" "Why, our Indian party, of course!" It started off as a joke, but soon the idea escalated.

By the end of our trip, we'd accumulated made-to-measure Indian clothes, several outfits each – we got a bit carried away – beyond-garish decorations, sticks of incense, lengths of brightly coloured cloth, stick-on *tikas,* the red marks of blessing worn on the forehead, a traditional cooking pot, and a whole bazaar of spices. Everything in our luggage smelled of curry, but that was a small price to pay.

We arranged a planning meeting at our house. Who to invite? How would we word the invitations? Fancy dress, of course. The Indian party was underway. Delivering one hundred invitations by hand is easy when there are so many maids around eager to oblige. Household staff in Indonesia love to chat and gossip with their friends and this would give them plenty to talk about. Ninety-two people accepted the invitation – a bit scary, as we were doing most of the catering. I did farm out the cooking of the rice and *naan* (on the barbecue). Apart from that, we did all the cooking in the weeks before the party. We met again to sample the food – pretty good; I guess the authentic spices helped. I still use some of these recipes today, although we're more likely to nip down to our local Indian restaurant. Except when we're in Provence, of course. No Indian restaurant yet in these parts. I watched Nigel Farrell and Reza in Channel 4's *A Place in the Sun*. There, in the Ardèche, just a bit north of Provence, they had, against all the odds, established an Indian restaurant. However, despite much hard work and the input of Reza's restaurant experience, the business soon folded. French people are very conservative when it comes to foreign food. In the Provençal supermarkets, it's still difficult to source Italian ingredients.

We talked about drinks for the party – pink gin was about the only exotic Indian cocktail we could come up with, and all agreed that this was pretty disgusting. Entertainment would be a continuous slide-show projected on to a large, white sheet, of our numerous holiday slides. I was a little doubtful about this – I had first-hand experience of how boring other people's holiday snapshots can be. Perhaps we needed something else?

Then our friend played his trump card. We would have party games. My heart dropped. If there's one thing I hate more than dressing up, it's games of any sort. In the cold light of day, the outlined games sounded pretty horrendous: a Ghandi speech-making contest; an Indian dancing competition; and, as the finale, a snake-charming competition. Our daughters would greet guests on arrival, decorate their foreheads with a stick-on red *tika* or yellow and white Hari Krishna stripes, and hand out envelopes with details of one of the three competitions. Of course, we would only give these to good sports, born exhibitionists.

I needn't have worried – the non-PC, Pythonesque party games were a smash hit. Everyone had come in Indian dress, some costumes run up in the local market;

others had required a trip to the Indian quarter in Singapore. Picture seven grown men dressed as Ghandi, in imaginative approximations of loin cloths, reciting such unsuitable speeches as *I had a dream, Ask not what you can do for your country,* and *We will fight them on the beaches,* in the persona of Ghandi, with Indian intonations and head rolling. Not very politically correct, I know, but everyone took it in good part, especially so our Indian guests.

The two Indian dancing troupes rivalled anything to come out of Bollywood, however, the funniest competition of the evening turned out to be the snake-charming competition. Two couples took it in turn to be the snake-charmer complete with wooden pipe and his snake, a female companion who had to emerge out of the giant rattan laundry basket we'd bought in the market just for that purpose. In India, every time that we stopped for a meal break, as if by magic a snake charmer and his snake had appeared out of the bushes. The first contestants performed very well; however, it was the second duo that brought the house down. I had been bemused when the beautiful, blonde, statuesque, Scandinavian 'snake' had asked permission to rummage through my drawers and use some of my underwear in her act. All soon became clear. At the first strains of the pipe, a long, sinuous arm pushed up the lid of the basket and began to wave a black lace bra in the air, in a slow, circular motion. Thank goodness she'd chosen something respectable from my drawers! It soon became clear that the snake was doing a striptease, as garment after garment was hurled from the basket. We fell about laughing. Of course, at the end the snake emerged fully clothed, probably much to the disappointment of many of our mesmerised male guests.

A memorable performance. People talked about it for months afterwards. Of course, these two stars won the prize.

The food was also a resounding success. Throughout the evening, we projected hundreds of slides from our trip, danced such traditional Indian dances as the Alabama Two-step, or lolled on the giant cushions we'd borrowed to replace our conventional furniture (which was carried to the house next door). Sweet incense filled the air, marigolds everywhere; and our garish, tinselled wall-hangings looked just right. We'd never repeat it; my idea of a party in England is eight people tops round the dining table, however, our house in Sumatra was enormous, kitchen help was easy to 'borrow' from friends and, most of all, people were really prepared to dress up and risk making a fool of themselves. It was rated the best party ever.

More Dressing-up, Magic and Scorpions

Yes, we have really fond memories of our time as expats in Sumatra. Of course, it took time to adapt to local ways. We learned that the Indonesians are a very gentle, polite people. They always greet you with a friendly "Selamat", reminiscent of the French "Bonjour", so much nicer than entering a shop or office in Britain and being studiously ignored. They are also very aware of rank and it took me a while to understand why my maid would stoop down low when passing anywhere close, one arm extended, almost dragging on the floor. She was showing respect for a 'superior'. It made us feel uncomfortable, but we couldn't dissuade her from the practice. Social occasions could be minefields unless you realised that the most honoured guest would always begin a buffet line. The host was expected to accompany his guest through the line and explain the dishes on offer.

On one memorable occasion, at a local wedding, we were the honoured guests. The mother of the bride was a member of WIC and although I didn't really know her well and had never met her daughter, I was the Vice President of the group and hence regarded as a VIP. I was told that my presence would be regarded as a blessing. The bride and groom, in elaborate national dress, sat enthroned on a raised dais (similar in fact to the thrones of Posh and Becks at their wedding), and I was led to the front of the receiving line to say a few words to the happy couple. The mother kept repeating that she was very honoured that I had accepted the invitation to the wedding. My presence was greatly appreciated. Very humbling.

Another custom that it took a bit of getting used to is the Indonesian view on privacy. Indonesians feel security and comfort in numbers. To them, privacy is a state of mind, not necessarily a physical condition. To be private is equated with being alone, and that is not a desired condition for an Indonesian. Attending an Inter-WIC conference in Jogjakarta, Java, I was looking forward to a spot of quality time. The programme seemed to allow plenty of opportunity for a spot of solo sightseeing or curling up with a novel. But it was not to be. Day and night, we did everything en-masse. I was advised which batik to buy and the best place to buy it. My Indonesian friends took charge of the haggling for the best price, ensuring that I wasn't going to be ripped off. They herded me to the best store for purchasing a *Kain songket*, a heavily embroidered antique, silk, ceremonial cloth or sarong embroidered with thick gold thread. Ironically, this came from Sumatra, but I'd had to come all the way to Java to find one; it now hangs framed in my study at home. We visited Borobudur, one of the world's greatest Buddhist monuments, built some time between 778 and

842 A.D., three hundred years before Cambodia's Angkor Wat, four hundred years before work had begun on the great European cathedrals of Amiens, Lincoln, Chartres and Rheims. By the nineteenth century, it lay in ruins and was restored mostly due to the intervention of Sir Stafford Raffles. It rises majestically from the arid plain, row upon row of cross-legged Buddhas sitting serenely. I would have liked to view the Buddhas in peace, to contemplate this guide to the path of enlightenment. However, my kindly Indonesian hosts kept me closely within their sight at all times, chattering constantly, adjusting their incongruous umbrellas erected to ensure a prized paleness of skin.

In the evening, my co-delegates crowded into my hotel room to chat, show me their purchases and get dressed for our dancing display. This took a while as the Achenese costume is extremely complicated: black silk trousers, *silue Aceh*, decorated with gold embroidery, an inheritance from Islamic South-East Asia; over this a sarong woven with metallic thread, since it is considered most improper for a female over the age of nine to leave her body 'uncovered', even though it is covered by the trousers!; a velvet, long-sleeved, fitted blouse; a vivid Lurex scarf, or *songket,* to be worn around both shoulders, secured with a large, elaborate, 'gold' belt; foot anklets decorated with tinkling bells; a mayoral 'gold' chain worn around the neck; and all topped off with a 'gold' tiara. I looked like the fairy on the top of the Christmas tree. My petite Indonesian fellow dancers looked exquisite, if a little tired. The complicated double-crown knotted chignon alone had taken about two hours to perfect. It was the kind of costume that you couldn't master by yourself; you needed an extra pair of hands. Our dance went down a storm, despite the fact that we'd only had two practice sessions (one in my hotel room at one o'clock in the morning, accompanied by bangs on the wall from the disgruntled guests next door), and lots of delegates returned home with photos taken with the Achenese dancing girls. Around two o'clock in the morning, reception phoned to tell me that the President of WIC was coming upstairs to share my room. "I thought you'd be lonely on your own," Ida greeted me when I answered her knock. I wasn't feeling in the least lonely, however, I **did** enjoy her company and her tales of growing up in Jakarta, where she had never slept alone, always surrounded by family and friends, before moving in to her husband's home.

Ida had been the one to introduce me to the Indonesian custom of never losing face, *malu*. I was co-chairing my first WIC meeting and feeling inadequately prepared. Ida, the President, had arrived late (this 'rubber time' is also very typical) and had not briefed me on the agenda. There was nothing written down. All seemed to be going smoothly when Ida, and about thirty other Indonesian ladies, suddenly stood up, nodded their apologies and left the room. The remaining one hundred odd pairs of eyes were now glued expectantly on me, sitting in splendid isolation on stage. Somehow, I stumbled through the programme. I'd been to a few meetings, knew that the various officials gave their reports, and answered questions from the floor, that there would be some sort of performance as the entertainment. I got through it, but only just. Ida later explained that she did not want to risk distressing me with bad news. The most high-ranking Indonesian wives had been commanded to attend a reception hosted by the boss's wife. Of course, it clashed with the WIC meeting; however, no one wants to be the bearer of bad news. Bad or contrary news is delivered so quietly and subtly that you may not even know what is going on. Hence, the silent nod and speedy disappearance from the stage, with no explanation!

Indonesians also try to avoid at every opportunity saying "No." They talk in circles. If you ask, "Do you have any children?" the reply will always be, "*Belum*," not yet, even if you are seventy-five! You 'do honour' by permitting someone to make a fool of himself, rather than risk the embarrassment of bringing it to his attention. Another, to me rather annoying, habit is to giggle while delivering bad news. Indonesians believe that this lightens the delivery of something you won't want to hear. So, when Asna, our maid, decided to wash my daughter's two-tone blue and white American baseball jacket and ruined it, the colour-run garment was presented to me with wide smiles and giggles. Of course, it made me feel less than happy and I found it very difficult not to react negatively. My daughter was furious.

In a corner of our house in Provence we have two magic medicine sticks, each about four feet high and elaborately carved. Asna was forever turning their 'faces' to the wall, fearing perhaps that they would bring bad fortune. We'd purchased one in nearby Lhokseumawe during a shopping trip. In the middle of the unpaved street a large crowd surrounded a medicine man, brandishing his magic stick, promoting his snake-oil or whatever he was selling to ward off evil spirits. And he seemed to have plenty of buyers. My Indonesian friends assured me that sometimes an Indonesian doctor would refer patients to a *dukun*, a native practitioner said to be skilled in healing bones and the treatment of psychiatric disorders. The other stick was purchased on Samosir Island, on volcanic Lake Toba, the largest lake in South East Asia, roughly the size of Singapore, about ten hours by road from where we lived. My husband had arranged the trip for our family and seven friends, eleven in all. As the road trip was particularly gruelling owing to the propensity of crater-like pot-holes, we flew to Medan, a trading centre and important harbour, the capital city of Sumatra. There we picked up supplies and the mini-bus which would take us to the ferry at Parapat, on the edge of Lake Toba. Fairly straightforward, but it wasn't always so. In the nineteenth century, exploration of the area was hampered by the head-hunting Bataks. Two missionaries who did find a way in were eaten, a common occurrence dealt out to law-breakers and enemies.

But we came in peace. Kathi and I went ahead with our children who were visiting from boarding school in Scotland. For us, this is one of the downsides of living abroad. It made boarding school necessary and we missed the children terribly. International phone calls were virtually impossible. Calls had to be booked days in advance, and it was touch and go whether you would get through. Their weekly letters and thrice yearly visits were very precious to us. Our mission was to track down emergency food supplies, just in case food proved elusive on the island, and, most importantly a plentiful supply of bottled water. Not as easy as you may think, however, we'd given the owner of the hole-in-the-wall, *Toko Ben*, in Medan, advance warning and he had rounded up such essentials as peanut butter, crackers and an impressive supply of water. My husband, the engineer of the trip, had calculated how much water each person would consume over the eight-day trip. He calculated two litres per day. It was always hot in Indonesia, between 32 and 34 degrees centigrade, and we did normally drink a lot of water. Somehow we managed to heave the boxes of water on to the ancient, rickety ferry. It did cross my mind that the boat was now probably officially overloaded. Well below the Plimsoll line. In fact, the boat had seen better days. We searched in vain for any signs of lifebelts or lifejackets. We docked safely, however, a few months later the same ferry boat sank in the middle of Lake Toba with about sixty people on board – no survivors.

An everlasting memory is of us arriving at the jetty on Samosir Island to be greeted by 'bearers' who cheerfully and uncomplaining heaved the enormous supply of bottled water on their heads, up the steep cliff to our hotel. It was like something out of *The African Queen*. Of course, you drink a lot of water when it is beautifully chilled. As temperatures rose, the water got warmer and warmer and everyone was reluctant to drink very much of it. When we departed the island, the scarcely depleted water supply was transported down the cliff, loaded on to the boat, unloaded into the waiting mini bus, and accompanied us to each destination on our itinerary. At the end of the trip, three large boxes of water remained. Rather than abandon them (the sensible thing to do), my husband had it loaded on to the company plane for the return trip to Lhokseumawe. Once in our fridge at home, the water suddenly became more attractive and was consumed in a few days. He never did admit that he had overordered and emphasised how comforting it was to know that we would have a plentiful supply of clean, safe water for the arduous trip.

The Batak people who live on Samosir Island on Lake Toba are descendants from wandering tribes of mountain dwellers from Northern Thailand and Burma and originally they were cannibals. Up until fairly well on in the nineteenth century, Sir Stamford Raffles, when appointed Governor of Sumatra, reported that for certain crimes a criminal would be eaten alive. In cases of adultery, the wife could partake in the feast, but usually only men could eat human flesh. Parents were eaten when they became too old to work! Now there's a solution the British government hasn't yet thought of. In the nineteenth century, the Bataks were introduced to Christianity by a German Lutheran missionary and today, basically, they are animists with a veneer of Christianity. *The Huria Kristen Batak* Church is presently the largest Christian congregation in Indonesia. However, Bataks still believe that supernatural beings inhabit all objects and govern their existence; everything has a soul. All objects and ideas, including animals, tools and natural phenomena, have or are expressions of living spirits. They believe in the existence of the spirits of their dead ancestors and sacred stones, trees and places. Their burial rites are very rich and complex and include a ceremony, *mangungkal holi*, in which the bones of your ancestors are re-interred several years after death. The Bataks still live fairly traditional lives, many in the *sopa*, communal houses found nowhere else in Indonesia. They are built on piles soaked in mud for years with not a single nail used, just rope and wooden pegs. The distinctive curved wooden ends (like a boat's hull) of these houses are richly ornamented with mosaics and outstanding woodcarvings of serpents, man-like figures, female breasts symbolising life-giving force, and elongated monsters' heads with bulging eyes – scary. The families' rooms are allocated by rank in this strongly patriarchal society. Elders still sit on an ancestral stone chair for council meetings and male priests and wizards, *datu,* are skilled in sorcery and the use of poisons. When I left Sumatra, my friend Ida honoured me by presenting me with a small, clay Batak spirit figure which had belonged to her husband's family for generations. Today, it sits on my mantelpiece, beside Ganesh, guarding the hearth. It is a mistake for foreigners to view spirit beliefs lightly. Spirits both good and bad are much more part of the scene in the East than they are in the West.

We had some other memorable experiences on this memorable trip. In Brastaggi, sixty six kilometres south west of Medan, the main town on the mainland, we climbed Mount Sibayak, one of two active (and still smoking) volcanoes in this highland village. Doesn't sound like much, but it was an arduous undertaking. To avoid the scorching heat, the climb had to be undertaken during the hours of darkness, so we set out at two a.m., led by a guide carrying several bamboo sticks. Turned out, these were paraffin 'lamps' to guide us through the darkness on our ascent. They proved to be extremely smelly and inefficient. I managed to step off the path early on in the climb and lost my trainer, never to be seen again. It took five hours to climb to the top, scrabbling up the last few metres of loose scree. We managed to miss the sunrise, supposed to be spectacular on a clear day, but this one was particularly cloudy, however, we did see lots of bubbling, sulphurous hot springs. It took another long three hours to scramble down the volcano and I'd never felt so exhausted. I abandoned breakfast in favour of a hot shower (apparently I used up the total supply of hot water) and bed. Later, we ventured down to the local, rather scrubby market, where I bought a carved figure which unscrewed to store 'medicine' in its base, from a peddler practising both white and black magic. Most of his brews promised to make the male powerful and enduring and the female over-reach local sex standards, but maybe it just lost something in the translation. Looking back, it was an amazing experience, one I'm never likely to have again. Years later, while looking through old letters and photographs sent to us after the death of an aged aunt, we came across an old, sepia postcard sent by her husband to his mother in 1926. The scene seemed familiar. Sure enough, it was Brastaggi, with the volcano looming over 'our' hotel. Our visit and climb had seemed very adventurous, but what hardships Uncle Tom must have faced on his business trip.

Just before we flew home, we visited the Bohorok Orang-Utan Rehabilitation Centre, on the edge of the Gunung Leuser National Park. We forded a river and walked for about an hour through dense jungle before we reached the rough planked feeding platform, twenty feet above ground, set up by rangers. The aim is to return 'pets' to the jungle and this was done in easy stages. Having a red-haired ape shambling around the living room is regarded by some people as a status symbol. Unfortunately, to procure these babies, poachers invariably killed and discarded the mothers. It was amazing to watch these huge creatures swing in from the jungle to feast on the bananas and milk provided as a kind of half-way solution. They are fed twice a day;

then left in the forest to forage for natural food. It takes three or four years to break their dependence on the feedings, but it has taken longer to convince urban Indonesians that keeping orang-utans as pets represents depredation of a rare treasure. Not quite like seeing the huge orange primates in the wild, but the next best thing.

In Provence, there are also many superstitions and magical practices. We always warn prospective visitors that we have scorpions in the house, and not just the odd one now and again. At first, I was terrified of them, with no idea what to do. In vain, we searched the shelves of the supermarket. One hundred and one remedies for getting rid of ants, flies, wasps, centipedes, termites, mice, and some pests we didn't even recognise, but not a single illustration of a scorpion on any of the packets and tins. One day, we found a small shop in St. Rémy which specialises in pest control. Shelves and shelves of remedies, but again we drew a blank on scorpions. I asked the shopkeeper in French: "Do you have anything to get rid of scorpions?" A Gallic shrug, an exhale of breath: "But they are not dangerous. Nothing to worry about. They will not harm you."

This should have been reassuring; however, they didn't **look** harmless. I researched scorpions, and in particular Provençal scorpions, on the Internet. The man was right. There is only one poisonous scorpion in Provence, a green one, and ours were most definitely black. They stood out clearly against the white walls. "The sting of a common, black scorpion," I read, "is similar to a bee sting. Nothing to worry about at all. Apply an ice pack to the affected area, however, if the patient goes into analytic shock, rush him to hospital immediately". Very reassuring. Finally, I plucked up the courage to enquire of our neighbours if they too had scorpions. Perhaps it was just our house which was over-run with them. "But, of course, it is *normal* . . .." No-one seemed particularly worried; no-one had been stung by a scorpion.

I continued to ask around. Dick, our only British neighbour, **did** have a remedy. Sheepishly, he related how shortly after moving in to his house he had phoned the *immobilier* who had sold him the house to ask how to deal with the plague of scorpions. "I know it sounds ridiculous," he continued, "but I was told to catch the next scorpion that appeared, scorch its tail over the gas flame on the cooker, and place it on the windowsill, as a warning to other scorpions."

He was convinced that it had worked, so we decided to give it a try. It didn't take long to round up enough scorpions, one for each window-sill. The scorching was rather unpleasant, but if it worked it would all be worth it. And surprisingly, it did work. From that day onwards we had fewer scorpions, very few. Now we see the odd one, however, I no longer fear them. My method of dis-patch is to use my spider catcher, a mini vacuum oper-ated by a battery which sucks up the scorpions, ready to be dispatched down the loo. My fearless husband favours long-nosed pliers. Visitors are surprised when, on their arrival, we issue them with a torch for the fre-quent power cuts and their own personal scorpion catcher. We have discovered that the scorpions don't like cold weather; they hibernate during the winter months and only emerge in early summer. Where they hibernate is still a mystery. We've also discovered that they really are pretty harmless. One dark evening, my bare-footed, unsuspecting husband trod on a scorpion lurking beside the loo. He described the sting as similar to a mosquito bite, an irritation but nothing to worry about. This didn't stop me shining a torch on him several times during the night to make sure that a mercy dash to hospital was not required. He seems to be the only person in the village ever to have been bitten by a scorpion. What a claim to fame! Our visitors always comment on the dead scorpions littering the window-sills, but hey! If it works, you can put up with a few scorched scorpions.

Life's No Beach Down Under

The Indian party was our swansong and by mid-1988 we were packing up and heading to what turned out to be a two year assignment in Adelaide, South Australia. We were sad to leave behind so many good friends; however, we were excited too at moving to civilisation. The only downside that we could see was that we'd be even further away from our children, still at Boarding School in Scotland. However, they visited us four times a year and we took some amazing trips together.

Adelaide is of course civilised, but you don't have to go very far to encounter superstitious beliefs, particularly among the aborigines. Not too many aborigines in downtown Adelaide, or only those who had become totally assimilated into urban living. However, venture out of town a few miles and you came across aboriginal people, many of them living in distressing squalor. When I made a trip with our teenage children to Alice Springs, en route for Ayers Rock, we encountered many more. About seventy percent of the population of Alice is aboriginal, many with alcohol problems, diabetes and

Aids. During a tour of the town, we were told by the guide that, like animists, they believe in innumerable spirits and Outback bogies which wander, especially at night, and can be held at bay by means of fire. Their beliefs are much more complicated than this and describing them as magic, or animist, or examples of totemism really fails to explain the true worth and significance. They believe in a supreme being, Biame, part human and part kangaroo or wallaby, and the ancestral heroes, their pastimes and everything associated with them, is encapsulated in the English language word 'Dreaming'. For a few weeks I worked as a volunteer guide at the Adelaide Art Gallery and herded Australians and tourists round the aborigine 'Dreaming' exhibition – a surreal experience, but I learned a fair bit about aboriginal culture.

After reading Neville Shute's novel *A Town Like Alice* at school, I'd always wanted to visit, and the town did not disappoint. Until seventy years ago, Alice was months from the nearest point of civilisation, Adelaide, from where all its supplies arrived by camel train. We took a train, the Ghan; however, the journey was a more manageable twenty three hours. We departed Adelaide at eleven o'clock in the morning and arrived in Alice Springs at ten o'clock the next morning. Of course, now you can travel all the way to Darwin on the Ghan, if you have two days to spare. Until I visited Australia, I had little concept of the huge size of the country, the enormous distances between places, the vast nothingness which makes up most of the country. Apart from one smallish town about an hour out of Adelaide, we encountered nothing, only mile after mile of flat scrubland with no visible habitation. My daughter spotted a solitary dingo, but I even managed to miss that. The train was a surprise: very comfortable cabins, classified as Red Kangaroo or Gold Kangaroo Accommodation – who says the Australians have no class system? – and a well-used piano bar where all the old favourites were trotted out. Plusher than British Rail; not quite the Orient Express.

Alice is delightful. It seemed well-ordered, a bit of a one-horse, Outback town but a pleasant place to live. Of course, we were there in winter; summer temperatures average 53 degrees centigrade! We did all the touristy things, except that they felt rather special and not too touristy at all. One of the highlights was a dawn camel ride in the sandy Todd River which hadn't seen rain for ten years. Pity we weren't there in late August when the Henley-on-Todd Regatta takes place. The river is as dry and sandy as a desert, nevertheless a whole series of races are held for sailing boats of every description. The boats are bottomless and the crew's legs stick out as they run down the course. Must be quite a sight. We took a trip to see the first Telegraph Station in Australia which when connected with the undersea line from Darwin to Java put Australia in direct contact with Europe for the first time; Anzac Hill; the Royal Flying Doctor Service; and, the highlight, the School of the Air. This has been broadcasting since 1951 lessons by radio to children living in remote parts of the Outback who cannot attend conventional schools. It provides a service for about one hundred and forty children living on properties or settlements covering over one million square kilometres of central Australia – mind-boggling. While there, we listened in to teachers speaking with their pupils and were told that the school's pupils develop a maturity and independence in study not usually found in the customary classroom situation. The pupils are supplied with instructional videos and individualised lesson packages, and once a year most of them gather together at the school to enjoy personal contact.

So Alice Springs proved more than just a stopping off place on the way to the star attraction, Ayers Rock. This too was very special; the rock has a mysterious air about it, however, it loses some of its magic when you are viewing it at sunrise and sunset with hundreds of other camera-poised tourists. The aborigines have claimed back (rightly) their Rock, and access is restricted. Accommodation is several miles away, so you are captive, dependent on transport laid on, and a prisoner to very high restaurant and hotel prices.

We flew home in a tiny plane that had to come down at Coober Pedy, Australia's 'Opal Wonderland', to re-fuel and pick up passengers. As we approached, the terrain was a swirling dustbowl, a lunar landscape. The terminal is a small, wooden hut with a corrugated roof – not much room for passengers in transit – and the children sat cross-legged on the runway to await take-off. Coming in to land, the town looks like a moonscape. Coober Pedy is the world's largest opal mining centre, however, the searing heat, on average 52 degrees in summer, means that residents live, work and play underground in the remains of former mining shafts carved out to provide a comfortable space and fitted with all mod cons – very strange. In addition to the homes, there are underground opal caves, gift shops, a Catholic church and even a bookshop. The town's name is an Aboriginal word meaning 'white feller's burrow', and it attracts dubious characters wanting to break with their past and hole up. The treeless terrain has hundreds of pyramids of upturned red earth and abandoned mines where hopefuls have rummaged through the landscape in search of riches. It has the look of an impermanent frontier shanty town, a war-zone littered with debris. Not a place I hope to re-visit.

Living in Adelaide for two years was not as pleasant an experience for me as I had expected it to be. Australia always has such a great press: beautiful scenery, eternal sunshine, barbecues, beaches and friendly people. All of these things are true. The countryside around Adelaide, mostly outback, is magnificent. However, you have to drive for seven hours to reach the beautiful, savage Flinders Ranges and experience the wonders of Wilepena Pound with its kangaroos, wallabies, koalas, emus, eight hundred year old gum trees, fragrant eucalyptus, vast natural amphitheatre surrounded by towering peaks, and basic, Boy-Scout camping sites. When I arrived in Australia, I asked a neighbour where to go at the weekend. "Oh, we drive out to Wilepena Pound. It's not too far, only a seven hour drive." I was amazed, yet eventually we spent three weekends there, and barely noticed the long drive through the hot, dusty red earth.

Another memorable trip we took as a family was to Kangaroo Island, at the tip of South Australia, about one hundred kilometres from Adelaide. Although it is the third biggest island after Tasmania and Melville Island off Darwin, it seemed to us to be completely unspoiled, underdeveloped, a nature paradise. It is sparsely populated by humans but extremely rich in wildlife. One of our most memorable experiences ever is of being led by a ranger (access to the beach is severely restricted) up close to a colony of sea lions complete with nursing cubs. We kept very quiet and tried to make as little disturbance as possible. It was a magical experience. We also saw our first echidna, a shy, porcupine-like creature, strolling across the main road. Plenty of venomous snakes in Australia, but we never saw one in the wild, only as part of the exhibit at a 'wildlife farm'. However, I did have a close encounter with two deadly red-back spiders which had sneaked into the house to enjoy the air conditioning.

A less successful trip was across New South Wales. We set off armed to the teeth with jerry cans of water, a reserve supply of petrol, a torch with spare batteries, warm clothes, a sleeping bag, and industrial strength insect repellent – everything we might need for survival if people's predictions came true and we broke down in the middle of nowhere. We had not been reassured by the Royal Automobile Association's safety and survival literature which warns readers: "If you break down, stay with the vehicle. A search party will come out eventually." Eventually! Crossing the vast state we felt as though we were in the middle of nowhere, certainly nowhere recognisable. On one stretch, we drove for six hours through the scrubby countryside without seeing another car or even passing habitation. It was so empty and featureless, completely lacking in charm. We drove for miles and miles, always expecting that around the next corner there would be something to look at, and there never was. I remember little about the one-shop, one-pub towns, but I do have vivid memories of going out to eat in the only venue possible in Mildura, on the Murray River, the place where we stopped for the night. It was a club full of hundreds of Aussies playing the 'pokies', slot machines. This form of gambling was illegal in South Australia, but we had now crossed into Victoria, and people took coach tours to indulge their habit. Adelaide did have a large, popular casino, memorable only for its dress policy of no blue jeans or trainers. It seemed that for many locals it was the place to go on a Saturday evening. We went once, out of curiosity. It was full of people enjoying themselves, but we're not gamblers. My only other foray into a casino was in Macau, a gamblers' paradise off the coast of China, about one hour by ferry from traffic-gridlocked, business obsessed Hong Kong. I was accompanying a school trip of teenagers from the international school in Singapore, and for some reason the tawdry casino was on the tour guide's list. The murky, smoke-filled rooms filled with desperate punters gave the place a real sense of evil, and the clutch of pawnbrokers full of Rolexes and heavy gold chains which surrounded the casino acted as a dire warning against taking up the vice. "My friend, he lose $3 million dollar in one afternoon," boasted the tour guide.

The Mildura pokies venue had communal dining tables set out in the midst of the machines, so no getting away from them. What a totally mindless activity, feeding coin after coin into a slot, and the food was appalling too. Mildura's other claims to fame are having the most of the biggest: the longest bar in the world (298 feet) at the Workingman's Club, where we ate breakfast as it was the only place open; the largest fruit juice factory in Australia; the largest deckchair ever built (in front of a main street motel); and the world's biggest talking Humpty Dumpty (at a poultry farm). Mildura is known as the Riviera of Victoria, but

I don't think that the Côte d'Azur has anything to worry about yet.

Sometimes, during our journey, to relieve the monotony, we'd turn off the highway, take a detour for miles down a dirt track, to follow a sign indicating a 'historic monument'. We never learned from experience: most often, the historic dwelling was a few wooden remains of a nondescript, gimcrack shack and a dunny (loo). In the red, rocky countryside, we stopped in Broken Hill which looms large in Australia's industrial history. Mining of the town's silver brought riches, but at great cost to the workforce. Today's mine workers still labour under terrible hardship conditions. Close by, is the Ghost Town of Silverton which has not survived. It has become a regular star in movies such as Mel Gibson's *Mad Max*. Australia's Hollywood. We did enjoy watching Australian movies: *Return to Snowy River*, *Ricky and Pete* and *Crocodile Dundee,* all were released during our stay. They exemplified the Australian love of the great outdoors, of wearing the rugged, all-weather R.M. Williams Akubra hats and Drizabone stockman coats, of physical, macho pursuits. The young girls in Adelaide, however, emerged summer and winter for the Saturday night visit to the pub, clad in strapless, full-skirted prom dresses.

One film that we waited weeks to see was *Cane Toads*. We were intrigued. No-one we spoke to seemed to know very much about this film, yet every time we tried to buy tickets we were told, "Sorry, mate. Sold out." Perseverance paid off and the film was hugely enjoyable, despite the unpromising plot. Basically, it's a documentary about the spread of sugar-cane toads (which live in the fields) through Queensland and then into the rest of Australia. It is a lesson in not interfering with nature as the toads had been introduced to eat pests present in the cane fields. Unfortunately, they didn't fancy the pests, but they thrived and reproduced at a tremendous rate. It was a real horror movie, with cane toads multiplying before our eyes, until the whole screen was filled with them. I don't think we could have taken more than the forty-six minute running time. A very different world was portrayed in the two French films which we watched at the cinema in Adelaide: *Jean de Florette* and *Manon des Sources*. I loved the Provence portrayed in the films and longed to visit. I must be careful not to turn into a set-jetter, visiting countries merely to gawk at the setting of a movie.

We didn't watch much television in Adelaide – too much beckoning outdoors, but we did enjoy the odd episode of *Neighbours* and a satirical programme called *The Comedy Store* whose Kylie character summed up all the aspects of the Australian character that I found it difficult to understand. It's healthy to be able to laugh at yourself.

Adelaide itself is a pretty, pleasant, sprawling, flat city of one million inhabitants, although it was difficult to know where they all were as the streets were frequently empty and parking a dawdle. You can walk across the city in about half an hour. Despite its open, airy quality, something about Adelaide was 'flat'. It is mostly low-rise buildings, many of them historical, and wide boulevards. After living on the edge of the jungle for so long, we chose to live in the city, a square mile, surrounded by pleasant green spaces which emphasised the claustrophobia of Singapore and London. I cycled every morning in the green, mercifully flat parklands and never failed to be thrilled by the huge, raucous flocks of pink and grey parrots called galahs (the locals regard them as vermin, much as we regard pigeons) and the brightly coloured turquoise and crimson parakeets squawking in the majestic gum trees. On one particular stretch of parkland, the rather surreal scene of groups of elderly green bowlers, dressed in immaculate whites, playing on immaculate striped bowling greens – at seven o'clock in the morning, to escape the sun, I suppose. On Saturday mornings, we walked through the parkland to Rundle Street and our favourite Italian café, *Al Fresco Gelateria*, for a cappuccino and *tartufo* treat, and some people-watching from the pavement cafes and Cinzano umbrellas. The café is a bit of a 1950's time warp – a good era for coffee bars – and the young, mostly Italian, females who met there to sip their cappuccinos for hours were treated to appreciative stares and much posing from a procession of slow-moving, flashy cars, driven up and down the street by the local talent. We liked it for its European ambience, its sixteen hours a day, seven days a week opening hours, and for its ten flavours of home-made *gelati*, especially the *perugina*, chocolate and hazelnut. On the way there, we passed court after court of adult netball players, again immaculately turned out. Netball is a big adult sport in Australia. Every two years, the Grand Prix took place in this parkland, spilling on to the streets surrounding our house. Exciting to watch, but a major inconvenience for residents.

The sun does shine for most of the year, although summers in Adelaide were blisteringly hot, 44 plus degrees for six weeks. Our family is very fair-skinned, so sun-block was necessary every time we ventured outside. Cool and tangy sea breezes at nearby Glenelg, Adelaide's most popular seaside suburb, but inadvisable to spend long hours sitting on the wide swathes of white sand in the unrelenting sun. Also boring; lying prone on the beach doing nothing is fine for a few minutes, but very soon I become restless. Glenelg's main claim to fame is that it is a palindrome, the only resort that is spelled the same way backwards. To reach Glenelg, you travel in a rollicking tram full of polished, creaking wood, leather hanging-straps and back-rests that can be released to face in either direction. The experience reminded me of the bone-shaker trams of my childhood transporting passengers from grimy Glasgow to the green suburbs. My grandparents lived at the end of the line and my treat was to help the driver ready the backrests for the return journey.

In Australia, skin cancer is a real threat. Yet, most locals seemed to visit the beach at every opportunity, even on Christmas Day, for a barbie. My husband's colleagues couldn't believe that we weren't tempted to join them and forego our turkey and Christmas pudding. On reflection, it does seem more sensible to have a barbie on the beach, but we had the last laugh. On Christmas Day, the long heat wave broke, the temperature plummeted twenty degrees, and it rained. We were very comfortable sitting indoors eating out traditional fare.

At first, the people I met in Adelaide did seem friendly. Within hours of arriving I received a huge basket of exotic fruit and orchids from my husband's Italian boss, Toni. Such gifts were commonplace when we lived in Sumatra and Singapore, however, I didn't realise how unusual this was in Adelaide. Never again was I given as much as a bunch of daisies. In Indonesia, I'd grown tired of the sometimes twice weekly, formal

126

social gatherings. I'd remarked to my husband, "I hope there aren't too many functions to attend when we move to live in Australia." I needn't have worried. In the two years I spent there, I was never invited to a company do; men only. Australia is still such a macho society. Friday night is sacred, a night to spend down at the pub with the boys. My husband became accepted as one of the boys after an incident at an Italian restaurant. He'd only been in the job a few days and was given the place of honour at the top of the long table. Standing up to give a short speech, he missed his footing and he and his chair toppled down the short flight of stairs behind him. Trying to maintain some dignity and ignore his considerable pain, he clambered back up, clutching his chair and smiling. It was the right thing to do. Before subsequent dinners, someone would quip something like, "Tonight will be a bit of a challenge, mate. The restaurant has a circular stair!" When we left Adelaide, he was presented with a custom-made model of a flight of stairs, complete with tipping chair at the top. At the base is a metal plaque inscribed: 'John Matchett, The Flying Scotsman'. It has pride of place in the study.

After a few of these social get-togethers, my husband excused himself. Australians have the right idea and work to live rather than live to work as I think we do in Britain. When we arrived, in 1988, the oil refinery worked a nine day fortnight. Every second Friday was a holiday, for workers and management alike. We enjoyed our new-found leisure and took the opportunity to venture into the Barossa Valley and McLaren Vale to taste and buy the excellent wines. On Saturdays, the shops closed at eleven in the morning. By the time we'd walked the mile in to the centre of the city, shopkeepers were putting up their grills and switching off the lights. My husband isn't too keen on shopping anyway. Worst of all, in the whole of Adelaide there was only one serious bookshop. I judge places by their bookshops, one of the reasons that Boston scores so highly. Harvard Square has a multitude of book stores, many of them selling excellent second-hand bargains. I had great hopes for the Adelaide Festival Hall which boasts better acoustics than the Sydney Opera House. It is home to the biggest arts festival in Australia, held every two years. Unfortunately, we'd just missed one, and we left Adelaide as the next festival was being launched. During those two years, Adelaide seemed to be suffering from post-Festival *tristesse*. The only culture running at the theatre was a rather tired version of *Cats*, oh, and a fascinating one-man show by visiting author Roald Dahl.

We had the wrong accent. The only British clubs were Working Men's Clubs. I went with my daughter to the local library to enquire about Women's Groups in the area and we were shuffled in to a private office to advise us on support groups for battered wives and their families! No book group. No discussion groups of any kind that I could find, except at the University, where I joined a stimulating creative writing class. I also learned new skills as I attended classes on Tai-chi, meditation and stained glass making. My pitiful attempts at the latter proved that I was never going to acquire the skill needed, but I had fun trying.

I didn't mope around. After being denied a work permit, I threw myself into voluntary jobs, at the university radio station, Radio 5UV. I spent one day a week re-organising the record library, commiserating with female colleagues who felt that their promotion opportunities were slim. Another day was spent working for Radio for the Print Handicapped, editing broadcast material, producing programmes and eventually broadcasting the lunchtime news programme. It kept me busy. I talked to 'real Australians' and on the surface people were very friendly. However, I felt that it was very much on the surface. Adelaide is a small community, more like a village than a city; people tend to be very 'small town', very insular, happy to ignore the rest of the world. There is a certain smugness about many Adelaide people who are quite convinced that they live in one of the last truly civilised corners of the world. I enrolled in an exercise class where it seemed that everyone had known everyone else since kindergarten. They seemed to lack the imagination to understand what it must be like to be far from home, without the support of family and friends. My parents, our aged aunt, our nephew and friends had come for extended stays on previous assignments, but this time we were on our own. There was no expat support system on this assignment. It was very difficult to break in. I felt very much the outsider. Years later, while watching Bill Murray in the film *Lost in Translation*, I realised that I too had felt disorientated and isolated in a strange country. Yes, they speak English in Adelaide, but it is a very different and unfamiliar lifestyle.

I kept my views quiet. I didn't want to be accused of being a whingeing pom, and yes, Australians do still use that term of endearment. If I'd been more into watching, playing and talking about sport, I would have felt less alienated. My husband didn't share my feelings about Adelaide. He was very involved in his job at the refinery, had a support system of male colleagues, and he enjoyed watching and playing sport, a necessity in this sport-obsessed society. I had an inkling of how other Australians viewed residents of Adelaide when I visited my relatives in Geelong, near Melbourne. They cracked jokes about people from Adelaide as we might about the Irish or the Polish, of course less so now that our society is so politically correct. I loved Melbourne, but then it is very British. I also loved Sydney, very vibrant and cosmopolitan, but we lived in Adelaide, very pleasant, but rather dull and flat, more mellow than vibrant. It did have outstanding restaurants. We lived in a mews just off Carrington Street where the restaurants were world class. Years later, I attended a cookery demonstration and lunch in the Singapore Hilton, given by the cookery writer and television personality, Ken Hom. It was held to promote his new cookery book *East Meets West*. He'd just been in Adelaide, so we had something in common, and he exclaimed how lucky I was to have lived so close to such wonderful restaurants, such as *Neddiez-tu* and *Mona Lisa* and a world-class Chinese restaurant called *House of Chow*, housed in an unremarkable bungalow. You could eat anything in Adelaide: outstanding, succulent steak, dished up in Australian man-sized portions; wonderful Italian food created by the large Italian population; Chinese food to rival anything in China; fusion food melding the very best of two cultures; crunchy fresh salad sandwiches, strangely, always with beetroot as an essential ingredient, served on delicious, muffin-textured, Yugoslavian bread, *lepinja*; local delicacies such as kangaroo (banned in several Australian states) which tasted like finest fillet steak; and late at night, the famous meat pie floater with mushy peas. We once plucked up the courage to taste this very popular local speciality which was sold from a twenty-four hour van in the middle of town. It sounded and looked pretty disgusting, but I have to admit that it was tasty. And Adelaide has the wonderful Central Market, buzzing with a dozen different immigrant languages, amazing smells and wondrous colours of gourmet delicacies. On Fridays, I competed with hordes of little old ladies dressed in black, fielding sharp, wicker baskets, to buy the fish, fresh from the nearby ports. Good practice for the fish stall in the market at Vaison-La-Romaine, Provence. Do only the British know how to queue? Most of the fruits and vegetables are grown within one hour's drive of the market, something I relish. To understand a country, you have to eat it. In Britain, we are catching up, with the growing proliferation of weekly Farmers' Markets and organic, locally sourced, healing foods in some supermarkets, but we still have quite a way to go. I re-visited Boston in the summer of 2006 and was amazed to find that the tiny *Bread and Circus*, the only shop I could find in 1992 selling freshly-squeezed orange juice, lentils, hummus and organic vegetables, had meta-morphosed into two huge wholefood stores stocking every wholesome food imaginable.

I thought that I was alone in finding Australia not quite as perfect as it is often depicted, until recently I read a very critical article by the Australian feminist Germaine Greer, deriding her homeland. The article was headed: 'Exodus from Oz – it's grim down under'. Her argument was that if Australia is so wonderful, why are twenty million Australians living abroad? Many Euro-peans especially have decided to leave Australia, to cut their losses, and return to Greece, or Italy, or Britain for a better life. Why? Greer puts it down to the fact that most of Australia is not rural or urban but suburban, full of replications of *Neighbours'* Ramsay Street, the cookie-cutter houses spreading out further and further from the central business districts. Everyone lives in identikit houses, lives identikit lives, yet people don't know their next door neighbours or ever read a book or discuss a movie. Yes, she exaggerates for effect, to make her point; however, her description very much matches the picture I have of life in Adelaide. Greer left Australia aged twenty five, bored, ungainly and bored by sport, 'which in Australia is a sure sign that you're a bad person'. My lukewarm approach to sport probably contributed to many of my negative feelings about Adelaide. Greer re-visits frequently and says that she loves her country; however, she does not want to live there. I guess that's how I too feel about Australia. It's a wonderful country, full of opportunity – just not for me. At Christmas, we receive cards from friends all over the world, people we've met on our travels and chosen to stay in touch with. Excluding relatives, we receive only one card from Australia, from the Italian who sent me my welcoming basket of fruit and orchids on my arrival in Adelaide.

Boston: Beyond Baked Beans

It seems that I've been a mobile wife for ever. When I learned in 1990 that my husband had been assigned to Boston, New England, I was really excited. Sure, I'd spent a few weeks in the States here and there – after all, my husband did work for an American company, but I was eager to see what it was like to actually live there. And if you've got to live somewhere in the US, Boston is pretty high on the list of desirable places to live.

My husband has always been very supportive. We both knew that I wouldn't get a work permit and he knew that I'd expressed an interest in studying for a Master's Degree. By the time I arrived, he'd sussed out classes available at Harvard and I enrolled as a full-time post-graduate student. Our son had just begun his university career; our daughter was about to sit her 'A' Levels and hopefully follow him to university. And now he was enthusiastic about me following my dream, only possible because we would again be expats and he would be earning an enhanced salary.

My first class was *Writing Herself – Women's Autobiography in the Nineteenth and Twentieth Centuries*. It made me think about my own life. Subjects ranged from well-known luminaries like Georges Sand and Vera Brittan – Shirley Williams, ex British and European MP, graced a seminar to tell us first-hand about her mother – to more obscure successes such as Lucy Lorcan, the Lowell mill-girl who wrote about her experiences growing up in a small mill town in Massachusetts. Yes, it was a hard life. Lucy went to work in the mill aged eleven, however, she also emphasises the positive side of the early years of the American factory system, where continuing education was encouraged and literary magazines flourished. On reading her autobiography, I was struck by her words: 'People can live and grow anywhere, but people as well as plants have their habitat – the place where they belong and where they find their happiest, because their more natural life'.

Until I fell in love with Provence, I thought that my habitat would always be Britain, although not Scotland where I was born and lived until the age of twenty four, but London. We have a house in Petersham, close to Richmond upon Thames, ten miles from the centre of London, but it could be the country. With the plague turning seventeenth century London into the place no-one wanted to call home, those with the financial means moved out. Many of them settled in Petersham and set about constructing a semi-rural idyll, touted as the most elegant village in England. They lived elegantly, close to the Royal court at Richmond.

We too think that it's a lovely village, despite the writer and critic A.A. Gill once describing it rather sneeringly in the *Sunday Times* as 'a ribbon of Grade II walk-through garages, cut, styled and blow-dried hedges, a sign on the road out of Richmond'. There are no longer any shops, but a spirit of village independence has survived and we do have London's only herd of cows grazing contentedly in the Petersham Meadows, and a one hundred year old village flower show at the beginning of July. We attended it recently after a long absence and were comforted to see that very little had changed. The same children's entries of miniature gardens, peppermint mice, colourful paintings and Victorian posies; the same jars of nostalgia-inducing, home-made jam topped by frilly, gingham covers, amazing, gooey chocolate cakes and unbelievable onions and leeks. The village's other main claims to fame are that in 1876 Vincent van Gogh preached at the Wesley Chapel in Petersham as a lay preacher, and that Charles Dickens lived here for several summers in seventeenth century Elm Lodge and Woodbine Cottage where he wrote most of *Nicholas Nickleby*. In the local history pamphlet available to buy in the library, there is photograph of him standing stiffly outside what was once the village shop. He enthused lyrically about Petersham and advised friends to, 'Come down, come down, revive yourself with country air . . . The roads about are jewelled after dusk with glow-worms'.

Once, we experienced a flutter of excitement when A. A. Gill reported that Michelle Pfeiffer was considering buying a house in the village. When the landlord of the nearby pub was asked to confirm that Michelle had popped in, he replied, "No idea. It was very busy that evening"! However, we **can** boast the authors Claire Tomalin and Michael Frayn and the actor Richard E. Grant as residents, and we used to have the pop singer Tommy Steele and (allegedly) Trigger from *Only Fools and Horses*, and George Vancouver the explorer and founder of Vancouver, Canada, lived for a few years in River Lane and is buried in St. Peter's Churchyard. Every year, on his anniversary, a representative arrives from the Canadian Embassy and in the company of local cubs and sea-scouts (the oldest troop in Britain) pays homage. Oh! And Peter Mayle once lived in Petersham for a short time, so I suppose we're lucky that he didn't write *A Year in Petersham*.

Tourists who visit London very rarely see the **real** London, the numerous 'villages' that have grown and expanded over many hundreds of years so that there is now very little division between one and another. It is in these 'villages' that most Londoners live, not in the world imagined by overseas visitors. In Richmond, you can have the best of both worlds: lots of green and trees, a large garden, caring neighbours, a sense of community. Yet, you are never more than a tube ride away from the teeming metropolis, with its world-class shops, restaurants, theatres, concerts, museums and galleries.

I've lived there now for thirty-one years, when I'm not being a 'mobile wife'. It has always been a familiar and comforting haven to return to. It's my kind of place. Other Scots have felt at home here too. Scottish lords created Ham House and Orleans Park; Sir Walter Scott wrote about the wonderful views from the Terrace; Scots too were responsible for Kew Gardens, buying the land, laying out the gardens, designing the Orangery and Pagoda. However, I enjoyed also every minute of living in the Boston area, where there are something like fifty five universities. Of course, some are more highly rated than others, but many are regarded worldwide as excellent. It was so refreshing to be in the middle of such an academic atmosphere. Everyone I met was taking classes in something – the hairdresser who cut my hair, the waitress in my favourite restaurant, *Legal Seafoods,* the guy sitting next to me at my first Red Sox baseball game, at Fenway Park. America does indeed seem to be the land of opportunity. People here still believe that they can pursue and achieve the American Dream.

In Britain we tend to sneer at American tinpot degrees in such subjects as ice-cream making. Many fear that with our current expansion in Higher Education and dumbing down of 'A' Levels' we will end up emulating the USA. We're not very far behind. Already, you can take a degree in football studies, golf management studies, lifestyle management and stress management. Certainly, many more students progress to a university education than in my day – but how can that be a bad thing? What is more difficult in Britain is to gain entry to university as a mature student. Yes, we have the Open University, and there are mature students in our universities, but Harvard, the oldest of the Ivy League colleges, founded only fifteen years after the Puritans landed, has an open entry policy. Classes are advertised everywhere. Access to courses is freely available. All I required for entry on to a post-graduate degree course was proof that I possessed a recognised first degree, and a short interview to assess my level of motivation. It would be tough to complete the required ten modules within my two year timeframe, but not impossible. Every encouragement was given. During my two years there, I worked really hard – if you dropped below a 'B' grade in the continuous written assessment you were out and off the course – but thrived in the wonderful facilities offered by the university. I would gladly have spent my whole life wandering through the corridors of Widener, one of Harvard's huge wealth of almost one hundred libraries. Harvard has the largest private library system in the world. In these days before the Internet, I had a modem called Hollis, linked to the Harvard library system. I would get up early (to see my husband off to work; Americans start work early, work long hours and have, on average, two weeks' holiday a year) and log-on to Hollis. By the time that Widener opened its doors as the Yard clock struck nine, I had done all my research, identified the books and articles I needed, and where they were situated in the maze of 'stacks', and was ready to check out the books or photocopy the relevant article. At the time, an amazing system.

I took four classes in American Literature and through studying this learned so much about American life. On trips home to England, when I told friends that I was studying American Literature, on more than one occasion they came back with the snide, "Is there any?" I must admit that this is a commonly held view. Certainly, during my first degree I studied only one American work of fiction, Henry James's *The Turn of the Screw*. At school, we read a few poems by T.S. Eliot and Robert Frost, but we were never exposed to the wealth of literature from the US, or any other country for that matter. Of course, we've moved on, become much more multi-cultural. Recently, I taught a module on Post-Colonial Literature – very fashionable at the moment– and another on twentieth century American Literature.

While at Harvard, I wrote a final paper on the American Dream – not bad for a Brit! In the Autobiographical History class I absorbed so much new information, particularly about slavery. Slave narratives were being re-published, or published for the first time – face up to your past. Facts about a country and its people seem so much more relevant when you are actually living in that country. Liberal Boston had been a place of refuge for slaves escaping from a harsh regime. I found my American classmates so articulate – speaking out, voicing opinions, was not something encouraged in Scottish schools when I was growing up – and I enjoyed listening to their ideas so much. Sometimes, I felt a gap of age and idealism. The young students in my class doubted that Betty Freidan's 1950's Happy Housewives, described in the American feminist bible *The Feminine Mystique,* ever really existed. Yet, I knew that they were still alive, both in Boston, and especially in its suburbs, and back home in Britain. My fellow company 'mobile wives', many of them from the southern states, were quite content to live the lives of the 1950's housewife. Many of them lived to shop, to have endless coffee mornings and lunches and Bridge games, to make sure that their husbands came home to a hot, home-cooked meal. I suppose that's the way they had been raised, and the husbands certainly expected that level of attention. They couldn't understand my thirst for learning.

How much better to **do** something with your life. People frequently asked me why I was trying to achieve a Master's Degree at Harvard. For your career? Promotion? I was doing it for myself, with no other end in view. Last time around, university had been more of a social experience. Over the previous twenty years, I'd given a lot of time to my husband and children. They were now seventeen and eighteen and no longer needed me as much as they once did, so I had to learn to let go. I feel very proud of them. My daughter has seen me working most of my married life and took it for granted that she would work to support herself. My parents gave me the best education possible, however, I was expected to do no more than marry 'well' and have children. My qualifications would be useful "if anything happened to your husband". These low personal goals were common both in the UK and the US in the late 1950's and into the 60's. My children have been raised differently; my son has been indoctrinated from an early age. He has always done his share of chores; he's quite a gourmet cook; he understands that women have rights. My daughter is fiercely independent and has forged a career in a competitive male environment.

And I have a wonderful husband who has always encouraged me to do my own thing. Of course, there has to be compromise. Because of the nature of his job, I find myself very mobile. But all of my memories of cultural and historic Boston and Cambridge are happy ones. Most of the southern company wives who'd grown up in places like Dallas, Shreveport or Lafayette were less keen on Boston: "The people are so rude and cold!" they complained. For them, Boston was a truly alien culture. I couldn't understand this at the time; however, a few years later, after a spell in the south, in Houston, Texas, I could see why they had formed that opinion. Certainly the check-out girls in the supermarkets there spent more time greeting you with a smile, asked how your day was going, and packed your bags as a matter of course. Sales-girls behind the expensive make-up counters in glossy

Neiman Marcus would think nothing of spending their time on discussing what creams or lipsticks were just right for you, urging you to try free samples of the latest products and fragrances. And business was always ended on a cheery "Y'all have a nice day, ye hear?" Somehow, they seemed genuine, as if they really **were** wishing you a pleasant afternoon.

Fortunately, I seemed to have the right accent for New England. Bostonians are great Anglophiles and interested in anything British. I do, however, pick up accents very quickly, and often find myself adapting my accent to the situation I find myself in. My children chide me about this, as they perceive it, condescending weakness. In Boston, I managed to distinguish three accents, some more attractive than others. At the Workers' Educational and Industrial Union in Down-town, despite the name I'd met mostly wealthy Boston Brahmins who lived nearby on Beacon Hill in fancy apartments overlooking the equivalent of London's Hyde Park. Most could trace their origins back to orig-inal settlers from the *Mayflower*, and it was as if they had never left Britain. One lady in particular always attended summer meetings clad in a Liberty print dress and flower-bedecked straw hat. They were eager to talk about Britain, but their perception was very much through rose-tinted, nostalgic spectacles. I spent a lot of time with the southern, expat, wives and enjoyed their company and unfailing support. At one rather upmar-ket luncheon in a restaurant in Downtown Boston, the rather patronising waiter asked the ladies where they were from, then he turned to me and simpered, "You're the only one here with a Boston accent." "Yes, and I'm from England!" I retorted.

It is a city rich in history. I duly walked the three-mile heritage Freedom Trail; watched the re-creation of the Boston Tea Party; visited Paul Revere's House and watched an enactment of *Paul Revere's Ride*; made regular visits to seriously authentic Little Italy in the North End, the only place to get a decent cup of coffee and traditional Italian foodstuffs. This was like walking through a time-warp, or a movie set filming *The Goodfellas*, or *The Godfather*. Sicilian Paolos were standing on every street corner, chatting loudly in thick accents, chewing fat cigars, eating slices of authentic looking pizza, planning who knows what. My husband once asked the Paolo (his real name) from the delicatessen if there was any real difference between the domestic mozzarella and the similar looking imported cheese. "Night and Day," came the terse reply.

Food is very important to Bostonians, ice-cream in particular. Bostonians are as serious about their ice-creams as Californians are about smoothies, and as opinionated about their preferences as New Yorkers are about their pastrami. Boston and Cambridge residents consume more ice-cream per capita than residents of any other city in the United States. Oddly, the bitter cold, snow-bound winters don't seem to make much difference to their addiction. There's even a separate guidebook on the subject: *The Boston Ice Cream Lovers' Guide*. But they don't just eat any old ice-cream; only the pure and unadulterated is acceptable to the Boston-bred connoisseur, and it has to come in unusual flavours. They argue over the merits of Herrell's Chocolate Pudding ice-cream over J P Lick's Oatmeal Cookie Dough with White Chocolate Chunks, or Ben & Jerry's Cherry Garcia (made in Vermont). Soon, I too was addicted and would walk miles to sample the delights from *The Old Fire Station* in Charles Street, or the venerable *Steve's* on Massachusetts Avenue, Cambridge. The highlight of the year is the Ice-Cream Festival, held in May on Boston Common, where for a miniscule fee you can taste generous scoops of up to fifty different ice-creams. I managed to devour two and a half; my diminutive friend Marie ten! She had to wear her woollen gloves to handle them, but this in no way spoiled her obvious enjoyment.

Bostonians are also fond of beans and fish and the city is sometimes referred to as Home of the Bean and the Cod or Beantown. Beans were the staple in the early American diet, and Boston started out as a fishing port. Decades before the Irish Catholic immigration which made fish on Friday a tradition, Boston Brahmins served the cheap and plentiful fish to their servants, saving the more costly beef and lamb for themselves. Today, everyone eats a lot of fish, especially clam chowder, although not the tomato-based red stuff so loved in Manhattan, but the one, 'true', white, cream-based chowder – truly delicious. The famous chowder from *Legal Seafoods* – motto: 'If it isn't fresh, it isn't Legal' – was served during President Reagan's inaugural week festivities. Bostonians also eat a lot of oysters, best at the legendary *Union Oyster House*, the longest continuously operating restaurant in the US. John F. Kennedy was a regular patron, and the menu boasts that Louis-Philippe, future King of France, once lived upstairs and taught French. Later, he became king but was exiled and ended up living in Claremont, Surrey, owned by the British Crown, where he died. Claremont eventually became the school where I worked for many years.

We ventured out from Boston to view Bunker Hill and further afield to the Plymouth Plantation on Cape Cod where the *Mayflower* voyagers had landed in 1620. We celebrated our first Thanksgiving there, sitting at communal tables with many of the townspeople dressed in the costumes of the original pilgrims. Who says America has nothing old? Here, you have living history, an authentic reconstruction of America's first settlement with its basic, one room, wooden shacks and high stockades. Actors enact the lives of the original settlers: hoeing, grinding corn and baking bread. When you stop to chat, they reply in character – unnerving. In Britain, we're just as good at national mythmaking, where sometimes a good story takes over from historical reality. Here at the Plantation, the organisers have succeeded in turning religious fundamentalists, who after all left England in protest at new-fangled ideas about religion, into heroes of the Enlightenment, the forerunners of democracy.

Plymouth's other claim to fame is its extensive cranberry bogs which are flooded before harvesting the jewel-like, red berries. This is probably where your Christmas cranberry sauce originated and your cranberry juice, as three quarters of the world's cranberries come from New England. The cranberry is one of only three fruits native to North America (others are the blueberry and the Concord grape) and its importance is evident in the exhibits at the nearby Cranberry World Museum. Long before the pilgrims arrived, Native Americans mixed deer meet and mashed cranberries to make *pemmican*, a survival cake that kept for a long time; they used the juice as a natural dye for rugs and clothing; and cranberries were used also in poultices to draw poison from arrow wounds. Really, cranberries are one of the first super foods, and a lot more palatable than broccoli! Recently, The Plymouth Bay Winery diversified into making cranberry wine: Cranberry Bay, a medium-sweet, fruity red wine, and Cranberry Blush, a light semi-dry, spicy blend of cranberry and white grape. So far, they only export to other parts of the US, so you'll have to pay a visit to sample it.

I visited nearby Salem, familiar to me from teaching *The Crucible* which was made into a movie in 1996 starring Winona Ryder. It had been a tiny rural backwater until a bunch of young girls started seeing spirits there in 1692, when it became a hell of witch trials. It was believed by many that Satan was attempting to overthrow New England by witchcraft. Native Americans too were generally seen as devil-worshippers, and their territories as Satan's kingdom. Today, Salem celebrates its past, but the re-enactments of the witch trials are tacky, and the stuffed witch figures swinging at the entrance to the exhibits are distastefully moth-eaten rather than scary.

I enjoyed my strolls across the river into Beacon Hill and cobbled Charles Street, a time warp of gas street lamps and Dickensian, small-paned, bow windows. Then, past the *Cheers* pub (the exterior is the shot used in the television series; however, the inside bears no resemblance to the 'bar where everyone knows your name'). Across Boston Common, always stopping to admire the tactile line of bronze sculptures in the Public Garden, *Make Way for Ducklings*. These characters appear in a charming, illustrated children's book by a local author, Robert McCloskey, which includes many Boston landmarks and I've bought many copies for appreciative children. Past the swan boats and the frog pond, frozen in winter and a mecca for skaters. Occasionally, a side trip to the Kings' Chapel Burial Ground on the edge of Downtown, whose most famous resident, Elizabeth Swain, is said to have been the source for Hester Prynne in the novel *The Scarlet Letter*, written by Nathaniel Hawthorne. Set in the 1600's, it tells the story of a woman who, while her husband is lost at sea, commits adultery with the pastor, bears a child, and is forced to wear a large, red letter 'A' stitched to the front of her dress. The novel addresses spiritual and moral issues from a uniquely moral standpoint and it is standard approved fare in all US High Schools. I came to it late, during my studies in Boston, but I found it extremely moving and thought-provoking. There have been four versions of the movie made, the last one in 1995, starring Demi Moore and Gary Oldman, but the work also made a recent appearance as a play at the Edinburgh Fringe Festival. Obviously the issues are thought to be still relevant today. Oh, and Elizabeth VerGoose, the author of the *Mother Goose* rhymes is buried there and her grave attracts hordes of young fans.

Cemeteries do hold a fascination for me and there were several to choose from in Boston. After visiting the impressive, cathedral-like Mother Church of the Christian Science Movement (which also houses the editorial offices of the respected magazine, the *Christian Science Monitor*), I was interested in reading more about its founder, Mary Baker Eddy, and I visited her grave in Mt. Auburn Cemetery, in Cambridge, about three miles from Downtown Boston. She was a remarkable woman, and in 1995 Eddy was elected to the National Women's Hall of Fame as the only American woman to found a world-wide religion. I am not a Christian Scientist, but I am in accord with their educational beliefs which are very child-centred and focus on the God-given potential of each child. When I returned to live in the UK, I took up a teaching post in a Christian Science school and taught there happily for eight years. Our travels can influence us in many different ways.

There are other famous residents of Mount Auburn, the first rural burial ground in America, including the poet Henry Wadsworth Longfellow, the artist Winslow Homer, the feminist Julia Ward Howe, and America's answer to Mrs Beaton, Fannie Farmer, who published one of the first cookbooks, *The Boston Cooking-School Cookbook*, in 1896. It is a very tranquil, green space and a favourite haunt of birdwatchers. You can tell the Puritan graves by their skull-and-crossbones motifs, for the Puritans looked upon death as dourly as they did life. On a recent trip to the Greyfriars Bobby Cemetery in Edinburgh, I felt disquieted by the eeriness of the same motifs. However, in Boston, the atmosphere is lifted by the cheery graves of the French Huguenots with their smiling angels and cherubs. Another of my favourite authors, Henry James, is buried nearby in Cambridge Cemetery. He too was an inveterate visitor to cemeteries and wrote about his visit to the Protestant Cemetery in Rome to seek out the graves of Shelley and Keats. I followed in his footsteps and also sought in Florence the burial place of Elizabeth Barrett Browning, the poet, who had eloped to Italy to marry fellow poet Robert. It must once have been a peaceful oasis, but now it resembles a traffic island, surrounded on all sides by a mayhem of screeching, polluting cars.

Further afield, in Amherst, Massachusetts, the poet Emily Dickinson is buried in the West Cemetery on Triangle Street. Every year, the museum there sponsors an Emily Dickinson poetry walk to honour the memory of the poet who died in 1886 after spending all her life in the town. At a series of locations significant in her life, students from the nearby college read her poems aloud, ending up at her grave. The poet was rather obsessed with death and the afterlife. When I taught an 'A' Level poetry class, the students grew more and more morose each week as we studied her many 'Death' poems.

I also made a pilgrimage to feel closer to one of my favourite authors, Edith Wharton. Her house is amazing, modelled on a French château and now home to a renowned Shakespearean Berkshire theatre group. At a time when many in Britain no longer see the relevance of teaching Shakespeare in schools, Americans just don't seem to be able to get enough of our bard. If you go to a West End UK production, most of the audience will be American groupies.

I did my own groupie thing and visited the house in Cambridge of the poet Henry Wadsworth Longfellow, where George Washington had later taken up residence; and the home of Louisa May Alcott in Concord. It is a well-preserved white cottage, intact with original furniture, including in the bedroom Louisa shared with her sister, the tiny half-moon, wooden desk built by her father, in the window recess, overlooking the orchard. She wrote *Little Women* and its sequels while sitting at this desk. The largest room in the house is given over to her father's study, complete with magnificent, huge, mahogany, green leather-topped desk.

Despite the fact that Louisa was the main breadwinner for the family, she never did have 'a room of her own'. Later, I learned that her father, a transcendental preacher, had founded a commune in a house on Ham Common, a five minute walk from where we live in England. In the nearby Concord cemetery, quaintly named Sleepy Hollow, are buried the families of Louisa May Alcott, Nathaniel Hawthorne, Henry Thoreau, Ralph Waldo Emerson and Walt Whitman. They're all grouped together, on top of a peaceful, little, wooded ridge, and a stone bench has been placed thoughtfully nearby for quiet worship.

As an admirer of all of these illustrious writers, I returned many times to Concord, archetypal New England suburbia, overflowing with white clapboard houses proudly flying the stars and stripes; store fronts little changed in hundreds of years; yellow school buses trundling along the wide, leafy streets; and the historic Colonial Inn close by the wooden Old North Bridge. This witnessed the start of the American Revolution, immortalised by Emerson, where 'the embattled farmers stood. And fired the shot heard round the world'. One of my Harvard professors, Sean O'Connell, had just published *Imagining Boston: a Literary Landscape*, tracing all the literary figures who had either grown up in the Boston area or had been attracted to join the literary figures already there. It seemed amazing to me that so many well-known writers either originated from or ended up in Boston. The city feels very literary and learned.

In Newport, Rhode Island, we rubber-necked the over-the-top, white, palatial mansions, which were always referred to as 'cottages' by wealthy occupants such as the Astors. New England's answer to Britain's stately homes, but a little grander and a lot more nouveau. The 1974 movie version of my favourite novel, F. Scott Fitzgerald's *The Great Gatsby*, was shot here. It tells of the betrayal of a handsome and enigmatic nouveau tycoon, played by a devastatingly handsome Robert Redford, betrayed by the American Dream during the Jazz Age of the 1930's. The shallow lives of the characters are destroyed by wealth. The film-makers probably didn't have to alter a thing. Fitzgerald's own life, his spiral into alcoholic and moral dissolution, is echoed in a poignant novel set in the South of France, in the decade after the First World War: *Tender is the Night*. The novel is his most autobiographical and charts the account of a caring man who, languishing on the Riviera, disintegrates slowly under the twin strains of his wife's derangement and the lifestyle that gnaws away at his sense of moral values. There are several versions of the film. In the 1962 version which I've seen, with Jennifer Jones and Jason Robards, the filming of the golden French Riviera and its sweep of expensive homes is magnificent, but there is little chemistry between the two main actors. Sometimes it's better to stick with the novels.

Boston and Cambridge are havens for bookaholics like me. Apart from in Hay-On Wye, I've never seen so many bookshops grouped together. In particular, Harvard Square had an amazing thirty three bookstores, many of them selling second-hand books or books at greatly discounted prices. Who could resist? Not only me but my whole family and many of our visitors returned to the UK laden down with irresistible bargains. Many of these were put aside for future reading and have found their way to Provence. At last I have time to read something other than the texts that I am teaching from the prescribed syllabus. We've become very popular in the village as the unofficial lending library of books in English. In one Harvard Square bookstore, a whole section was given over to Scottish poetry. In January, we signed up for a Burns' Supper, not knowing quite what to expect. It was so popular that the event had to be held over two evenings for about five hundred people. Bagpipers and Highland dancers had been flown in from Scotland; all the usual recitations and refreshments were there. Slightly surreal and it made us feel a little homesick.

Harvard Square is a must-see if you travel to Boston and neighbouring Cambridge. I spent some time there almost every day that I lived in Cambridge. It's so vibrant, always something going on, a bit like London's Covent Garden or Edinburgh during the Festival, with buskers singing, tap dancing, juggling, fire-eating, putting on a magic show. Like Covent Garden, performers must audition, such is the demand for 'spots'. It's a bustling place, crowded both day and night with students taking a break from class, dropping in to the legendary Coop store for stationery, textbooks and college sweatshirts; panhandlers milking the crowd watching the acts; rubberneckers observing all life from the outside tables at the fashionable café *Le Bon Pain*. This café is a Harvard institution. There are always a few stalwarts playing chess, the most serious playing against a clock; and people of all ages sipping cappuccinos or lattes outside, even on the coldest day. When I arrived in Boston, the first time that I'd lived in the States, I dreaded entering a coffee shop. It seemed that you had to know all the language, just the right expressions, to gain your cup of coffee. I soon learned the jargon: "A regular decaf skinny cappuccino with a twist on the side to go, please." Nowadays, British high streets are full of designer coffee shops: Costa Coffee, Starbucks and their clones, but in 1990 all this was new to me.

Also new to me was the weather. I'd got too used to living in the soft south. True, I'd grown up in Scotland, not renowned for its Mediterranean climate; on several occasions our school bus had been dug out by the snow plough. But in Boston you get *real* snow. In our first winter there, snow fell on fifty-five days. And that was just when the snow **fell**. From November to March, it never really went away. Layer upon layer built up. Huge machines cleared the roads and pushed the mounds of snow into high banks at the side. I purchased a whole new survival outfit, thereafter referred to as my Boston clothes: sheepskin boots, thick wool tights, a heavy wool coat, a serious hat, scarf and gloves. Years later, these clothes came in very useful on freezing Christmas trips to Munich and Prague. The whole outfit had to be donned even for the shortest trip to buy the breakfast bagels; then the whole lot had to be removed in the overheated, stifling shops and classrooms. Bostonians live for winter; the city truly embraces the season. Of course, the locals snorted at our discomfort and assured us that this was a mild winter, nothing at all. I waited and waited for a real cold snap when locals told me that Harvard Yard would fill up with snow like the fairy tale scene in *Love Story*, when Ali McGraw and Ryan O'Neill lie on the ground and make angels' wings. With only four months left of our stay in Boston,

I set out on a coast to coast train trip. When I returned, people told me of the serious snowfall I'd missed, showed me photos of the Yard under three feet of virgin snow. Three years later, in 1995, my husband returned to Boston on a business trip and the snow was so deep that it had completely covered the cars, so perhaps the Bostonians were being truthful after all and it wasn't just another of those: "When I was a boy . . ." stories to instil awe into the listener.

I have fonder memories of the fall in New England. When I first arrived I was sceptical. Surely autumn was autumn, even if it was called fall? After our first trip to view the leaf peep, I had to admit that I was wrong. Mile after mile in New Hampshire, Vermont and Maine we encountered every autumnal tone imaginable. The maple leaves provide a wonderful rich red rare in the UK. The locals take their display very seriously and weather reports are given daily, with regular updates so that people don't miss the best foliage. It's something that I would recommend – a holiday to New England to view the fall. Almost as spectacular is autumn in Provence, as the vines take on their autumnal hues shortly after the harvest, the *vendange*. On a more mundane level, on your US leaf-peeping expedition you can take in a few factory outlets where designer clothes are a fraction of the regular store price. Visit L.L. Bean, an American institution in Maine, and stock up on plaid shirts and everything imaginable for the great outdoors. Better than splashing out on designer approximations by Ralph Lauren. When we lived in Indonesia, one of our American neighbours sustained himself by a daily reading of the store catalogue. I think he got to know it off by heart and he would come home from his vacation newly kitted out by L. L. Bean, clutching the current catalogue.

Studying still left time for exploring Boston and its surroundings. Boston is a walking city – you can walk everywhere in relative safety. This is pretty unusual in most US towns and cities. Years before, on a visit to friends in Dallas, I'd risen early especially to stretch my legs after a long trans-Atlantic journey. : "Where are you off to all dressed up in your walking gear? You can't walk in Dallas. Everyone climbs into the car, even to go to the store on the other side of the highway. There are no sidewalks!" I wasn't convinced and set out around the block, however, after a few blocks I had to give up and admit defeat. Apart from the lack of sidewalks, the relentless humidity in summer precludes any serious walking. A common sight at the malls is that of women (for some reason it seems to be a female pursuit – perhaps they combine it with shopping) power walking, clad in the latest designer sports gear. They can window shop as they exercise. Seemed like a good idea to me. It was my first exposure to the American retail institutions of Lord and Taylor, Macys, Neiman Marcus and Bloom-ingdales.

A complete antidote to retail is a visit to Martha's Vineyard. Almost traffic free with wide cycle lanes; no fast food chains or garish neon signs; tasteful restau-rants; excellent book stores; picture-perfect clapboard houses, including the beach-hut like 'Gingerbread' houses built to house those who flocked to the popular nineteenth century religious Revivalist meetings. They are now greatly prized and cost about as much as a cottage in Dorset or a seaside beach hut; empty, golden beaches; and friendly people. What more could you want? It's full mostly of affluent yuppies, dressed in crisply pressed walking shorts, logoed polo shirts and Timberland deck-shoes, and their Ralph Lauren-clad children – quite similar in fact to Rock, in Cornwall.

Another unspoilt destination is Stockbridge, home to the artist Norman Rockwell, famous for his depictions of small town America. Even though you don't recognise the name, you've probably come across some of his best-selling posters. One of the most famous is entitled *The Runaway* and shows a diner with a policeman and a little boy sitting on high bar stools. The boy has a Dick Whittington red bundle on a stick beside him, and you just know that the policeman is reassuring the boy that nothing is as bad as it seems. The diner is to be found in Stockbridge, the subject of another famous painting *Stockbridge Main Street at Christmas*, where the village either resembles Toytown, or lets you wallow in the nostalgia of a perfect American community. The town really is picture perfect. We stayed overnight in the *Red Lion Inn*, a Historic Hotel, one of the few remaining American inns in continuous use since the eighteenth century. It was like a step back in time: painted and stencilled wooden beds, patchwork comforters, antique painted chests and closets, original Rockwell drawings on the walls, and rocking chairs on the verandah overlooking Main Street. Later, we sought out *Alice's Restaurant*, immortalised in the folk song by native son Arlo Guthrie. The lyrics describe how he and his friends visited *Alice's Restaurant* for Thanksgiving dinner; collected her garbage as a favour; drove to the dump, closed for the holiday; abandoned the garbage; were tracked down by an eager policeman who had spotted an addressed envelope at the bottom of the gulley; arrested, charged with littering, and jailed. Before he enters the cell, his belt is removed in case he hangs himself, for littering! It gets even more bizarre. Years later, Guthrie is about to enter the army to serve his country in Vietnam. He passes all the medicals and tests until he comes to the final question: "Have you ever been arrested and charged with a crime?" Thus, the littering prevented him from serving his country. Guthrie sees it as an example of American blind justice and has been making a living ever since by singing the tale. We heard the sad story at a concert held in Boston. Give it a listen, but allow plenty of time as the sorry tale goes on, and on, for at least twenty five minutes. In fact, almost the whole concert. *Alice's Restaurant* no longer exists, but the old Trinity Church where she once lived is now the Guthrie Centre and a shrine for cultural and educational exchange.

All too soon, it was time to leave Boston and move to Singapore where the facility that my husband had helped to design would be built. In my last six months, I completed my last class, a psychology option. I liked the fact that the degree was so wide; it reminded me of the educational system I had grown up with in Scotland. In addition to four classes in my major, English, I had to take two English seminars, two history classes and something completely outside my field of study. I chose a course on late nineteenth century French painters. This was taught by an American with perfect French. He had lived in Paris for four years and was an ardent Francophile. I felt a little out of my depth; everyone else seemed to have an art background. Our end of term paper, twenty-five typed pages, was to be an in-depth study of a significant painting from the era. I discussed my concerns with him and he suggested that I write the paper on a work of Literature, Guy de Maupassant's *Bel Ami*. This is a satire of the period and concentrates on one painting: Manet's *A Bar at the Folies Bergère*. It wasn't until I got back to London that I was able to visit the Courtauld Institute and view the painting in all its glory. However, Boston Museum of Fine Arts has an outstanding collection of nineteenth century French art. Americans on the Grand Tour snapped up the Impressionist works of art that were receiving so much criticism at the time and not highly prized by the French. Since then, I've sought out the Impressionist paintings we studied. In 2003 and 2004, when my husband spent eighteen months working in Paris, as a consultant to his old company, I became a regular visitor to the *Musée d'Orsay* and the *Louvre* and we visited Monet's wonderful garden at Giverney. Recently, The Royal Academy in London held an excellent small exhibition of nineteenth century Impressionist paintings, either by French artists such as Monet, Pisarro and Renoir, or by American artists who had visited Giverney and been inspired to paint in a similar style. I recognised many of the paintings from my wanderings round the world-class Boston Museum of Fine Arts which had loaned the paintings for the exhibition.

My psychology class helped me with my thesis entitled: *Macbeth, James I, Maternal Deprivation and Patriarchy*. Catchy title, isn't it? It began as a working title, but my advisor rather liked it and so it stuck. I'd been inspired to attempt a Shakespeare thesis after taking a seminar with Professor Marjorie Garbor, a renowned Shakespearian scholar and author. I found her intimidating, but boy did she know her stuff, and she liked the preliminary ideas for my thesis. As part of her class, we researched obscure facets of Shakespearian connections. I discovered in the rarefied theatre archives that Sarah Bernhardt had not only played Hamlet on stage but actually thought that Hamlet had been a woman! In my professor's book published while I was in Boston: *Vested Interests: Cross Dressing and Cultural Anxiety*, she mentions this fact, but I looked in vain for my credit. It makes fascinating reading; almost anyone you can think of in the media is, according to Garbor, a cross-dresser – including Elvis, Theodore Roosevelt, and Peter Pan.

I completed my thesis working under the direction of the curator of the Harvard Theatre Collection. Wearing white cotton gloves, I was allowed to handle precious articles, ancient theatre programmes and first folios. Nothing was too much trouble. I wanted to view several versions of *Macbeth*; they were ordered in for me. I wanted to read a thesis from Chicago University; a copy was sent by return of post. Remember, this was in 1992, before the wonders of the Internet. My adviser had doubts about a piece of my research, gleaned from reading Antonia Fraser's work on Mary Queen of Scots: "I'll just check it out this weekend. I'm going to a party over in England with Antonia and Harold." It was such a rarefied world. We attended a 'black and white' costume party to celebrate the acquisition of Andy Warhol's black and white theatre portraits. Harvard is so wealthy compared to British institutions.

My completed thesis was dedicated, bound in standard Harvard Crimson leather, and a copy placed in the hallowed Widener Library, the largest privately owned library in the world. In the US, only the Library of

Congress and the New York Public Library have more than Widener's three million volumes (and that does not include the holdings of Harvard's ninety or so departmental libraries elsewhere on campus). When I re-visited a few years later, the thesis co-ordinator had a copy of my thesis on her book shelf. Said she showed it to students and it had inspired three new Shakespeare theses after a long, dry period. To my surprise, I received an 'A' grade for my thesis, and a distinction for my completed degree, and the highlight was the graduation ceremony, known as Commencement. So much pomp and ceremony. Thirty thousand participants crowded into Harvard Yard, decorated for the occasion with banners and bunting. Each year there is a key speaker and my favourite living author, John Updike, was that year's guest. He is one of the authors who have moved to the Boston area to become part of the literary scene. Bands played, reunion classes marched proudly, the medics behaved uproariously. My parents attended and I think they felt proud of my success and glad to be part of such an illustrious occasion. My first stint at university in Scotland had been more of a social experience. If I had not been a mobile wife, I would never have had the opportunity to attend Harvard, to widen my reading, expose myself to new literary theories, and mix with students much younger than myself. I'm a different person because I had that experience.

I've kept up with a few of my classmates; returned to Boston for a Harvard Club wedding and a reunion; re-visited my neighbour Marie and old haunts. Once you've lived in Boston, it never quite lets you go. Friends we made during our expat stay there visit us in London and Provence, where we sit up late reminiscing about mostly happy times. Boston will always be one of my favourite places, as it was of Charles Dickens who visited in 1867 and stayed at the Parker House before giving readings from his work at the nearby Tremont Temple. He had such celebrity status that the hotel had to keep a guard outside his door to fend off curious fans and autograph hunters. I love watching television series set in the Boston area, such as *Ali McBeal*, *Cheers* and *Boston Legal*, and the numerous movies, such as *Good Will Hunting*, *Mystic River*, *Little Women*, *Love Story* and *The Firm*. Film makers seem to love the area as much as I do.

Back on the Rails: Amtrak Adventure

In the spring of 1992, just before we left Boston, I took a trip from the east coast to the west, across the States by train. Friends were horrified when I outlined the journey. "But nobody travels by train!" What they meant was, "People like us don't travel by train." However, they were wrong. I had finished studying for my degree, was waiting to graduate, and had time on my hands. I'd flown many times within the country; however, you don't see much of the terrain travelling that way. I wanted to see the bits in between. "But there isn't anything! Just miles and miles of plains and wheat fields!" Then that's what I'd see. My friend's husband, Bill, was envious of my twelve-day trip, coast to coast.

He'd never left the US, had no desire to do so, and considered my journey the perfect holiday. We tend to forget that he is fairly typical and that only around 11% of Americans hold a passport.

I didn't know quite what to expect. The Amtrak train ticket certainly wasn't cheap; it didn't equate to a Greyhound bus. I decided to treat myself to a first class sleeping berth, with private shower and loo. It was sheer luxury, a double cabin all to myself, where the banquette folded down at night to create a luxurious bed made up with fine, crisp, cotton sheets.

Riding the rails provided an ever-changing cast of characters. The people on board were a revelation, full of helpful information about their own backyard. Travellers were seated in the dining car as they arrived, in groups of four, so my travelling companions changed at each unexpectedly good meal. On the whole, the passengers were affluent and retired, and they had chosen the train as the most enjoyable form of transport. It wasn't just about getting somewhere but about travel. In addition to this trip from Boston to Chicago, then on eventually to reach Los Angeles, they'd travelled on the Californian Zephyr, passing through Denver, the Rockies, Salt Lake City, to San Francisco. One couple had taken the southern route on the Sunset Limited train from Orlando through New Orleans, San Antonio and El Paso before arriving in Los Angeles. All the names seemed magical to me, a train virgin. There were no beige people on this train. Why did they choose to travel this way? They enjoyed meeting like-minded people with a thirst for travelling; they enjoyed the legroom; the privacy when desired; the huge picture windows; and, for some, the laptop sockets.

All I had taken with me was a notebook, a pen and a stack of reading material. However, I spent hour after hour just staring out of the window at the passing countryside. In a way, my friends had been right. There wasn't much there, in the middle of the US, but it was good to see it for myself and it helped me to appreciate the vastness and history of America. We passed through a town 'Famous for the invention of chewing gum'. Another was 'The home of Pillsbury baking mixes'. The smallest, one-horse town has its claim to fame.

And there was plenty of time to 'stand and stare'. This is no TGV, capable of topping one hundred and sixty miles per hour. Rather, we ambled along at about seventy miles per hour, no faster than British Intercity trains, but a lot more punctual. Amazingly, the train arrived at each destination more or less on time, with the exception of a one-hour delay in reaching Flagstaff, Arizona, due to bad weather and snow on the track. In Britain, we can't even cope with leaves on the track. Trains are a pretty reliable indication of a country's character.

My first overnight stop was Chicago, just long enough to do a mini-tour of the city, see the Frank Lloyd Wright architectural wonders and explore one world-class museum. A lightening stop, but it gave me a flavour. The highlight came in the evening as I entered the lobby of my historic hotel. Such a crowd of people! My enquiries revealed that it was a party for Bill Clinton, who had just been adopted as the Democratic Presidency candidate. I didn't know much about him then, but I heard him give a brilliant speech and with his charisma it was obvious that he was going to go far.

After a long haul, we pulled in to Lamy, near Albuquerque, New Mexico, and I took a bus to Santa Fé.

For years, American friends had raved about this town, beloved of artists, and I'd wanted to see it for myself. While living in Boston, I'd read a coffee table book on Santa Fé Style, basically Spanish colonial, or South Western. Most of the buildings, including my hotel, are adobe, made of mud and straw bricks covered in pink mud plaster, giving the buildings their sensuous, curving walls. Adobe is one of the oldest building materials known to man, and Santa Fé in particular is awash with it. Actually, I learned later that most of these buildings have a wooden frame and faux adobe stucco, but they looked charming none the less. It was quite different from anything I'd seen before. The town claims more fascinating characters, more art, and more multicultural energy than any other city in America, with the possible exception of New York, one hundred times its size. And the town lives up to its claims; it's a unique experience.

Santa Fé is more than a little kitsch, very expensive, and, surprisingly, one of the culinary capitals of America. Apart from New Orleans, it is the only town that has evolved a broad and distinctive regional menu. Anyone for crab and mango on tortilla spaghetti with habañero chile sour cream? No, I didn't make that up. Notice the spelling: not 'chilli' as in Texas. And all washed down with chile-spiked beer or jugs of salt-crusted margaritas. Years later, while visiting my husband who was living in Houston, Texas, we set out to re-visit Santa Fé. It was eighty five degrees and humid and I was clad in bare feet and sandals and a cotton skirt. Unfortunately, when we reached Santa Fé, a sudden change in the weather meant that the temperature had plummeted and there was

eighteen inches of newly fallen snow. I was totally un-
prepared.

My husband refuses to be daunted and, despite the
inclement weather, we ventured out to try and find the
famed Coyote Café. "Oh, you'll never get in. You have
to book months and months ahead," we'd been
warned. I had to wear my seen-better-days trainers, a
pashmina and a headscarf for ploughing through the
snow – hardly glamorous. To our surprise, we were
greeted with smiles and led to an excellent table where
we could watch the proceedings in the kitchen. So
much for the doom-mongers. I remember eating rabbit
confit enchilada with molé poblano sauce and orange-
jicama salsa. Perhaps I wouldn't remember the meal so
clearly if I hadn't framed the menu. Rather a naff thing
to do, but it hangs on our kitchen wall in Provence and
brings back happy memories of a wonderful nouveau
New Mexican meal, spiked with Christmas red and
green peppers. French dinner guests peruse the framed
menu hanging on the kitchen wall with puzzlement and
much shaking of the head, unable to recognise anything
even vaguely familiar.

In addition to the wonderful, spicy food, I overdosed
on the art and bought a Georgia O'Keeffe poster of a
giant orange poppy which now hangs framed in our
salon in Provence. It seems to fit right in, looks very
Provençal; the two cultures have similarities. Both areas
have wonderful light, big skies and scenery that attract
painters and writers. O'Keeffe bought a ranch close to
Taos, a few miles from Santa Fé, in the 1920's and
painted the animal skulls, flowers and churches that she
discovered around her home. Four miles south of Taos,
she painted again and again the mission church of San

Francisco de Assisi; its adobe buttressed back is regarded as one of the purest architectural forms in North America. The same church inspired Ansel Adams to abandon his plans to become a concert pianist and take up photography.

I had made a side trip to Taos to follow up the D. H. Lawrence connection. At the time, I was teaching *Sons and Lovers* and on researching Lawrence's life discovered that he and Frieda had spent several years living in a ranch in New Mexico, writing, but also producing ten paintings. He had been searching for something spiritual in New Mexico and also hoped that the dry desert air would heal his tuberculosis. Unfortunately, it did not and he died in 1930, in Vence in the South of France, aged only 44. I tracked down an exhibition of his paintings in Taos Plaza, in a rather run-down, cowboy-style hotel called *La Fonda*. I was lucky. The exhibition had only been open for a few days. The hotel's owner had deemed the paintings lewd, pornographic and had kept them locked in the cellar, well away from the public. However, he'd died a few weeks before and his heirs had decided that the paintings needed an audience. To be honest, I thought them of poor quality. I love his novels and his poetry, however, his paintings, which have now been obtained by Nottingham University, are an acquired taste.

We visited Taos Pueblo, one of the most famous architectural monuments in the United States, two miles out of town. Begun about 1200, it has been inhabited continuously for almost eight hundred years. It is amazing, a series of adobe 'apartments' piled one on top of the other, the topmost reached by a series of ladders. Yes, it is a well-worn stop on the tourist route, but it seemed unspoilt, in no danger of becoming another Disneyland. The inhabitants still have no electricity, piped water or phones. There are a handful of artists' studios, mostly selling rather fine pottery, and we bought from an Indian named Nighthawk a 'healing bear', a very tactile stone bear with a hole in his middle and coloured feathers tied to his back. Years later, when we owned our house in Provence, we wandered into a well-known artist's studio in Vaison-la-Romaine. Among the usual paintings of lavender, sunflowers and olive trees were a series of paintings of what we recognised as Taos Pueblo. We spoke to the artist and he was brimming over with enthusiasm for the wonderful adobe buildings in New Mexico, the fusion of Indian, Hispanic and Anglo culture, and the special light that reminded him of Provence. Most things in New Mexico are above 1500 metres which does give everything an amazing clarity.

What about the fascinating characters? No shortage of those in either Santa Fé or Taos. Pueblo and Navaho Indians sit under the portico in front of the General's Palace, displaying their beautiful weavings and chunky silver and turquoise jewellery. This is the genuine article, heirlooms of the future with a sacred spiritual significance. And the residents who choose to wear Santa Fé style are just as colourful. For the women, this means a full, tiered skirt encircled by a large silver *concha* belt, tan suede embroidered waistcoat, dangling Navaho earrings, three or four silver and turquoise bracelets and the ubiquitous cowboy boots. The men wear equally colourful dress of fringed buckskin jacket, big silver belt, cowboy boots and a chunk of turquoise worn round the neck on a thong. Very colourful, but everyday dress for them.

For a few days, we stayed in the *Taos Inn*, a historic hotel dating from the 1600's and furnished with antiques and local art. The cold weather was kept at bay with a wonderful log fire in the traditional *kiva* fireplace. Originally, a *kiva* was a sacred shelter used by Pueblo men for ceremonial rites and social or political gatherings. It was entered by a smoke hole in the roof; the *kiva* fireplace is modelled on this and we copied the design for our fireplace in Provence. Our bookshelves are painted adobe pink. Actually, the tin said 'National Trust Book Room Red', but they're very pink. When we went down to the hotel bar in the evening, we were amazed by the 'fancy dress' of the regulars. Several Doc Holliday look-alikes in string tie, long frockcoat and black hat. Others seemed to have modelled themselves on Kit Carson, another local resident. The women in their hippie-chic were even more ornately dressed than the ones I'd seen in town. I felt very ordinary and dull.

Back to my train ride. I made a short trip to Flagstaff, close to the Grand Canyon. On everyone's list of places to see and very worth seeing. I woke up in the morning in my hotel room on the edge of the canyon to a foot of snow and unbelievably spectacular views. I had time for a day tour round the perimeter; with more time, I would have liked to sign up for a three-day hike into the bottom of the canyon.

My coast to coast trip finished in big, bustling Los Angeles, my least favourite destination. I did all the touristy things: gawked at the stars' homes in Beverley Hills; the shoppers on Rodeo Drive; Universal Studios; and the cemented hand-prints outside the Chinese Theatre. But there was a feeling of unrest and the place seemed to have no centre, no soul, certainly no sidewalks for walking. I was glad to leave and fly back to less pretentious Boston, the American city where I feel most at home.

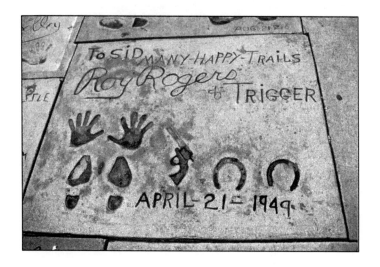

Singapore Sling

But soon it was time to move on, to uproot and move to Singapore. We lived there from 1992-1994, while the chemical plant designed in Boston was added to the refinery; however, we got to know the country quite well while we were living in Sumatra in the mid-80's. Trips to Singapore then were frequent and exciting. We loved living the simple life on the edge of the jungle in Sumatra, but Singapore represented civilisation and excitement. It was here that you could catch up on favourite television programmes or see the latest blockbuster movie. Most of all, we loved the opportunity to stay at some of the best hotels in the world, eat wonderful food in restaurants ranging from Michelin star standard to simple hawker stalls. *Raffles Hotel*, symbolic of the grace and style of the colonial area, was still in its original state: non air-conditioned, depending on ceiling fans and open-side 'walls' to keep the customers cool. In the past, the hotel had been a haven for rubber planters down from up-country Malaya, a meeting place for the rich and famous. When the Japanese took Singapore in 1942, many British made their last stand in *Raffles*, dancing the night away. We played the tourists and sipped our Singapore Slings in the Long Bar and ate the traditional curry *tiffin* for lunch. The hotel lived up to its carefully nurtured legend and we listened avidly to tales the barman told of the last tiger being cornered in the billiards room in 1902; visits by Joseph Conrad and Rudyard Kipling; and Somerset Maugham gossiping all evening and writing the resulting stories in the morning.

Years later, when we came to live in Singapore, *Raffles* was magnificent, but almost unrecognisable: acres of gleaming white marble, neo-classical columns, air-conditioning and a mini-mall of expensive designer boutiques. Tourists still sipped their Singapore Slings, but not in the original Long Bar. It was **called** the Long Bar but had moved several floors away from the original. The *tiffin* was as magnificent as ever: a buffet of sixty or so curries and accompaniments, but this venue too had changed. There was still a strict dress code – my nineteen year old, self-conscious daughter was once kept standing for several long minutes at the entrance to the tea room while worried staff debated over whether she was wearing knee-length black linen shorts (unacceptable) or culottes (would just pass muster). Fortunately, they decided on culottes. What **has** changed is the entry policy. In its heyday, *Raffles* was a white, male, officer-class preserve. Lowly other ranks, Chinese, Indians and Eurasians were all banned. Even today, locals with long memories refuse to give *Raffles* their custom. My Canadian friend Colleen with whom we were having tea that day, is married to a Chinese Singaporean who refuses to set foot in the place. *Raffles* may be in for another dramatic change as it has just been sold by the Singapore Government to a US investment firm as part of a £495 million package. Many Singaporeans fear that the national monument described by Somerset Maugham as a symbol 'for all the fables of the exotic East' will be Americanised by the new owners. Let's hope it doesn't end up looking like Disneyland.

In Singapore, we also shopped for food. Yes, all the necessities to survive were available in Sumatra: good rice, fish, vegetables, fruit; however, sometimes you yearned for something from home. For the American expats, this would be something like Hershey bars, or chocolate chips for baking cookies. As a Brit, I longed for homely ingredients, all non-essential, like Worcester sauce, oatcakes and marmalade. Singapore could provide all these and more.

When we first moved to live in Singapore, an early visitor was a young, well-fed Chinese who introduced himself as Richard. Richard was Mr Fixit. Anything you desired, Richard could procure for you. I don't mean anything illicit; rather, he came armed with a portfolio of coloured photographs of everyday food items to jog your memory. You ended up ordering things you didn't even know you wanted: Ribena, no problem; peanut butter, easy. He was a godsend, especially as I worked full-time and had no way of getting to the early morning markets to buy the choicest fruits and vegetables. Richard's many helpers would do this for me, choosing the ripest pineapple, asking for it to be peeled, the eyes removed (a difficult and messy business). I never received any second-rate produce. My box of ordered shopping would arrive at the door minutes after my return from work, saved until the last delivery to ensure freshness and payment. How he managed all this was a mystery.

One day, we visited an outlying area in search of a sofa and purely by accident came across Richard's business empire. He was working out of a hole-in-the-wall. Dozens of cardboard boxes full of recognisable expat favourites lined the alley in front of his shop. How he procured the goods, who knows? What an efficient operator! What an entrepreneur! He probably runs a business on the internet now, similar in scale to Tesco's.

Richard could procure almost all the ingredients necessary to celebrate Christmas, bar the English sausages and party crackers. Silly really, but I just had to have these, so the children were given a shopping list of British essentials to bring out on the plane with them at the beginning of the school holidays. Of course, the sausages were a Customs non-starter. The crackers made it to Singapore, but not before the authorities pulled out the 'cracker' in each one. On Christmas Day, we pulled the crackers in unison while shouting, "Bang!" Apart from the obvious fears about combustion on the plane, Singapore in the 90's had a law banning firecrackers of any description. In fact, Singapore had a long list of banned items and activities: jay walking, litter, smoking in public places, graffiti and vandalism in general, chewing gum, failing to flush a public toilet and drug taking of any kind. Singapore is a city state ruled by a kind of benevolent authoritarianism. How dreadful, I hear you say, yet the country is well-ordered, happy, crime-free, a marvel of efficiency, cleanliness and prosperity.

Everyone has a roof over his head, albeit in uniform tower blocks of identikit apartments. You never see any beggars. Public transport is clean and efficient. The streets are safe. When the mayor, Ken Livingston, was looking for ideas on how to improve London transport, where did he turn? Yes, he and his advisors made a trip to Singapore to study the excellent Mass Rapid Transit rail system which runs on time, is clean and efficient, not a piece of graffiti in sight. Probably he came up with the idea for his congestion charge in Singapore. Certainly when we were living there, cars could not enter the central zone during peak periods unless they displayed a disc showing that a tax had been paid for that day. An inconvenience, but it certainly eased congestion. And jay walking really is a crime. If you attempt to cross the road in an unauthorised zone, one of the many police on duty will fine you on the spot. What Singapore is short of is land: too many people in a very small space, however, the government introduced measures to deal with this.

The streets are impressively clean. When we lived there, dropping litter could result in a fine equivalent to £400, and repeat offenders were forced to join rubbish collection teams wearing jackets proclaiming "Corrective work order." Perhaps they were just ahead of their time. Moves are afoot in Britain to 'name and shame', to make offenders bear some responsibility for their anti-social behaviour.

And the no smoking in public policy is refreshing, quite a change from the incessant intake of distinctive clove-scented cigarettes by every male in nearby Indonesia. It's good to enter a restaurant and not have to worry about someone lighting up a cigar as you're half-way through a meal, or chain smoking throughout the meal. How do they taste the food? Dividing restaurants into smoking and no smoking areas just doesn't seem to work. In Britain, we now have no smoking in the workplace, hence the common sight of workers hunched over with cold, lighting up outside the office building. Moves are afoot to ban smoking in all public places. And in Ireland, they have banned smoking in pubs and restaurants, with little fall in trade.

Graffiti is endemic in the affluent area where we live in England. Slogans painted over are soon defaced again. However, recently, community police have taken a hard line, identifying offenders through their 'tag' and insisting that when caught they clean off the graffiti when caught. Perhaps Singapore had the right idea. In 1993, the western press, America in particular, was outraged by the harshness of the punishment meted out as the result of anti-social behaviour to a young American schoolboy and his associates. Joyriding in his mother's car, he and his friends spray-painted buildings and, worst of all, cars. I say that because cars were prohibitively expensive and you had to obtain a 'right to buy' permit before you were even allowed to contemplate purchasing one. This also helped to keep the traffic flowing. As he was the only one old enough (16) to be prosecuted, he was convicted of vandalism and sentenced to both a term in prison and flogging. Younger participants in the crime were spirited out of the country by influential parents. Many in the liberal west were shocked by the perceived barbarity of the punishment, but it certainly acted as a deterrent to others.

I believe that the ban on chewing gum in Singapore has been rescinded recently, just as we in Britain are realising that we have a huge problem on our hands as streets and schools are covered in gum.

For a long time, Singapore has had a zero tolerance stance on drugs of any kind and therefore the city has few of the problems associated with a drug culture. Perhaps Britain should have learned something from Singapore and we wouldn't have the problems we have today.

The 'nanny knows best' way of thinking led Singapore to organise a Great Singapore Workout, designed to mobilise Singaporeans for the National Healthy Lifestyle Programme. It made it into the *Guinness Book of Records* for the largest mass aerobic session when more than 26,000 eager citizens joined Cabinet ministers for an exercise session. When we first visited Singapore, in 1985, we never saw an overweight Singaporean. Any food available was Chinese, Malayan or Indian, based on staples of rice and noodles and healthy. By 1993, the streets were full of overweight children, partaking eagerly in the plethora of fast-food chains that had grown up. The ethos of after-school tutoring in a multitude of subjects leaves little time for exercise and leisure pursuits. Singapore was quick to address this problem, by introducing compulsory exercise in schools, encouraging a healthy, low fat, traditional diet. Sound familiar? *Jamie's Dinners* may not have been necessary if we had copied Singapore sooner.

Fifteen years ago, Singapore already had in place a strategy to make it easier for people to meet, marry and produce offspring. Graduate matchmaking agencies were commonplace, just as they are in Britain today. We may not have the horribly named 'Breeding for Brilliance' campaign, however, there is some concern that our largely single and poorly educated London immigrant population is reproducing faster than any other group.

Of course, Singapore is not perfect. I found the huge masses of people and lack of green spaces claustrophobic. If we had lived in Singapore before our assignment in Australia, I would have appreciated the wide open spaces more. On our frequent forays to Changi Airport, a flawless utopia of perfect palms, orchids and cascading waterfalls lit by neon, you could hardly move for families having a day out. Even more bizarrely, pupils in school uniforms relishing the green space and air-conditioning to complete homework and study for exams.

The food is good, the water drinkable, the telephones work, our house was surrounded by palm trees and orchids; however, there's got to be more to life than shopping in immaculate, white-tiled, air-conditioned plazas, and Singaporeans live to shop. It's very much a consumer culture. The huge array of designer-name boutiques and department stores cater to fashion-conscious locals as much as to tourists. When we lived in Sumatra, there were no recognisable shops. You knew that there was little to buy and you accepted it. Clothes had to be made by a local dressmaker. Apart from staples like rice, vegetables and fruit, food was in short supply. The company commissary received a shipment of imported supplies, in theory every six months; however, on one occasion we waited for nine months, and when the shipment was opened there were unexplained gaps. Corruption was rife. On frequent trips to Singapore, I stocked up with homely British essentials, and even more bizarrely, on one such visit I managed to catch six episodes of my favourite period television series ever: *Brideshead Revisited* – sheer nostalgic escapism. In Singapore, our expectations were raised as the shelves in the supermarkets were groaning with food; however, you soon came to realise that the choice of goods was limited and perhaps not what you wanted to buy.

There was also strict censorship. Sometimes, a publication would not appear at all. At other times, you could buy foreign newspapers or magazines; however, the censor's pen would have blacked out some offensive story. Films, too, were often difficult to follow as essential episodes were deemed too violent or pornographic or critical of Singapore and had been cut by the censor. I would find it difficult to live in a country where individual liberties, some of the freedoms we take for granted, are placed below the welfare of society as a whole.

I loved my job in Singapore, teaching English and English Literature at a private international school, to pupils who were mostly British, Canadian, Taiwanese, Korean and Japanese. In fact, we had twenty two nationalities. I worried that through the literature on offer, we were teaching these pupils an ethnocentric view of life in America and Britain. Many of my female Japanese students were worryingly passive and had ambitions to be housewives – American housewives. On my recommendation, my brightest Japanese pupil gained a place at Smith, an illustrious Ivy League American university.

We've kept in touch for many years; I'm not sure that she was very happy there or that the US lived up to her high expectations. Her American experience made it difficult for her to fit back into conformist Japanese society. The Korean students were a tougher bunch. They came from a society where hard work was expected and caning the accepted punishment for low academic performance or misbehaviour. They became enraged when I refused to be bullied, or bribed, to raise their grades to an 'A'. Gradually, I earned their respect and many of them did achieve the all important top grade. We taught in tandem a British curriculum, leading to GCSE's, and an American accredited programme. Pupils could dip in and out of both, much like the British government's proposed new educational system, and most of them gained entrance to universities of their choice. However, I co-edited the school Yearbook and some of the pupils graduating could not compose two or three lines for their entry. I worried about how they would fare in the real world. In Singapore, many of them were the sons of rich businessmen or diplomats. They drove BMW's, Mercedes and had expensive mobile phones (still rare at that time). When they moved to the US to pursue a business degree in California, the most common ambition, would they have the same status?

We all rubbed along well together in the multi-cultural English Department. Department meetings were held frequently downtown in the *Hyatt Hotel*. Business was discussed, policies implemented, minutes taken over a Ritz-like afternoon tea accompanied by a piano tinkling in the background. Or occasionally over a jug of ice-cold margaritas in a surreal Tex-Mex bar. Very civilised. Despite there being around 48,000 expats in

Singapore at that time, it seemed like a big village. On Saturdays, during forays to Holland Village, a shopping area a little out of town where small Chinese emporiums co-existed amicably with a Haagen-Dazs ice-cream parlour, or on strolls down the main thoroughfare, Orchard Road, I always bumped into someone I knew, from school or the larger expat community.

As recently as the 1960's, Singapore was a cesspool of filth and poverty. Many of the predominantly Chinese population were living in villages without water or sewerage. Gang fighting was commonplace. Today it is unrecognisable. The country's stunning economic turn-around, initially under the premier Lee Kuan Yew, left Singapore with the highest standard of living in Asia and it has continued to grow and prosper since we left, with a few blips in the economy.

When we first visited Singapore, in 1985, Chinatown was huge. You could wander through the slightly threatening, very exotic streets for hours. We bought Chinese cooking bowls and spices from old shop houses and lit incense in backstreet temples. By the time we came to live there, in 1992, most of the old Chinatown had been razed to the ground in the name of progress, to make way for the new, super-efficient metro system, and replaced with towering glass and concrete shopping malls. Eventually, the government realised that they had lost something, that tourists didn't necessarily want a completely sanitised city. So the Mysterious East is being put back into their island, without re-creating the squalor. Amazingly, having eradicated Bugis Street, the centre of the Red Light district and the haunt of transvestites, they've introduced a sanitised version and employed lady-boys to strut their stuff and titillate the

visitors. Little India and Arab Street are newly promoted; visits to the Chinese mythology park at Haw Par
Villa, the Chinese Gardens based on the style of Peking's
Summer Palace in the Sung Dynasty, and the theme park
on Sentosa Island are encouraged. The old, crumbling
shop-houses down on the once-seedy waterfront have
been restored and gaily painted, turned into thriving,
buzzing restaurants and bars. You can view the statue of
Sir Stamford Raffles as you dine – I think he would have
approved. On Sunday mornings, you can still visit Chinatown and listen to the concert as hundreds of prized
caged birds show off their repertoire, outside the street
cafés. The owner's status is reflected in the jade-en-
crusted carvings or the simple rattan enclosure. Old
men bring their pets for an airing, to enjoy a few hours
of almost freedom. A delicately carved wooden birdcage
now hangs in our conservatory at home, but the bird inside is painted wood.

We were as guilty as anyone of sometimes longing
for a sanitised version of Singapore. You can eat the
excellent Chinese, *Nonya* (a combination of Chinese
and Malay), Malayan and Indian foods at open air
hawker stalls. They are government inspected and very
clean. However, the heat and humidity often seemed
less attractive than the restaurant in the air-conditioned
American Club where you could eat only slightly toned
down versions of the same food. Perhaps a strange
choice for us to choose to join the American Club, but
it was the best club in town, with wonderful sporting
and social facilities. My husband works for an American company, and many of our closest friends are
American. Our only gripe about the club was the dress
code: no blue jeans in the dining rooms and men must

wear jackets. In a tropical climate, that just seems nonsensical.

Other attractions, such as the beautiful, state-of-the-art Bird Park and zoo remain unchanged, but I read recently that grim Changi Prison has been knocked down and a new, modern correctional facility built. Our family visit there on Christmas Eve was one of the most moving experiences of our stay in Singapore. The makeshift prison chapel where prisoners prayed, under the cross carved from a shell-casing by Sergeant Harold Stogden; the museum with postcards, drawings, lockets, murals and heart-rending, photographic records and testimonies from prisoners interred during the Second World War; and the posted messages from visiting Japanese, ashamed of the atrocities committed by their countrymen. All these really touched us. We should not forget. Our visit to Bukit Larangan, Forbidden Hill, was also memorable. In the old Christian cemetery, weathered tombstones, almost indecipherable, hint at a tougher past when tropical diseases took their toll. The epitaph on the gravestone of Charles Chalk, 26, says simply: "Who came here in search of health and died." At the immaculately maintained Kranji War Cemetery, in the north of Singapore, is the major war grave for the Asia-Pacific region, where 4,467 are buried. A further 24,000 names of soldiers and airmen whose bodies were never found are inscribed on a palm-shaded memorial. Singapore was running out of space even in 1944, so perhaps now some of the old burial grounds have been bulldozed to make way for more identikit flats, more glass shopping malls.

We like watching and taking part in festivals and Singapore has more than thirty, linked to the lunar calendar. I remember vividly Chinese New Year with its feasts, dancing dragons and lions, stilt-walkers and jugglers; the Hindu festival of *Thaipusam,* during which devotees pierce their bare chests with hooked chains hanging from a frame which they carry through the streets to proclaim their faith. We saw this celebrated both in Singapore and Bali, and in Provence we have a photograph in our gallery of a young, Balinese man in a trance, physically supported by two of his friends; and the Moslem festival of *Hari Raya Pusa* at the end of Ramadan; and the pilgrimage to the island of Kusu, attended by both Chinese and Malays, who go to the site where a turtle transformed itself into a safe landing place for ship-wrecked sailors. The turtles in the lagoon are still worshipped today. When my parents visited, I worried that they'd find little to marvel at in western-ised Singapore, but I was wrong. I was used to being surrounded by orchids, hibiscus, bougainvillea and palm trees which ran rampant in the stultifying humidity. They were not. I took them on a trip to Kusu and my mother especially was enchanted. As she stood on the Bounty-white beach, holding a coconut, she exclaimed, "It's a paradise; just like being on a desert island!"

Three quarters of the population is Chinese, but the city is multicultural and people seem to rub along in harmony, while accepting differences. I like the story I once heard that summed up the attitude of Singapore's races by saying, if you told a joke the Malays laughed; the Tamils tried to work out its spiritual significance; and the Chinese placed bets on whether you could tell another just as funny. I took taxis every day, to get to and from work; shop downtown; enjoy the nightlife. Taxis were cheap, clean and plentiful, a godsend if you happened to get caught in the almost daily monsoon-like rainstorm. The drivers were friendly, inquisitive and shared the latest jokes. Several times a week, when I gave directions to the taxi driver taking me home from work: "Regency Park, please", the retort would come something like, "How you afford live in such fancy place on teacher's salary?" A fair point. "I have rich husband," seemed to satisfy them. In their eyes, this was a perfectly satisfactory explanation.

Crusty *Baguettes* in Vietnam

In 1994, just before we left Singapore, I took a short trip to Vietnam. This was before the American trade embargoes were lifted, before the introduction of 'progress', of Coca Cola and McDonald's. My daughter visited very recently and found a country almost unrecognisable from my descriptions. My stay there was brief but memorable. Vietnam is very different from Singapore, or any of the neighbouring Asian countries we have visited.

I had read Graham Greene's *The Quiet American* which he wrote while staying in the *Continental Hotel*, in Saigon. This hotel was favoured by journalists covering the Vietnam War, while the nearby *Rex Hotel* housed army officers. Apart from these two historic hotels, there was very little accommodation on offer, apart from the run-down waterfront *Majestic* and the luxurious and super expensive *Saigon Floating Hotel*, opened in 1989 after being towed from its previous location on Australia's Great Barrier Reef. So, being a romantic, I plumped for the *Continental* with its French colonial façade, hoping to find something remaining of 1930's Saigon. In reality, the hotel, while it looked grand and colonial from the outside, had a long way to go before it reached the standard of services found in other more developed tourist destinations.

The room rate was extortionately high and had to be paid in American dollars. In fact, small currency dollars were the only thing to use on the street; you would have needed a wheelbarrow to transport the thousands of Vietnamese *dong* required to pay for anything. The room itself was functional but dark and dreary, over-furnished with over-stuffed red velvet chairs and a sofa. I searched in vain for references to the famous writer but failed to find any. Nothing in the hotel blurb about the illustrious history of the hotel; no equivalent of the blue plaque; not even a copy of Greene's novel in the small shop in the foyer. I ate breakfast in the cavernous, echoing restaurant which looked as though it could once have been the ballroom and wondered if Greene had sat here to sup his morning coffee, to order a boiled egg from the old lady in the white hairnet and overalls whose sole job it was to immerse the eggs in boiling water for the required minutes, and jot down notes for his novel.

Things got better. I had arrived at the airport the day before, unclear who was going to pick me up. The Singaporean travel agent had been vague; "Someone will be there to meet you when you arrive in Ho Chi Minh City

(always referred to as Saigon by everyone I met there)."
Well, someone **had** been there as there was a handwritten sign propped up at the exit to the airport with my name on it. However, no-one claimed the sign. Eventually, my diminutive guide appeared, apologising profusely for his failure to welcome me. He introduced me to the driver who would escort us around the city and north to the seaside town of Vung Tau, the Bay of Boats, and the hill town of Dalat. They were the most gentle and courteous of people and went out of their way to look after me and ensure that my trip was memorable. Apart from reading Graham Greene, my only exposure to Vietnam had been through American made movies such as *Apocalypse Now* and *The Deer Hunter*. More than four hundred films have been made about the Vietnam War, although only one during the actual conflict: *The Green Beret*, starring John Wayne as a gung-ho American. It was released in 1968 and reviled by critics and audiences alike. Many of our images and opinions are shaped by what we see on film, but I was sure that there was more to Vietnam.

Everywhere we went, people whizzed past us on bicycles, rickshaws, a few scooters and very few cars – traffic mayhem, almost impossible to cross the road on foot. Hustle and bustle everywhere. I marvelled at the traditional dress worn, mostly by the women, the sea of bobbing conical hats. I'd only seen them worn during a holiday to Bali. High School girls cycled past on sit up and beg bicycles. They were beautifully and pristinely dressed in flowing white dresses with high side-slits, wide-bottomed, white trousers and elbow-length, white gloves. "To protect them from the sun; they wish to have pale skin," my guide informed me. Most surprising of all, bundles of long, crusty *baguettes* for sale on every street corner, along the wide boulevards, leftovers from French colonialism which stretched from the late nineteenth century to 1954. The colonial footprint is stamped most heavily into the culture in its food and architecture. Yes, locals do eat rice, but this bread is also an important staple, something I'd never seen anywhere else in the Far East. And you can still get excellent *café noir* or *café crème* in the smallest café, sublime *kem caramen* (*crème caramel*), *bit tet* (the French *bifteck*) and a *boeuf bourguignon* cooked in rice wine rather than red Burgundy – true fusion cooking. Café proprietors entice you inside with a soft, "*Madame, s'il vous plaît.*" The fusion of Vietnamese and French cuisine makes for a magical combination. Locals are ambivalent about their French colonial past, "They were a good thing. They left us beautiful buildings and boulevards. They brought us culture, taught us how to enjoy life." "The French exploited us. They taxed us heavily and they kept us in our place. No matter how hard you worked, you could never rise in station."

Proudly, I was shown round the austere, brutalist style building, the Thong Nat Reunification Hall, which housed the Party headquarters. It had replaced a French Governor's mansion, almost certainly more beautiful. Room after room, each stuffed with the same red velvet, boxy furniture of my hotel room (obviously a local speciality). I think the eager-to-please guide sensed my lack of interest, failed to understand how under-whelmed I felt and we moved on quickly to the highlight of the tour – *The Exhibition House of Crimes of War and Aggression in Vietnam*. In fact, my guide called it *The Museum of American War Atrocities*. The museum has since been re-named; however, probably it contains the same gruesome, memorable exhibits. I wasn't prepared for the horrific mutilations on show: the foetuses in jars to demonstrate the devastating effects of Agent Orange; photographs of victims of napalm and the My Lai massacre of 1968 where 504 people were killed; others showed US soldiers before 'torn up' bodies of the Vietnamese victims; heaped up bodies from the 1970 Binh Duong Massacre; a US plane spraying toxic chemicals in South Vietnam. A leaflet thrust into my hand outlined the 'war of aggression' against Vietnam by the United States; the 7,850,000 tons of bombs dropped; the 75,000, 000 litres of lethal chemicals sprayed on villages, rice-fields and forest; the carpet bombing of densely populated areas; and the land where nothing can be grown, even today. It was all very one-sided, but very shocking and moving. An American visitor was sobbing uncontrollably as she read of atrocity after atrocity. Outside, to emphasise what had brought about the destruction, there were twisted heaps of rusting American tanks and helicopters. Propped in a corner was a French guillotine brought to Vietnam in the twentieth century and still in regular use in the 1960's. Why had they taken me there? Perhaps it was the easiest way of explaining the shocking, grisly atrocities that had been committed in their country.

Next day, we ventured further afield and en-route passed the American Embassy which I'd only seen in news clips and movies, where frantic people rushed to escape on the whirling Huey helicopters on the last flight out of Vietnam before the fall of Saigon. We stopped while I took a photograph, but my hosts were uneasy. Crowds of young men were milling around in a kind of holding pen adjacent to the embassy. According to my guide, these were the mixed race offspring left behind after the American invasion. They were desperate to go to the US, the land of opportunity, and to escape a country which shunned their obvious difference. Every day, they turned up, hoping to be called and informed that they had been granted a visa. Since then, the embassy has been razed to make way for progress, perhaps to erase sad memories.

We drove to the Cu Chi underground tunnels, an area that played an important role in the wars against both the French and the Americans. The intricate network of tunnels stretches for one hundred and twenty four miles, a subterranean village on three levels, the deepest level much too narrow for the western frame to penetrate. Down there, during the Vietnam War, there was a whole infrastructure of hospitals, canteens, sleeping quarters, the entrances almost impossible to spot. The tunnels seem to sum up the tenacity and ingenuity of the Vietnamese. When I visited, it was already a bit touristy. I was offered Vietcong scarves, 'genuine' American GI water bottles, grenades and cartridge belts. Perhaps they **were** genuine, and the sellers were only trying to make a living. The land between the tunnels and Saigon, about twenty two miles, was still contaminated by Agent Orange and nothing could be grown. The food I ate in the city was delicious, but vegetables were in very short supply as none were grown locally.

In Saigon itself, I found very little to buy. A few rather charming sepia postcards, depicting a bygone era, a few silk artefacts, some lacquer work of rather dubious quality. Most of the shops were almost empty of goods, but the shopkeepers were smiling and polite, eager for you to purchase something, but with no real hard sell. In Provence, two Vietnamese lacquer trays are in constant use, transporting food and plates from one level to another. The postage stamps are kept on the kitchen mantelpiece in a tiny, lacquered brown and black box.

My visit to Vung Tau was a bit of a non-event. Vietnamese find it romantic. Certainly it lived up to its name, Bay of Boats, although many of the vessels were commercial, and the stalls and bars lining the grey, silted beach were tacky. It had been used by the Americans for 'R & R' and the Russians now working at a nuclear facility in the town had taken over the amenities left behind, including the massage parlours and the bar traffic. The music blaring from the bars included such well-known favourites as *The Young Ones* and *Oh Carol*, perhaps left over from another era? It seemed a bit of a time warp. Someone offered to take my photo standing next to a Vietnamese cowboy or a mangy, stuffed peacock – all very surreal.

Dalat, Vietnam's most popular mountain resort, lived up to expectations. Nestled among pine-clad hills, it is green and fertile with a much more pleasant climate than the city. The cool temperatures and tranquillity attracted the French who built their holiday villas there. The town still has a French feel to it. Everywhere, the fields were full of fruit, flowers and vegetables. Many of the vegetables we are familiar with in Europe can be grown here and Dalat's wonderful flowers are exported all over Vietnam. My driver and guide tucked lustily into delicious looking, crisp lettuces and tomatoes bursting with ripeness. They couldn't understand my reluctance to overdose on the first vegetables we'd seen since leaving Saigon. I'm afraid I've had too many stomach upsets in the past to ignore the warning: "In foreign climes, avoid salad at all costs!" Politely, I declined too the enticing *digestif* of wine poured from a jar containing a curled-up snake.

The town was a time-warp. People still travelled on foot, horseback or in carts pulled by horses or water buffalo. There were almost no cars around and it was a relief to be able to wander around the traffic-free streets, full of ethnic minorities in their traditional dress who had come from surrounding villages to sell their produce. And not just food: beautiful handicrafts such as jewellery, bamboo handbags, rattan boxes, pressed flowers, fur hats and wonderful lengths of woven cloth coloured with vegetable dyes. In an 'antique' shop run by an old Frenchman, I bought a small stone lion, symbol of Vietnam, which now sits on the mantelpiece. Vendors transported their wares in swinging baskets strung on wooden yokes stretched across shoulders. The town is charming, so vibrant and full of colours, sounds and smells. During the war, there was a tactic agreement between the two sides not to bomb Dalat, or to engage in any military activity there. Unofficially, it was a haven of respite for generals of both sides. Today, it is popular with honeymooners who bask in the beauty of the cascading waterfalls, the flower gardens and the rather tacky swan boats on the Lake of Love. Dalat also attracts retirees and my driver shared his dream of earning enough money to buy a small piece of land in this paradise and build a home.

You can still visit the summer palace of Vietnam's last Nguyen emperor, very faded French grandeur both inside and out. What I really wanted to see was the palace on the lake where one of my favourite writers, Edith Wharton, had stayed during her travels. I had read that it was being restored and was to open as a luxury hotel for the expected flood of tourists. We found the palace; however, sadly restoration was clearly still in progress and I stayed in a small, comfortable guesthouse overlooking the lake, protected by a mosquito net draped over the bed. Recently, while staying in a hotel in Versailles, I flicked through the bedside brochure and there was the lake palace in all its splendour, now named the *Dalat Sofitel*. It probably attracts a lot of visitors. My daughter took a trip to Vietnam in 2004. She loved everything about the country, however, it had changed so much in a few short years. A multitude of hotels to stay in, fast food, shops bulging with attractive goods, neon signs . . . progress?

When I left Vietnam, I wished that I could stay longer and explore more of this beautiful country and its gentle, friendly people. Customs took away for examination my ten dollar blue and white vase, vigilant against possible smugglers of their ancient heritage.

The Lone Star State: Everything's Bigger in Texas

In 1996, when we first began our search for a house in Provence, my husband was on assignment in Houston, Texas, designing a petro-chemical plant for Saudi Arabia. At that particular time, my heart was not completely into being a mobile wife because I'd resurrected my teaching career and was working happily as Head of Department in a local private school. I'd also resurrected neglected friendships, lived close to our children and aging parents, and was enjoying the proximity to London theatres and galleries. However, I've always been supportive and we decided that I would commute to Houston during school holidays. Half-term every six weeks, two weeks in October, three weeks at Christmas, and of course the long summer break. So, I didn't actually live full-time in Houston, but I got to know it quite well.

Texas doesn't sound very exotic, however, it may be the most foreign experience I've ever had. My only experience of Texas had been an epic six-hour session of watching *Lonesome Dove* on a video borrowed from our Texan neighbours. Basically, it's a story about two former Texas Rangers from the tiny town of Lonesome Dove who decide to seize the day and move their cattle from the south to Montana. Another example of striving for the American Dream, undertaking a journey of discovery, themes present in most of America's Literature. Bizarrely, the viewing had been in Sumatra, where we relied on taped material to get us through the occasions when homesickness struck. Our tapes, recorded by our next door neighbour in Petersham, were of light-hearted, familiar programmes such as *Yes Prime Minister*, and *Only Fools and Horses*. These proved very popular with the American expats; surprising, as I've always thought that our sense of humour was poles apart. Perhaps they recognised similar characters in their own culture.

Texans take a huge pride in their lone star state, illustrated by this old saying: "Never ask a man where he's from. If he's from Texas, he'll tell you and if he ain't, you don't want to embarrass him." Houston especially is like no other place I've ever been to, quite different from any other city in Texas or the US. It epitomises the frontier ethic and southern gentility and for many people it is where the American Dream is still alive; a place where the values and traditions that built the nation are still a part of the culture. Houstonians have an underlying belief in themselves and the idea that anything is possible. This is admirable but it can come across as arrogance.

The city was established in 1836 on a bayou, a marshy inlet infested with alligators, but at first glance there seems very little of this left. As your plane comes into land, skyscrapers loom and multiple highways twist and turn. Since the discovery of oil, the city has boomed. Houston is the oil field service and design capital of the world and the world centre for the petrochemical industry.

My first question was, where is downtown, the centre of the city? It wasn't obvious. On our first visit, a business trip, we'd stayed in a hotel which was part of the Galleria, a vast shopping mall modelled on the Milan Galleria. Truly amazing, with an indoor skating rink in the middle. When jet-lag forced us to rise at five o'clock in the morning, we wandered down to the skating rink, without stepping outside, and watched the serious skaters having private lessons. No matter what time you went, there would always be skaters.

I soon learned that the Galleria was the hub of Houston, rather appropriate in such a consumer culture. I already knew several people living in Houston whom we'd met on earlier expat assignments abroad. My next door neighbours in Sumatra, Yolanda and Xavier, who had become close friends, were living there, like my husband on assignment with Mobil Oil; a teaching colleague from Singapore; people we'd known in Boston. Really, it's a small world. Everyone was pleased to hear from me and we would arrange to meet – at the Galleria. We did a bit of shopping, ate lunch in the

French café, *Madeleine's,* or *The Cheesecake Factory* (wonderful salads as well as cheesecake of twenty varieties), and reminisced about old times. There's a lot of shopping and lunching in Houston, and there's got to be more to life than that. You can choose to eat junk food, but you can also have wonderful Texan beef and fine dining of every description.

However, there is another side to it. Our apartment was in an area of Houston called Sugar Land, about twenty miles from the Galleria; twenty minutes on the free-moving freeway. As the name suggests, the fields had once been full of sugar cane, and the Imperial Sugar Plant still operated on locally grown sugar. More recently, rice had been planted in the paddies, and we were still surrounded by miles of open countryside. A few miles down the road, one October holiday we went in search of the famed Texan pecans. An old man sat at the side of the road beside his shack. He was dressed in bibbed dungarees, a checked shirt, cowboy boots and hat and we couldn't understand what he was saying in his incomprehensible dialect. He didn't find our brand of English too easy to understand either. He pointed to three sacks, three different sizes and grades of pecans: large, small and broken pieces. After a tasting, we bought large quantities of each which I carted back to England. After giving a bag to a friend she retorted that until then she'd never realised how lacking in freshness, how almost rancid, supermarket pecans taste. The Texas pecans were really special, and they kept for months in the freezer. When a friend from Houston visited us in Provence last year, she was surprised when I asked her to bring out some local pecans – truly delicious. In addition to the pecans, we brought home from Houston a cream sofa, now in Provence – looks elegant but isn't very comfortable – and a custom-made, fine leather, wing-backed chair – not very elegant looking, but supremely comfortable.

Further down this road, cotton still grows in the fields, and alligators still lurk in and on the banks of the Brazos River which floods the land and leaves rich soil in its wake. The town, Richmond, is poor, some of the buildings like stage-sets for a Wild West film, and bail bond facilities are advertised everywhere. It still has the feeling of small-town America circa 1920. Somehow it is reassuring to find a corner drugstore, a hardware store and a five-and-dime within the shadow of the old court-house. And it also has our favourite restaurant, the quaintly named Quail Hollow Inn, run by a Swiss couple. Bizarrely, the food served is mostly French, but the décor is pure cowboy.

However, there are still gracious plantation homes, leftovers from an age when cotton was a big industry here, worked by black slaves. This is one of the first permanent settlements of the original three hundred colonists. Not all of Houston is big and brash and afflu-ent. This is a visual antidote to Houston's skyscrapers. I couldn't help noticing that most of the lower-paid jobs were done by Mexicans who form a large part of the population. There are also blacks descended from slaves, Germans, Czechs, and a big Indian population. However, the majority of Houston settlers are southern whites who came in search of a new life after Recon-struction. They brought their old southern ways with them. You will still be addressed as "ma'am" and "sir", even by children. People have an unfailing courtesy. They also seem to have great faith in themselves and believe that anything is possible. Bearing this in mind may help you to see where President George W Bush is coming from.

Nearby, is the Brazos Bend National Park with hiking and nature trails and photography platforms for focusing on the park's exceptional wildlife. It isn't a theme park; as well as snakes, deer, armadillo, nutria and turtles, there are alligators at every turn, some of them serious alligators. In the summer, they submerge themselves in the murky water and try to look like logs; in the spring, they like to sun-bathe on the river bank, so you have to be vigilant. Most of the locals have an alligator story to tell.

There isn't much in Houston that is historical, with the exception of the San Jacinto Battleground, now a State Historical Park. The park marks the site where Texas won its independence from Mexico in 1836. San Jacinto monument is the world's tallest at five hundred and seventy feet and there is an interesting museum of regional history. Like the Tower of Pisa, the monument is sinking. You can ride in an elevator to the top for a view of the towers of downtown Houston on one side and a spaghetti bowl of oil pipelines on the other.

Apart from this, there's the world famous NASA Lyndon B. Johnson Space Centre; exciting baseball at Minute Maid Park. The evening we went to a game, the Houston Astros unexpectedly thrashed the Los Angeles Angels 5-0 – huge excitement and an electrifying atmosphere; you can go to a rodeo, a concert, a multitude of movie houses. Houston is easy living, easy parking, year-long sunshine (although there are frequent tornados, one really bad one while we were there that ripped the side off the shopping mall a few yards from where we lived and tossed cars and animals into the sky), but there's got to be more to life than that. I enjoyed my visits, but I only ever met one couple who had come to Houston to spend a holiday; the city is a trifle bland, a bit lacking in culture, always unbearably humid so that people are forced to drive even short distances. I'm not sure it will ever be on the list of must-see places for European visitors.

But there's more to Texas than Houston, and on one October holiday we drove across Texas to Santa Fé, New Mexico. My second visit to Santa Fé but my husband's first. Texas is a world in itself: 692,300 square kilometres, larger than many nations in the world, including all those in Europe; a vast emptiness. You cannot cross the state from Beaumont to El Paso in one day by road, hence the ditty: 'The sun has riz/ The sun has set/ And here I is/ In Texas yet.' In my ignorance, I had the impression that Texas was all the same: flat and boring, however, nothing could be further from the truth. Texas is full of a great diversity of geography, people and cultures. It has sophisticated cities, tumbleweed-swept, one-horse towns, beautiful beaches, searing hot deserts, sleepy border towns, wide open plains, bottomless canyons, dramatic mountains, almost empty highways and big, big skies. In both geography and culture it is a microcosm of the entire country. On the whole, these are rural communities, very 'cowboy', making a living from ranching and cattle. However, the Panhandle area has oil and a gas field, first discovered in 1916. By 1930, it was the world's largest (just before oil was discovered in Arabia).

One of the stars of Texas is San Antonio, large, bustling, very Mexican, probably the nearest you can get to Mexico without actually going there. We stayed in the luxurious *Mansion del Rio*, sunk into the River Walk, a man-made entertainment and shopping area on both sides of a meandering stretch of water. Sounds tacky, but we found it buzzing, exciting and quite classy: good, mostly Mexican or Tex-Mex food, jazz concerts, street entertainers, opulent tropical vegetation. At the hotel brunch buffet, I was reminded how unsophisticated some Americans can be. A group of diners hesitated, with no idea how to proceed. Some heaped shrimps, eggs and chocolate cake on to the one crowded plate. The suspicious looking sushi lay untouched. The bird labelled 'capon' was a mystery to many. "Is it a fish?" asked someone. On being told what it was, he retorted angrily, "Then why not just call it chicken!" I had to agree with him. Sometimes restaurants are too pretentious.

San Antonio is a great place to shop: lots of small boutiques and the market, the *Mercado,* is full of brightly coloured, attractive Mexican handicrafts at rock-bottom prices. I was tempted into buying yet another nativity set – I'll soon be competition for the nativity displays in the *santons* shop in Séguret, Provence – twelve hand-painted ceramic figures for $4. Mary, Joseph and Jesus look very Mexican, and there seem to be more donkeys than usual. Bizarrely, I found a set of blue and white painted ceramic canisters emblazoned with *Thé, Café, Sucre and Farine* – ironically, I'd searched all over Provence and never quite found exactly what I was looking for.

Of course, San Antonio meant for my husband following in the footsteps of his childhood hero, Davy Crockett, and a visit to the Alamo. Probably even more exciting than visiting the final resting place on the summit of Lookout Mountain, Golden, Colorado, of

Wild Bill Hickok. He had been killed by Jack McCall in Deadwood, Black Hills, but his last wishes had been to be buried in this beautiful, peaceful spot overlooking the valley. The Alamo is a shrine for Americans and two and a half million people visit the complex every year. We were amazed to find that it is open every day of the year except Christmas Day, and that entry is free. Most visitors come to see the old mission where a small band of Texans held out for thirteen days against Mexico's proclaimed dictator, General Antonio Lopèz de Santa Anna. The Alamo has come to symbolise the cradle of Liberty. To the last man, the Alamo defenders died, among them household names such as William Travis, Jim Bowie and Davy Crockett. *The Alamo* is the first movie I remember being taken to see as a child.

It was crowded but very well enacted and extremely moving. The only trashy element came in the gift shop where on offer were commemorative bricks of three dimensions: patio bricks for $100; bigger limestone bricks for $1000; and for the seriously rich or seriously patriotic, Pillars of Texas for $5000. We weren't tempted by any of these, nor the more modestly priced souvenirs: an Alamo golf ball, bank, hero figurine, dog bowl, plastic etched glass, butter spreader, baseball cap, or even Alamo bottled water! My husband did waver over the acrylic Davy Crockett coonskin hat with genuine racoon tail, but I hurried him away. I understood the attraction, absolutely. As children, playing cowboys and Indians, my brother and I had fought over whose turn it was to wear the rabbit fur Davy Crockett hat to defend the Alamo against the baddies.

After you've left San Antonio, towns are small and rural. We spent the night in the hill country town of

Fredericksburg, as its name suggests, a very German town, where we drank wonderful German-style Texas wine and admired striped and fringed Navajo blankets. We stopped in Valentine, Jeff Davis County, intrigued by the name. As we stuffed ourselves in the intriguingly named *No Name Café* with the $1-99 All U Can Eat pancake special, we read about the town from a card thoughtfully placed on each table. It was founded on February 14, 1882, when a Southern Pacific Railroad crew building east from El Paso reached the site. Romantics can request a Valentine postmark for their Valentine Day's card. "Place your St. Valentine's Day card(s) correctly addressed to the proper recipient(s) in a pre-stamped envelope. Place it (them) in another envelope and mail it to: the Postmaster, Valentine, Texas 79859, USA". In case you are tempted, valentines for foreign delivery have to be posted by 1 February to ensure sufficient time to reach the loved one.

Fort Davis, in the Big Bend National Park, was another charming stay. This had been a military post to fight back against the raids of Apaches and Comanches along the San Antonio to El Paso trail. As we stood where the settlement was now functioning as a Living Museum, it was easy to imagine how terrifying it must have been in the nineteenth century to be attacked by the tribes of painted 'savages' hurtling down from the craggy, cacti covered hills above. We stayed in the *Hotel Limpia*, a two-storey, wooden, historic building dating back to 1912, complete with verandas and rocking chairs – a good way to relax and enjoy the by-gone era of Texas. The hotel has its own cookbook, featuring recipes on offer in the rather fine restaurant. The buttermilk and honey biscuits (don't be misled: a kind of scone) just might be an old, traditional recipe, but I'm not so sure about the Burgundy marinated roast beef or the raspberry vinaigrette. The charming town seems little changed from its Wild West days and the unspoiled vistas have been used in several films: *Lonesome Dove, The Streets of Laredo, Dead Man's Walk* and *Dancer, Texas, population 81*. Other claims to fame are to being the highest town in Texas and the site of the McDonald Observatory, belonging to the University of Texas.

El Paso couldn't be more of a contrast. It's the largest border city in the US, with a blend of Spanish, Mexican and thoroughly western heritage found nowhere else in Texas. A catchy Marty Robbins tune called *El Paso* came to mind, about a West Texan town where *cantinas* are filled with lawless gunfighters and beautiful *señoritas*. Actually, it's a ballad, rather than a song, and you can just imagine similar shoot-outs and crimes of passion happening in downtown El Paso today. The atmosphere was threatening; the car park where reluctantly we left our car for a day-trip across the border to Juarez, seedy. It wasn't the best introduction to Mexico – no border town ever is. We couldn't understand why the bus-driver announced our arrival at a downtown pharmacy. As everyone else got off here, we followed, very curious. We discovered that in Mexico you can buy prescription medication (without a prescription) at greatly reduced prices. As long as you know the name and the dosage, it's available. Americans make pilgrimages across the bridge separating the two countries to stock up. We resisted, however, next door we were tempted to buy a lop-sided ceramic bowl which the 'antique' dealer assured us was authentically ancient. It sits now on our kitchen mantelpiece in Provence, and the first person to rise in the morning raids it for change to buy the croissants in the village shop.

After Santa Fé, we rode the romantic Route 66. It doesn't appear on modern maps any more, so you need good directions before heading out on the old two lane highway. The US Highway, 'Route 66', was commissioned in 1926, the year that US numbered highways came into existence. It ran for 178 miles from Amarillo to the New Mexican state line and is considered the Mother Road of American highways, the old Main Street of America. However, we knew it better from the Beach Boys' song. Known as the Panhandle, the area is flat, arid and under-developed. It is centred in Amarillo and Lubbock, where ranching, cotton and sunflower seed harvesting are the major occupations. And Amarillo also supplies the world with helium. Of course, Amarillo is now on the tip of the tongue of everyone in Britain with the re-release of the old, catchy Tony Christie number *Is this the way to Amarillo?* helped to become a hit by the video appearance of the comedian Peter Kay.

West of Amarillo, on Route 66 (now Highway 40), is one of the area's most celebrated sights: ten red Cadillacs nose down in an orderly row. I'd seen pictures of the sculpture, but it looked truly amazing as it loomed suddenly into view, in the middle of nowhere. Even more remarkable in a state where if you don't drive the ubiquitous pick-up truck you're considered a bit gay.

Another highlight, at least for my husband, was Lincoln, whose most famous resident was William H. Bonney, aka Billy the Kid. It's a one-horse town: two historical markers, two general stores, a post office, café, school and the famous old Evergreen Tree at Lincoln Fertilizer Plant. We re-lived our childhood cowboy films as we watched an enactment of the shoot-out between the famous outlaw Billy the Kid and the sheriff, Pat Garrett. I had become aware of my husband's fascination with the mythical Wild West when he brought to our marriage his three most prized possessions: *Lone Star Texas Ranger*, *Desert Gold* and *Riders of the Purple Sage*, all written by Zane Gray. I managed to resist reading them until I was confined to bed two years later. I must admit, they were pretty riveting.

We paused at Waco, more famous these days for the fifty-one day siege of David Koresh and the Dravidian religious sect who eventually committed mass suicide. In the Texas Ranger Hall of Fame, we viewed the actual pistol that Pat Garrett had used.

As we travelled along, the temperatures were sweltering and the terrain rugged and rather monotonous, but there was a certain romance in listening to the local country music on the radio. The Panhandle is proud of native sons Waylon Jennings, Roy Orbison and, of course, Buddy Holly. I only vaguely remember Buddy Holly, perhaps from a revival of his music. He had hits in the 1950's with such songs as *Peggy Sue, Maybe Baby, True Love Wins, Oh Boy, That'll be the Day*, and countless others. However, I do know that Holly, who was born in Lubbock in 1936, is regarded as having influenced virtually every aspect of the musical entertainment industry, from rock and roll, to country and rock-a-billy. He continues to inspire artists, musicians and song writers to this day. Unfortunately, he died aged twenty two while travelling on a light aircraft after a concert in Clear Lake, Iowa. We'd seen the movie *The Buddy Holly Story* and knew some of his life story from that. Curious, we took the time to gawk at his statue and to visit the museum whose collection includes Holly's Fender Stratocaster guitar; an original itinerary from his last tour; the singer's lyric notebook with handwritten lyrics and margin notes; and a pair of his maroon and black stage shoes. You couldn't help but be moved. People from all over the world make the pilgrimage to Buddy Holly's grave, in the City of Lubbock Cemetery, on East 34th Street.

Yes, it was a real nostalgia trip, but we're glad we did it. Otherwise, I might have gone home thinking that Texas was Dallas and Houston, big, skyscraper cities, full of business men in cowboy-yoked suits and ten-gallon hats. Texans are still cowboys at heart and the majority believe strongly in the Second Amendment, the right to own and bear arms. Recently, a friend from the North East of the US sent me an e-mail poking gentle fun at Texan obsessions: 'Due to the popularity of the Survivor shows, the network is planning to do its own show entitled *Survivor, TEXAS STYLE*. The contestants will drive throughout Texas in pink Volkswagen cars with large bumper stickers that read, 'Cowboys are cry babies; John Wayne was a sissy; I'm a vegetarian; Deer hunting is murder; I'm here to confiscate your guns; Barbecue is disgusting; and Hillary in 2008. The first one who makes it back to Houston alive wins.' Rather silly, but it does sum up many Texans. They really believe in the bumper sticker which proclaims: 'Life's too short not to live it as a Texan.'

Laissez les Bons Temps Rouler: Let the Good Times Roll

During one of my trips to Houston, we made a side trip to New Orleans, searching for authenticity before I taught Tennessee Williams' *A Streetcar Named Desire*. Does the 'A' Level syllabus influence my travels, or my travels influence the choice of syllabus? A highlight on our way there was stopping off at Lafayette, Louisiana, for a magical trip on the bayou and some Cajun culture. We stayed on the Charles Mouton Plantation, dating from around 1820, and listed on the National Register of Historic Places. It just isn't true that there's nothing old in America and that all hotels are plastic chains. The house had survived the Civil War and had been the home of the first Democratic Governor of Louisiana and two mayors of Lafayette. We actually stayed next door at Bois des Chênes, the carriage house for the mansion, in a Victorian testered bed. Guests were given a tour of the mansion, but the main attraction for us was the promise of a boat trip into the Atchafalaya, guided by the owner, a heavily bearded and pocketed naturalist and expert on flora and fauna. In season, he led fishing and hunting trips; however, his main interest was showing off the nearby bayous, a vast wilderness swamp and an overflow area for the Atchafalaya River. It really was a wilderness, not a place to venture into without a good guide.

The two-hour, late afternoon trip took us into a different world as Mr Voorlies pointed out to us a jungle of plants such as hibiscus, lotus, elephants' ears, huckleberry, willow and oak. Great swathes of dripping French moss brushed against our faces as we moved silently through the water, adding to the eerie atmosphere. The most exciting things were the wildlife: muskrats, opossums, otters, turtles, nutria (a large, furry rodent also known as coypu), a huge owl sitting in the fork of a tree so close you could have reached out and stroked its feathers, herons – and, of course, alligators. At first, we couldn't see any of the promised 'critters', but after the guide had pointed out a few 'logs', we got our eye in. Really scary when one, maybe fourteen feet long, slid almost silently into the water alongside the boat. "Makes great eatin'!" our guide assured us. "Don't rightly know whether 'gator or turtle is my favourite barbecue food."

We weren't tempted to try either, but that evening we took his advice and travelled in to town to a Cajun dancehall which served local specialities: crawfish, crab and shrimp dinners, *boudin* (a kind of sausage stuffed with spices and rice), gumbo and dirty rice. The food was outstanding, the Cajun and Zydeco music, a merger of rhythm and blues, jazz, rock and roll and gospel, foot-tapping and difficult to resist dancing to. The French spoken all around us was like nothing we'd heard before, but still recognisable. The predominantly Catholic French Arcadians from Nova Scotia were forced to leave Canada in 1755 and settled in Louisiana. One song, rendered in English, was Hank Williams' *Jambalaya*. The famous line, 'Son of a gun, gonna have fun, in the Bayou' took on an added dimension in this setting.

We found the area fascinating, the people friendly and very laid-back. Apparently, shopkeepers often shut up shop on a whim and leave a sign in the window saying 'Gone fishing.' Something in common with the shopkeepers of Provence! Perhaps that's the right attitude to life. New Orleans couldn't be more of a contrast. There, people are into partying big time: "*Laissez les bons temps rouler.*" The city draws people from all over who are hoping to find themselves as artists, musicians, writers, painters and sculptors. The rumbling of the streetcar outside his window on St Charles Avenue supposedly inspired Williams to write *A Streetcar Named Desire*. Now, there's only a bus named *Desire*, which doesn't really have the same resonance. However, the streetcar still runs to *Cemeteries,* mentioned in the play. The spartan wooden seats lack comfort, but the wide windows let in a constant flow of air to ease the stifling heat and humidity. The cars are crowded with locals, and you'll be riding a piece of romantic history.

There's a tremendous energy to New Orleans, a crush of humanity both day and night in the streets of the French Quarter, *Vieux Carré*, the site of the original city founded in 1718 as a military outpost. It's six blocks by ten, with rows of nineteenth century houses, antique shops, galleries and boutiques. In the black and white film version of *A Streetcar Named Desire*, starring Marlon Brando in perhaps his best ever role as Stanley, the impression of New Orleans is of a hot, steamy, languorous jungle, the violence simmering just under the surface. And that's the impression we got. It's the only city in the US where I've seen heavy bingeing of alcohol, at all hours, in the streets. People, mostly young people, stagger around with huge plastic beakers of lurid cocktails with names like Hurricane, hell-bent on having a good time. Perhaps we'd arrived twenty years too late.

We did enjoy much about New Orleans: the quaint, narrow streets, the shuttered Creole townhouses, the lace (decorated cast ironwork) balconies, the wonderful jazz music found on every street corner and belting out of every café and club, most of all the food. We crowded into Preservation Hall, a unique institution, standing room only, to hear the real old-timers of jazz. Here jazz is found in its purest form, uncluttered by such niceties as air-conditioning, drinks or even a place to sit. Later that evening, we braved the streets and walked to the farthest dark corner of the French Quarter, to *Donna's*, a city hotspot, or so we'd been told. You would never have found it by accident. The bar and grill looked so unimposing that we wondered if we'd been misinformed, but inside the place was jumping. For hours, we listened to a brass band playing jazz, unique party music which has its origins in the music played at jazz funerals, while people danced and supped their ice-cold beers.

A really memorable experience, and we had many. We sat in Jackson Square, a throbbing performance space, and listened to more jazz; we watched buskers perform, and were mildly harassed by tarot readers and psychics intent on revealing our fortune. We ate in the *Café du Monde*, an institution open twenty four hours a day since the 1860's, famous for its *beignets*, warm, square doughnuts covered in icing sugar. Locals and tourists alike breakfast on delicious strong chicory coffee and *beignets*. The place is full of characters; we shared our table with a very chatty lady of the night. Later, we lunched on *Muffuletta*, a giant sourdough sandwich stuffed with tissue thin slices of ham, wedges of runny cheese, spicy sausage, olive oil and olives, very similar to the *pan bagna* you can buy on the streets of Nice. Dinner was in *Antoine's*, the oldest restaurant in North America, operated by the same family since 1840 and famous for its Creole cooking. Creole dishes were developed by French and Spanish city dwellers and feature delicate sauces, much like French cooking today. The restaurant has fifteen small rooms, the most discreet in the rear. We were given a table in the front room, the least prestigious and least favoured, but it did have the advantage of a great view of all the celebrities being ushered to their favourite tables out back. The next morning, Sunday, we experienced a jazz brunch with friends Doug and Laura from our days in Sumatra, at Arnaud's, an institution since 1918. With its languidly turning antique ceiling fans, mosaic tiled floors and dark panelled walls, it did have a bygone air. Our friends, very positive and upbeat people, had not altogether enjoyed their stay in New

Orleans. They had found it to be a city in conflict with their Christian beliefs, a decadent, immoral city, full of heavy drinking, drugs and witchcraft.

We were there at Halloween, but the city is a 'city of spirits' all the year round. There are plenty of people of all races who still draw from both Christian and African religious traditions in the practice of their faith, and the mixture of the two is voodoo. The only authentic voodoo house of worship is the Voodoo Spiritual Temple. On Thursdays, the 7.30 pm service is open to the public and visitors are welcomed by Priestess Miriam Chamani and her staff. You can have an African bone reading there – we resisted – or visit the birthplace or burial site of the nineteenth century voodoo priestess, Marie Laveau. People leave gifts and offerings on the tomb of the Voodoo Queen. A nearby shop, Vodoo Authentica, sells more than a hundred types of voodoo doll and *gris-gris,* bags for potions.

It's the only place we've ever visited to offer official cemetery tours, which are very popular. Owing to the swampy nature of the ground, New Orleans tombs are built above ground, on streets with names, so it's easy to see why they became known as the Cities of the Dead. These miniature cities even have their skyscrapers, since upper floors would be added as members of the same family died. Around the perimeter, you'll see rows of wall vaults, 'ovens', which hold the remains of the city's poor. Rather gruesome. You can catch them as a backdrop to scenes in the films *Easy Rider* and *Interview with the Vampire.*

Even more gruesome is the Halloween Parade, the biggest celebration apart from Mardi Gras. A crush of humanity fills the streets, thousands of ghosts and ghouls parade: a quartet of Druids, Elvis, the King, in his Las Vegas persona, the Invisible Man body swathed in white, a family dressed in cardboard boxes painted as breakfast cereals, wielding large kitchen knives – aka cereal killers! Holy-rollers appear at Halloween, and apparently at Mardi Gras, to save Carnival revellers. They carry crosses with electric displays of: 'Sinners repent!'

The streets in the centre of town do have an aura of decadence about them, even without the carnivals, the more than twenty festivals every year. Voodoo shops' candles flicker from store-fronts; *gris-gris* amulets strung up to put a spell on passers-by. We'd seen these voodoo shops in a filmed version of John Grisham's *Runaway Jury*, starring Dustin Hoffman, Gene Hackman and John Cusack. The character played by Cusack bought a St Catherine candle in a voodoo shop, to help his prayers that the flawed jurors would reach the 'right' verdict. In Bourbon Street, doors swing open to reveal scantily clad exotic dancers strutting their stuff on the bar. Probably no worse than Britain's Soho, but nevertheless seedy. There's a chaotic twenty four hour street party atmosphere. And if you fancy a more intimate experience, New Orleans boasts a drive-through daiquiri bar.

But there's another side to New Orleans, of genteel, grand mansions and faded plantation houses. We rode the streetcar to the Garden District with its embarrassment of beautiful Victorian homes, some of them in an advanced state of decay. Many are Disney-like, similar to Sleeping Beauty's palace. One is even called *The Wedding Cake*. Ann Rice, queen of gothic horror novels, lives here. We located her house by following the hordes that had come to pay homage at this Halloween celebration. It was completely over the top, decorated with witches, skeletons, cobwebs, ghouls, giant pumpkins and broomsticks. Oh, and an incongruous, life-size statue of a panting Alsatian dog. An eager fan shared with us that every Halloween Rice holds a party for fans in one of her houses decorated for the occasion. A chamber music ensemble accompanies white-faced ghouls clad in formal attire, dancing waltzes. Walking back to the French Quarter, hot and sweaty, we stumbled across *Emeril's*, an institution, run by New Orleans' answer to Gary Rhodes. Despite our rather dishevelled appearance, we were squeezed in. We had the best seats in the house, perched on high stools, overlooking the amazingly hectic kitchen. Another memorable meal, of Creole food. We're glad to have experienced New Orleans, but the 'good times' are a bit too much for us.

In 2005 Hurricane Katrina halted the music for a while, but New Orleans is now back on track, living up to its name as the party city. You can take in the Hurricane Katrina Tour, or spend a few days as a volunteer on re-build projects.

Mayan Magic: Tequila Sunrise in the Yucatán

I don't think we'd like to live in Mexico either, at least not in a border town anywhere near El Paso, nor in the Yucatán which welcomes more visitors than any other part of Mexico. Actually, I'm being a bit unfair here. Most visitors spend their time on the *Riviera Maya*, particularly Cancún, a mega beach resort. The familiar names for shopping, dining and sleeping ensure that you are not even aware that you are in Mexico.

As you'll have gathered by now, we've decided that life is not a beach, so at Easter 1998 on a side trip from Houston, we opted to fly inland to the colonial Mérida, gateway to the Mayan heartland, hire a car, and drive to the sites of Chichén Itzá and Uxmal. Hardly ground-breaking stuff, but fairly adventurous and slightly scary as we had been warned by well-meaning American friends that driving around the countryside is ill-advised.

Car hijackings and kidnappings are common, but that can happen in France, Italy or Spain.

The Aveatica flight attendants were less than helpful in completing our first challenge: the landing forms, written completely in Spanish. Nor was it reassuring when the Captain cracked jokes about how many men does it take to change a light bulb, and using a compass to find north. Perhaps he was just nervous. And things didn't get much better. Our colonial style hotel, built round a central courtyard filled with tinkling fountains, fragrant frangipani, bougainvillea and hibiscus, marble floors inset with decorative painted tiles, and comfortable plantation chairs couldn't be faulted. However, a notice prominently displayed in the lobby informed guests that at 12:30 all shops and museums would be closing for a five-day fiesta. A bit of a blow, as it was now 10 a.m. and we would only be in Mérida for three days. No time to unpack then; no time to admire the hand-woven curtains and bedspreads. We may not have shopped till we dropped, but in the short window of opportunity available to us, we managed to buy a few mementoes, including soft, pliable panama hats and a guidebook, written in English, on the Mayan ruins. We admired the omnipresent cotton string hammocks, not just tourist lawn furniture but actually still used by many locals in preference to a bed. In hotels that cater to Yucatecans, you will always find hammock hooks in the walls because many will travel with their own hammocks; and I yearned for an embroidered *huipiles*, the beautiful, colourful smock-like garment worn by many Yucatán villagers. Actually, from past experience, I know that these indigenous garments are best left in their indigenous habitat. Local garments rarely look as good on large Westerners walking down Bond Street.

We were able to admire from the outside the beautifully decorated buildings. A good example of an early colonial city, Mérida lacks the severe baroque and neoclassical features that characterise central Mexico. Most of the seventeenth century buildings are finished in stucco and painted light, pastel colours, like some of the houses in Provence. The numerous plazas are all built round huge trees, left unpruned to grow as high as possible, and the flowers grow in wild profusion rather than in serried, municipal rows. The town had a laid-back, relaxed feel to it, full of people sitting on benches, talking with friends, getting ready for the fiesta. But the traffic is horrendous. The main museum, when we tracked it down, was closed for eighteen months anyway, for restoration; a long time to wait.

The town is charming, a good introduction to the area, but we would never get used to the food. The whole family – amazing how keen the by now grown-up children were to join us on holiday when they heard the destination – had been expecting a diet of beans and corn (we like beans and corn), but were surprised to find a diet high in meat, in particular, turkey. In some restaurants, practically the whole menu was based on turkey, cooked in such a way to render it heavy and slow to digest. The meat, whether chicken, pork or turkey, came coated in *achiote*, a red, paste-like mixture of ground *achiote* seeds (from the *annatto* tree. No, we'd never heard of it either), oregano, garlic, flour made from maize and other spices used in Yucatán cuisine. It sounds quite interesting, but it is a very acquired taste, and it is used liberally on everything, so no matter what you ordered, it all ended up tasting the same. I wasn't tempted to bring home a jar of *achiote*. Other foods are Caribbean-influenced, and fried bananas and yucca root were on every menu, with bottles of dried chillies on every table, to add if the already tear-brimming food wasn't sufficiently hot.

Most of the food that we think of as Mexican, such as tacos and fajitas, actually owes more to American Tex-Mex which we had so loved in the *Border Café* in Boston and similar restaurants in Houston. Rather unhealthy food – even the beans are fried in lard – but at least it tastes good.

So we consoled ourselves by filling up on nachos and salsa and drinking generous, ice-cold jugs of margaritas and tequila sunrises, in the courtyard bar of the *Casa del Balam*, our hotel. After dinner, we were persuaded to try the quite delicious Yucatecan liqueur, *Xtabentun*, made from fermented honey and flavoured with aniseed. Perhaps we could introduce it to Provence where there is an abundance of both. As we drove out of Mérida, we were amazed to come across a large mall with signs advertising *TGI Friday's*, *Pizza Hut* and *McDonald's*. Is it only the tourists who plough their way through the traditional Yucatán delicacies?

If the food wasn't exciting, the festival certainly was. I think the area is a bit like Provence: there's always a festival or celebration going on. The city is vibrant, the streets full of people, especially on Sundays when the streets are closed to traffic and food stalls spring up everywhere. There are comedy acts, jazz, folk and classical music concerts, and at night in front of the Town Hall, hundreds of people dance with great energy to mambos, rumbas and cha-cha-chas. We were lucky enough to be there on a Sunday and be part of the fair called *Mérida en Domingo* (Mérida on Sunday) and thoroughly enjoyed the dancing, the music and the lively flea-market. Passers-by greeted us constantly with a smile and a *"Buenos días!"* Their politeness to complete strangers reminded us of the importance of the *"Bonjours"* in France. On Monday, there was another festival, the *Vaquerias* feast, associated originally with the branding of cattle on Yucatecan *haciendas*. Among the performers were dancers with trays of bottles and filled glasses on their heads – a sight to see. During our stay in Uxmal, the hotel put on a similar display. If we hadn't seen the 'original' in Mérida, we would have jumped to the conclusion that the dance had been made up especially to entertain the tourists.

We were sorry that we were going to miss the two-day celebration of the Day of the Dead. Only recently, in Provence, I learned about this celebration honouring saints and ancestors. The week before, all the shops and garden centres were full of autumn-hued chrysanthemums, huge yellow and rust blooms in terracotta pots. I considered buying some as my hostess gift to take to French neighbours that evening. Or, I could bulk up the fading summer plants on the terrace by introducing a few pots. Fortunately, I never got round to it. Later that day, we were surprised to see crowds of people making their way up the hill to the churchyard – carrying pots of chrysanthemums. Bemused, we followed them and spied a family we know from the local restaurant *Les Florets*. "Monsieur Bernard, why all the chrysanthemums?" "Why, to honour our dead," he replied solemnly. My grandparents are buried here, and my great grandparents."

In Mexico, they take it a bit further. Relatives gather at cemeteries, carrying candles and food, and they often spend a tequila-fuelled night beside the graves. They bring with them bread formed in the shape of mummies, loaves decorated with bread 'bones', sugar skulls emblazoned with glittery names, and photographs of the deceased. Children dress in costumes and masks and carry mock coffins and pumpkin lanterns, much like our Halloween, except that they are expecting donations of cash rather than a few pieces of candy.

Chichén Itzá was our next stop; the ruins are pretty hyped, but they are the Yucatán's best-known ancient remains, probably dating from the ninth century, and really worth seeing. The Mayan city is so vast that despite the tourists sometimes it appears empty, and you can be alone to contemplate the sheer scale and wonder of it all.

The site occupies four square miles, so it takes all day to see the ruins, and we returned later that evening for the spectacular sound and light show. Extremely atmospheric.

Our hotel too was interesting: a beautiful XV1 century colonial hacienda which in 1923 became the Carnegie Institute, a Mayan expedition headquarters. The picturesque cottages built for the Carnegie staff had been re-modelled as guest-rooms, but the remodelling hadn't run to glass in the windows. A minor inconvenience. The surroundings were serene, broken only by the squawks of the brightly coloured parrots in the tropical vegetation outside, or the chatter from a troop of monkeys swishing through the trees. The food wasn't much better than we'd experienced in the city, but we had long ago realised that this holiday wasn't going to be a gastronomic experience. While my energetic family climbed the twenty three metre high pyramid, *El Castillo*, I admired it from the base and read that it had been built with the Mayan calendar in mind: the four stairways leading up to the central platform each have 91 steps, making a total of 364 (the platform makes it 365). On either side of the stairway are nine terraces, which makes 18 on each side of the pyramid, equalling the number of months in the Mayan solar calendar. There are 52 decorated panels, including the mythical jaguar figure. The ruins are mysterious and many defy interpretation.

You could overdose on temples right here, but each one is different and interesting. What I liked best was the ball-court, originally one of nine but now the only one standing. Carved on the walls are Mayan figures decked out in heavy protective padding. The most gruesome depiction is headless and kneeling, with blood gushing from his neck. Another player, holding the head, looks on. Using only their elbows, knees and hips, players had to knock a rubber ball through the 'basket', a stone ring placed high on the two walls. The losers were sacrificed to the gods – quite an incentive to play your very best! Especially as the Mayans ripped out the still-beating hearts of their sacrificial victims.

The sound and light show actually started five minutes early, at 8:55. What happened to the infamous Spanish timekeeping? It was exceptionally good, tremendously atmospheric, as the booming voice re-told the stories of mythical animals and gods, such as Chaac, the rain god, Ah Kinchil, the sun god, and Ahmakiq the god of agriculture who locks up the wind when it threatens to destroy the crops. We've all got the t-shirts, not as tacky as it sounds as they depict Mayan mythical figures. I also bought a small pottery Mayan priest who guards my hearth, along with Indian Ganesh, the Batak spirit figure, the Brastaggi medicine man, and the Vietnamese stone lion – I'm covering all bases.

En route to our last stop, Uxmal, we passed traditional villages of tiny, one room, thatched-roofed houses; the hammocks of the occupants were clearly visible through the open doorways. We caught glances of peasant women wearing the traditional embroidered *huipiles* that I'd admired in the city shops, cooking tortillas on flat iron pans set over fires in front of the houses. In the gardens were growing swollen squash, fat, ripe tomatoes, abundant beans and chillies, staples in the Mexican diet. The cooks drew their water from *cenotes*, sinkholes or natural wells that exist nowhere else. It had struck us that driving through the countryside, we had seen no rivers or lakes.

Uxmal is spectacular, possibly the most splendid archaeological site in the area. Despite the Mayan builders possessing neither metal tools nor any detectable transportation, they built these rich, geometric stone facades, all skilfully decorated with delicate carvings. The age of the Maya ended in the fifteenth century with the arrival of the Spanish conquistadors. Military conquest and old-world diseases decimated the Mayan population. A new social order and a new religion replaced many of the ancient beliefs. They became a lost civilisation. The food was the usual tough, almost inedible meat, this time beef. How many prime herds had we passed on our road journey? The

Yucatán peninsula is magical, unique, unlike anywhere else we've visited. There is no other place like it. I've never seen the area depicted in a movie, but I look forward to watching Mel Gibson's *Death-Wish* style revenge thriller *Apocalypto* (a Greek word meaning an unveiling, a new beginning, apparently), which is set in Mexico six hundred years ago and has been filmed in the Mayan dialect Yucatec, employing Mayan villagers. I just hope that he allows subtitles.

Life could be a Beach: California Dreaming

Being a mobile wife does have its perks. While assigned to Houston, I accompanied my husband on a business trip to the idyllic resort of Laguna Beach, California. Raised on the harmonies of the Beach Boys, I was enthusiastic about the visit. California is usually portrayed as the Golden State, Paradise on earth. Television programmes such as *Baywatch* show California as the home of youth, physical beauty, good health, and laid-back lifestyles; yet, it has one of America's largest and fastest growing populations of retired people. Perhaps it had something to offer. True, I'd found little to like in Los Angeles where I'd ended my coast to coast train journey. However, in my twenties I'd visited San Francisco and loved it.

Arriving at John Wayne Airport, Irvine, we splashed out and hired a huge, finned convertible to enjoy the full Californian experience. Actually, as we soon discovered, the roads are pretty choked, so I'm not sure we got the benefit. But it was fun! Laguna Beach hugs the coast for about nine miles and started as a *Plein Air School* artists' colony in 1917. I spent hours browsing in the ninety or so shops and galleries full of high quality paintings, on sale for serious prices.

The highlight for us was our boutique hotel, the *Inn at Laguna Beach*, situated on a cliff, right on the beach. So different from the chains of faceless, over air-conditioned, corporate hotels in which we usually stayed. At night, we opened the French doors and fell asleep to the sound of the waves crashing on the shore. I've never slept so well. Later, I was given a gift a CD of surf sounds – soothing, but not quite the same. 'Our' beach, was pristine, swept clean every morning, and sparsely populated at the end of the season. If you tired of that beach, you could take your pick from the quaintly named Shaw's Cove, Sleepy Hollow, Ailso Creek, Wood's Cove or Thousand Steps Beach. The fire-fighters' basket ball team, the surfers, and the lifeguards were indeed beautiful people, fit and tanned. I lunched on freshly squeezed Orange County oranges – I could have chosen around fifty different combinations of juices blended to order; large, healthy salads with wonderful, locally grown tomatoes; and ocean-fresh seafood. I visited nearby Newport Beach with its claimed nine thousand yachts; and at the other end of the spectrum, car-less that day, I took two local buses to San Juan Capistrano Mission. I attracted stares, probably because I was the only white face on the bus. Definitely a mode of transport for the less affluent. The mission is renowned for its swallows which return every March 19, St Joseph's Day. It has some interesting artefacts from the Indian, Spanish and

Mexican eras and I bought a replica ceramic bell to hang on our Christmas tree.

During my few days in Laguna Beach, I talked to some of the local people, all very friendly, very philosophical, very flaky and brimming with interesting information. They were proud of the town's reputation as Southern California's premier seaside artists' haven; of their famous former residents: Bette Davis, Mary Pickford, Judy Garland, Charlie Chaplin and Mickey Rooney. All had maintained homes there. The quaint 'cottages' framed by tropical gardens which cascaded down the hillside above the beaches were probably worth millions of dollars. They told me about the Laguna Beach Festival of the Arts and the Film Festival; the oldest Playhouse in the US, offering five plays each season; and the magnificent, big sky sunsets. Laguna Beach is affluent and up-market. Since its launch last year, the teenage soap opera *Laguna Beach: The Real Orange County* has turned the community of 25,000 into a global brand synonymous with the young, rich and beautiful. It is picture-postcard perfect; it has a unique small-town charm I've rarely found anywhere else in the US. However, I'm not sure that it would sustain me for ever.

Business completed, we finished our road trip by driving along the coast towards San Diego and inland to Palm Springs, an artificial green oasis in the middle of a major desert. We passed miles and miles of tomatoes growing, and miles and miles of churning, less picturesque windmills. Palm Springs, an hour's drive from LA, became a winter escape for Hollywood stars of the 1930's. I knew that stars such as Bob Hope and Frank Sinatra had homes there. They'd been attracted by the dry desert climate, the opportunities to play year-round golf, and the mineral hot springs. Didn't really sound like our sort of place; definitely not my sort of place. I've always thought of Palm Springs as a destination where you go to play golf or die, but we might as well have a look while we were there.

We did see numerous lovely resorts, lots of lovely hotels, but we hadn't booked ahead and unfortunately a large motorbike convention was in town that weekend. We'd been expecting to see genteel geriatrics. Instead, convoys of burly, tattooed, leather-clad Easy Rider bikers zoomed past us, hollering greetings to their buddies. They were also shooting a film, or maybe a television soap, *Poodle Springs*, or that's what it sounded like when I asked an extra what was going on. And all the hotels were full. No room at the inn. So, we ended up staying at a very ordinary, rather run-down motel on the edge of town, far from anything that was happening. Actually, I'm not sure that very much **was** happening. The town seemed rather tacky – lots of amusement arcades with migraine-inducing video slot machines; casinos with bingo, poker, horse-betting – a strange combination I thought; ubiquitous fast-food joints; ads for celebrity homes' tours, presumably like the one I'd taken in Los Angeles.

About the most interesting thing around is the Palm Springs Desert Museum which has a rich collection of Native American basketry, pottery and jewellery. The Agua Caliente Band of Cahuilla Indians (no, we'd never heard of them either) own over twenty per cent of Palm Springs land and much of the surrounding territory. Their developed land parcels are the most valuable around. We were glad to hear it. I'm sure there's a lot more to Palm Springs than this; it just wasn't our sort of place.

It gets cold at night in the desert, very cold, and we were driving a convertible, dressed in summer clothes. On our way out of town, we stopped at a large Factory Outlet mall, one of the high points of American shopping. There, designer well-known brands can be purchased at a fraction of the original price. My husband kitted up in a huge, padded, fur-trimmed and hooded parka; I made do with a woollen scarf. Unfortunately, our stylish arrival at the airport hotel in Irvine was marred by both the doors of the flashy convertible sticking and the zip on the parka refusing to budge. It was now around thirty degrees, sweltering, so we looked more than faintly ridiculous as we struggled to get out of the car, *California Dreaming* still playing on the radio.

Anyone for Tennis?

Now, I think that our days of expat living are over. All the hard work of restoring the ruin is forgotten and we spend most of our holidays in Provence, enjoying our *maison secondaire* and gradually getting to know some of our neighbours. At last! A social occasion where the majority of guests are French. A daunting prospect, but quite exciting too. When my daughter telephones from England I tell her the latest news: "Daddy joined the Gigondas Tennis Club last week and now we have been invited to a tennis club party!"

"Wow! How exciting! You'd better start researching how to say, "Pass the dip, please, in French.""

"Not sure they go in very much for dips . . . the hostess has been cooking for three days . . . sounds a bit over the top for dips." I had gleaned this information after I had been roped into the preparations. Rather, my impressive range cooker had been roped in to cook an elaborate looking terrine, as my new state-of-the-art oven was deemed to be the most reliable in the village. "Just place the terrine in a bain-marie and cook at 180 degrees for one and a half hours. Then leave it until it is absolutely cold and place carefully in the fridge for twelve hours." Golly! Just as well my cooking skills are finely honed and I understand the make-up of a bain-marie.

Carefully, I followed the minute instructions; however, as the raw terrine had been delivered in the late evening, I realised that if I followed the instruction to the letter I'd have to stay up half the night. I'm ashamed to say that the terrine entered the fridge while still fairly warm. Imagine my relief at the party when I spotted it, looking magnificent, on the groaning buffet table.

Before the *soirée* I did leaf through my French phrase books. The trouble is they're either aimed at furthering brief encounters or providing such useful information as booking a hotel room, or ordering a coffee in a café. But the section on the weather might just prove useful. I've noticed that the French, certainly in this area, seem about as obsessed as the British about the weather. Perhaps it's because most of them are involved in the wine business. Every little nuance is worthy of comment. Does it look like rain? Perhaps there will be *un temps de cochon*, literally pig's weather, rain so torrential that you can't see the lines on the road. Very occasionally we do get such weather, when the rain cascades down the steep lanes of the village; it is sometimes a relief after a period of relentless heat, an excuse to curl up with a book. The *vignerons* rejoice that their grapes will receive some welcome sustenance. Will the *mistral* come up later in the day? How many days will it last? The previous week there had been a new weather phenomenon on which to comment: snow – in April! Unheard of! "*Normalement....*" There we had this expression again: something exceptional, out of the ordinary, unexpected, unheard of. As though I would think less of their country if it snowed in spring, when tourists expect blue skies, swathes of scarlet poppies and bone-warming sun.

It's the same with holidays which result in shops closing their doors to customers. France has more holidays than any other nation in the world, including one hundred and ninety seven saints' days, Brigitte Bardot Day (March 1) and National Guillotine Day (November 12). In May alone there are four national holidays: Labour Day, VE Day, Ascension Day and Pentecost. Then there are the *ponts*, the bridges. If a holiday falls on a Tuesday, the sensible thing to do is to *faire le pont* and take Monday too as a holiday. If it falls on a Thursday, why not add Friday? Add these to breaks for lunch, bouts of family illness, births, weddings, funerals and annual holidays and it's a wonder that shops manage to open at all. On many occasions we've made a special trip to buy something essential from a small shop, only to be greeted by a locked door and a sign proclaiming *fermeture exceptionelle*, literally 'exceptional closing', something out of the ordinary. In the nearby Séguret *santons* shop (little Provençal nativity figures), the owner has a bank of printed index cards encased in a plastic holder on the back of his door. He has at least ten different reasons for the shop not being open. How does he choose? When you arrive and the shop is unexpectedly open, you feel so grateful that you buy more *santons* than intended.

We set out intrepidly for the party. So many social minefields. When should we arrive? The invitation stated 6 until 8 – not a big window. If we arrived fashionably late by British standards, we might miss the speeches, the toasts (we were celebrating a member's impressive sixty years of playing tennis). *Quel faux-pas*! We decided on ten past six as the optimum and set out. Most guests seemed to have beaten us to it, so there were lots of introductions to get through. Tricky. Surprisingly, the French are much more formal than we Brits in everyday situations. We rather enjoy the customary "*Bonjour!*" that greets us every time we enter a shop, every time someone walks past our house, panting, stopping momentarily for a rest before scaling the last few steep steps leading up to the church. People come across as very polite, a welcome contrast to the rudeness frequently encountered in Britain. The challenge when entering the village *épicerie* is to sum up quickly the waiting customers: men, women, a combination? Is *monsieur* serving alone today, or is *madame* helping him? Has *madame* left her husband snugly tucked up in bed? How many customers are present and of what sex? This affects whether your greeting is "*Bonjour, monsieur*", or "*Bonjour, madame*", or "*Bonjour, mesdames*", "*Bonjour, messieurs*", or more probably "*Bonjour, messieurs-dames*" to cover all sexes present.

Arriving at the tennis club *soirée* was even more daunting. Not only *bonsoirs* and firm handshakes, but three kisses on each cheek for the sixteen or so people assembled. At least, I joined in all the kissing. It seemed my husband only had to kiss the women present, not the men, so he was let off lightly. In Provence, three kisses are *de rigueur* in social situations. Rather a charming custom, but it does involve a lot of kissing. The kissing was repeated as each guest made his *au revoirs* – no slipping out un-noticed as we'd made a pact to do if the social situation proved too much for our limited French.

Now I had a whole new circle of acquaintances to greet with a hearty *Bonjour*! each time I spotted them in the village. I'd started off by greeting everyone I met with what I supposed was the correct form, only to be told disapprovingly, with much wagging of the finger, that I should only say *Bonjour* to the people I know. I didn't really know anyone to begin with, however, after a few weeks many people in the village looked vaguely familiar and deserving of a *Bonjour*. Apparently, you greet **everyone** present in the *épicerie*, gift shop, or *café*, but you don't *Bonjour* the customers in the nearby *supermarché* – easy once you get the hang of it. Another possible trip-up is greeting someone with a handshake and a *Bonjour* if you have already greeted him/her earlier in the day. What a lot to remember!

At the party, I did talk about the weather – the rain, apparently good for bringing out the escargots, and we salivated as *monsieur* shared his secret recipe which contained an unbelievable amount of garlic. Of course, rain was also beneficial to the vines at this stage in the proceedings, while in late August it could prove disastrous. Apparently, it had been a cold winter, and concern was expressed over the fate of the peaches, the lemons, the cherries, the apricots. *Normalement*, winters in Gigondas were fairly mild and plants such as geraniums survived to bloom again in the spring. But not this year. When we'd arrived at the house at the beginning of

April, the geraniums were black and slimy and many of the terracotta pots had cracked with the frost. Truly an unusual winter – *exceptionnel*. And ten centimetres of snow in Malaucène last week! Unheard of – snow in the next valley, in April. But none in our village, just the other side of the mountains. We've yet to see snow here, but there is a photograph on the Post Office wall of Gigondas looking even more picturesque than usual with a sprinkling of snow.

Party conversation quickly progressed from the weather to politics – quite a leap. Fortunately, I felt fairly well-informed about both the upcoming British General Election and the French vote on the European Constitution. True, I'd gained most of my facts from reading the English *Sunday Time*s, but at least I had some views and I understood vaguely what was going on.

The champagne toasts and speeches were soon over. We congratulated our hostess on having played for sixty years, really quite an achievement, and she was presented with a wine decanter and six wine glasses. Probably to improve her game. The previous summer I'd attended a tennis doubles match – Scotland and Denmark versus France – as a spectator and learned a few new words of French, probably best not repeated in polite society. At around half-time the game was interrupted and a cool-box was opened to reveal, not the British oranges, but three bottles of chilled wine. How civilised! I'd been instructed to bring a bottle and had carefully chosen a fine, gutsy red – another *faux-pas*! The post-master gently informed me that the French never drink red wine as an *apéritif*. In Provence, *rosé* is the norm, maybe white at a pinch. However, no-one seemed to have a problem scoffing the socially incorrect red. They probably wanted to spare me the burden of carrying the bottle back up the hill. Now, I could walk a few metres to the recycling area and safely deposit the empty bottle in the bottle-bank.

The imbibing and scoffing of *canapés* liberally spread with olive paste, *tapenade,* in no way seemed to affect the second half of the game, except to give the players a new burst of energy. Perhaps we should adopt this French habit? Maybe thus we could finally produce a British world tennis champion? The French take their tennis playing very seriously and we miss having a friendly game of mixed doubles where no-one cares who wins.

At the tennis *soirée*, as I'd predicted, there were no dips in sight, but a groaning table of the most elaborate dishes. The French certainly know how to eat. No standing around nibbling finger food here. Several tables had been laid end to end with colourful local tablecloths; every chair in the house had been mustered and places set for all guests. It was a wonderful repast with many toasts, even one to *Les Anglais.* Despite all the barbs in such recently published books as Agnes Poiriers' *Les Nouveaux Anglais* about our doubtful dress sense and severe hang-ups, the French tennis players were genuinely welcoming. They were interested in why we had bought a house in their village; what we thought of Provence; how it compared to life in London. In our limited French we tried to answer their queries honestly. London has many obvious attractions, but we love the quiet of the French village, the customs and traditions of the area, and we'd found the Provençal people very friendly and welcoming, offering us help and advice at every opportunity.

Table-hopping seemed *de rigueur*, much like the fashionable restaurants in New York or London, so we were exposed to conversations with many of our neighbours. The local post-master, the president of the Gigondas Tennis Club, laughed about our initial reluctance to equip our house with a letter box. We'd feared receiving a deluge of junk mail, *publicité*, left hanging out, advertising our frequent absences. But, of course, the post lady, Brigitte, doesn't deliver *pub* when we're not in residence. Not like the locum post deliverer. Recently, we became aware that Brigitte must be on a well-deserved holiday when our mail box began to fill up with unwanted *pub*. Yet, puzzlingly, no personal mail for two weeks. My birthday passed – no cards. I couldn't have offended everyone. The mystery was solved one week later when the mail box bulged with seven envelopes, some franked three weeks earlier. The post-master explained that the postal delivery system had broken down due to the temporary worker's inability to distinguish where residents actually lived. When we had first come to live in the village, I had expressed concern about how the postman would know where we lived. A Gallic shrug was followed by the customary *pas de problème,* and it was explained that even a letter addressed to *Matchett, le village* would reach us with no difficulty. Not always true, as we'd discovered. Our mail had been sitting in an alien letter box for several weeks until the owner of the *maison secondaire* arrived on holiday from Paris. It was still a delight to open the belated birthday wishes; however, we welcomed the return of the super efficient Brigitte who in summer delivers the mail straight to our breakfast table on the terrace.

As more and more of the excellent local wine flowed, the postmaster went on to tell anecdotes about previous owners of our house: Madame M. and Madame C. Like many *Gigondasiens*, he spoke like a machine gun, *une mitraillette*, but I picked up the gist of what he was saying. *Madame*, I'm not sure which one, had told him about the presence of a ghost, *une phantome*, roaming our rooms. Had we seen it? Felt its presence? I have felt a presence now and again, especially when I've spent time living on my own, during thunderstorms and the frequent power cuts. I'd put it down to an overactive imagination, but who knows? I do sense something in the original kitchen, when I'm tapping away at my computer, but it's a friendly presence. Perhaps it approves of us painting and shelving the old cheese cupboard and filling it with books. Perhaps someone is glad that the ruined house has been restored, brought back to life and loved again.

The eight o'clock watershed passed and guests showed no signs of departing. We hadn't even reached the all-important cheese course. The passing around of the laden cheese *plateau* took about as long as the kisses and speeches. Cheese certainly plays a much larger part in the life of most French people than it does in Britain. President de Gaulle is often quoted as having said, "How can anyone be expected to govern a country with 325 cheeses?" There are probably many more today. In the nearby town of Vaison-la-Romaine, we are fortunate to have the cheese shop run by the lady who was recently awarded a medal by President Chirac as the best *ouvrier* (literally worker) in France. It is a joy to enter her shop and leaf through the Patricia Wells cookery books where she receives a warm mention. I only discovered the shop, rather hidden in a narrow street off the main square, through the American cookery writer's recommendation. She has a farmhouse and vineyard near Vaison, runs cookery classes, and has embraced fully the Provençal life. It's fun to search out a recommended honey or cheese-maker, search the country lanes for a suggested *domaine*. Her standards are high and she rarely disappoints. I've also learned a great deal about Provençal cooking, customs and traditions from poring through her books.

Garden of Eden

Adjoining our house in Provence is a small, triangular piece of land, steeply meandering down the hill and bordered by heaps of limestone stones, once part of an enclosing wall. The land is heavily overgrown and wooded, covered in spindly trees that spring up every summer like weeds. The provenance of this land is vague:

"Madame M, the owner of your house, kept her goats on the land."

"I remember it as a garden, full of beautiful flowers."

"The land used to belong to your house."

The last point is particularly interesting as, when we bought the house, the land belonged to our neighbour, Madame J. Rumour had it that it had once belonged to 'our' house but the owner had not paid the taxes. Seizing the day, Madame J. had begun to pay the peppercorn taxes, and in ten years the land became officially hers. Who knows?

When we bought the house, I wrote a very flowery letter, in the French style, to Madame J, extolling the potential beauty of the land, promising to create a paradise of flowers to be enjoyed by all, if she would only allow me to purchase the land. Surely this would be an improvement? (I didn't include this in my begging letter). In its present state, the garden was an eyesore, wildly overgrown, the interior barely visible through the dense trees.

Shortly afterwards, I received a very polite, equally flowery, reply from *Madame*. She was *désolée* but the land was not for sale. A neighbouring house that she owned but in which she did not live was up for sale and she wished to keep open the option of selling this land with the house.

What a disappointment! Each spring when we arrived in the village, the land appeared stark and bereft. The wood only sprang to life, like the beanstalk in *Jack and the Beanstalk*, towards the end of April. Without the trees, it was easier to see what plants still survived – not many: a few straggly rosemary bushes, two spindly fig trees, half a dozen or so ubiquitous purple irises; and a tangle of wild flowers that I couldn't identify by name.

For four years whenever we sat on our terrace we eyed up this land, making plans for a garden if we should ever manage to persuade *Madame* to part with it.

Get rid of the weedy trees and plant soothing olives and cypress trees; build an *abri*, a shelter, to shade us from the sun; a small fountain to create coolness; fill the garden with native Mediterranean plants which require little water to survive. At a *brocante* fair, we'd found an old, sepia postcard which seemed to show – although very blurred – a wall enclosing the garden, goats grazing, a door leading from our house on to the land. Perhaps people's memories were sound?

No matter; it wasn't ours now. Madame's stance had hardened. She had allowed us access across her land to restore our house and bring in our furniture – very generous of her. However, now she was adamant: "Do not step on my land!" Or words to that effect. On the whole, we respected her wishes; however, when we needed a major alteration to our fireplace, to solve the problem of clouds of smoke billowing into the room every time we lit a fire, the huge stones to reduce the volume of the space had to be carried across the land by the builders. By now, the trees were so overgrown that the builders had to hack down the undergrowth to beat a path to our door. Unfortunately, *Madame*, who hardly ever entered the village, chose that day to visit her property. From the open bedroom window I heard her screams of indignation. You didn't need to be fluent in French to understand the gist, the tone. I was a complete coward and remained hiding in the bedroom, leaving my husband to confront the extremely angry neighbour. She waved her walking stick in the air for emphasis. Words to the effect that our actions were unbelievable, inexcusable . . . The tirade went on and on. This was not going to help our campaign to purchase the land.

Undaunted, every so often I would write another letter to *Madame*, enquiring politely if the land was now available for us to purchase. On each occasion, her son, whose English is excellent after two years living in California, would communicate a definite *non*. Years passed and *Madame's* house was not sold. Too much restoration required? Too expensive? It appeared to us that the vendor was not even sure that she wanted to sell the house, inherited from her sister. It was now let to holiday-makers as two *gîtes* and would thus provide a reasonable seasonable income.

Then, a year ago, out of the blue, *Madame's* son approached us as we sat on our terrace and announced that he was thinking of selling the land. Were we interested in buying? Adopting nonchalance, our response was guarded; however, inside we were very excited. At last! The projected garden was within our grasp.

But, nothing happens quickly in Provence, as we'd discovered when we bought and then developed the house. A year passed and we reminded *Monsieur* that he had offered us the chance to buy the land. Over a few glasses of wine in our kitchen, a deal was struck – not exactly a bargain, but we really wanted that land. We parted very amicably and a few weeks later the sale was confirmed at the office of the *notaire* in the next village. *Madame* was present. Now advanced in years, she had no recollection of ever having met us, or having screamed abuse at our transgression. This was good news for us. We smiled and simpered. I told her how much I loved her village and Provence; how young she looked for her avowed 81 years. The son was now in charge and conducted the legal business, only including *Madame* to obtain the required signature. Within an hour, the paperwork was completed and we were well on our way to owning the garden. The contract, the *compromis,* was signed by all parties, and a few months later the papers of ownership arrived from the *notaire.* We now officially owned the land, all 84 m2 of it.

It was a good feeling and we began to plan our Eden. As we would not be there to care for it all year, a Mediterranean garden would be ideal. We contacted an architect recommended by a neighbour. He specialised in garden design; his wife had a building company – seemed ideal. *Monsieur* and *Madame* drove us to Grignan in the Drôme to view one of their projects. The garden was truly lovely: not quite on our scale as it was vast with a blue, mosaic-lined swimming pool flanked by changing rooms and a Versailles-style water feature. However, the drought-resistant planting was what we had in mind for our plot.

Impressed, we began to plan our garden with the architect and after many e-mails to and fro we had computerised plans and a virtual garden. On paper, it looked magnificent. This was December. It should have planning permission by January, we were promised, and should be completed by March. Just in time for the summer!

Of course, it was not to be. Had we forgotten so quickly the struggle to have the house restored? Planning permission was not granted.

At frequent intervals our neighbour visited to console us. "Don't worry. These things take time. Even if you don't manage to develop all the land, you could plant a few flowers, make it pretty. Not perfect like the garden of our Swiss neighbours, but good enough." But I want a garden like the Swiss neighbours'!

Things really galloped apace when we changed horses and employed two young architects who had just set up their practice in the village. They are enthusiastic, full of interesting ideas, and, most importantly, Laurens is a local – her family have lived in the area for generations. Soon we had full planning permission and the builder started work a few weeks later. We employed tactics learned from reading Peter Mayle's *A Year in Provence*: "Our son is getting married in May. Possibly the wedding party will be held in the new garden."

In fact, our son married in Vernazza, on the Italian Riviera, but at the end of April we did celebrate my birthday there. The sun shone on us as we shared an English afternoon tea with a dozen of our neighbours. Our heroic efforts to prepare the land for planting had attracted many admiring looks. Not many people have to buy a second pick-axe handle! We barrowed in the stones for a dry-stone wall and a rock garden, the topsoil, the compost and finally the cypress and olive trees and the plants. Friends have given us plants and bulbs and a bird house. There's something in bloom at every season of the year and we and the passers-by get an enormous amount of pleasure from the garden. It's full of colour, bees, butterflies and cats, and our wonderful *Parisienne* neighbour, artist and friend, Catherine, waters when necessary and pulls out the odd weed, *mauvaise herbe,* masquerading as a flower. For us, it truly is a Garden of Eden.

Home Sweet Home

Our Richmond conservatory has a full complement of Sumatran rattan *mama sans, chaises longues* and coffee tables. Rattan is very light, so our dining table and chairs have been all over the world. Company shipments are weighed; no restrictions on volume. Now, our Sumatran dining table has come to rest in Gigondas, complete with a new glass top. This table has been to Adelaide, Boston, Singapore, Houston and back to the UK with no problems. However, on this final trip, to Provence, the glass broke. How to get it replaced? By enquiring around, we discovered the local mirror business, the *miroiterie*.

Two men from the shop agreed to come to the house the following day, and meticulously they constructed a template from the intact shards. "*Pas de problème!*" How's that for service? Within a week, the table-top was back in place and it fitted perfectly.

Just in time for my first guests. One of the things I enjoy most about our house is filling it with visitors. People who are reluctant to drive all the way round the M25 for dinner, no matter how good your cooking, think nothing of driving for the best part of two days to your 'château' in Provence. Despite our protestations that we own a very simple village house, some people choose to imagine something much grander. "I'm sure you're being very modest!" Actually, the *maison secondaire* had turned out a great deal bigger and grander than we had anticipated. Tumbling down the hill over four levels, including the two cellars, *caves*, the square footage is quite impressive. We don't have a forty foot sitting room in cramped, expensive London. Yes, we have the three bedrooms, but three bathrooms? My Gigondas kitchen is home-made, but it looks so impressive that neighbours have asked for the name of the designer and want one just like it. My husband constructed the shelves and worktops from pine floor-boards. He couldn't locate better wood and the lengths fitted comfortably on the car roof-rack. We have the big, pine, farmhouse table and the fancy range stove – not much room for these in our bijou London residence.

I don't really know exactly what people expect, but most are pleasantly surprised – by the lightness and airi-ness of the huge rooms, the (restrained) Provençal décor, and most of all by the view. The view was the factor that convinced us in the first place that this was the 'one'.

Many of our visitors when they think of Provence
think of the Côte d'Azur – golden beaches, yachts,
crowds. Vaucluse couldn't be more different. People
come to this area for the vigorous outdoor pursuits: the
rock-climbing, hiking, mountain biking, and of course
the outstanding food and wine. The markets are sensational. On my notice-board in the kitchen I keep a handy
list of market days in the surrounding villages. Some
markets are very local, very simple, merely one or two
stalls heaped with fresh produce, however, others merit
the early rise. It takes a lot of persuasion to convince
weary visitors looking forward to a lie-in that it's worth
rising literally at the crack of dawn to catch the market.
In summer, markets get going very early – arrive after
8 a.m. and the crowds are thick, parking impossible, for
of course the market is held on the village car parks. It's
an enigma where the shoppers are expected to park their
cars on market day. And cars are an absolute necessity in
this countryside almost devoid of public transport.
Shortly after mid-day, everything is gone, packed up for
the next destination on the circuit. It took me a while to
realise why some of the stall-holders seemed familiar. Of
course! The organic bread seller at Carpentras market on
Friday was the same man who'd joked to me about
Britain's adoption of the euro in Vaison-la-Romaine on
Tuesday. To me, it seems a hard life, but the stallholders
all seem very cheerful and they take great pains in setting
out their wares to advantage: whole stalls selling nothing
but twisted tresses of new garlic, or onions of ten varieties. I didn't even know there **were** ten different types of
onions. Stalls selling quilts of many hues and patterns,
the stall-holder patiently unfolding and displaying
the beauties on request – how many quilts could you get

through in a lifetime? Heaps and heaps of brightly coloured *indienne* print tablecloths: square, round, rectangular, oval – twelve napkins to match; very cheap. You can only use so many tablecloths, but I find myself seduced into purchasing far too many. Best of all are the produce stalls. There are few tastier experiences than wandering through a Provençal market. You soon learn who has the finest, plumpest tomatoes, the first wild strawberries, picked early that morning, the most luscious purple figs, bursting with ripeness. One man may sell only raspberries; another, the first *girondelles* mushrooms I imagine found that morning in secret places, knowledge probably passed down from father to son. I'd been tempted to forage for my own wild mushrooms – it couldn't be too difficult, could it? I'd been told that in France you can take your mushrooms to the local pharmacy for identification, to avoid mistakes. However, my enthusiasm was curbed when a local told us how he'd picked a whole basket full of promising looking specimens, only to have all but two rejected as *bon* to eat. Quite sobering.

The vegetables and fruits growing in sun-drenched Provence do seem exceptional. They're not blemish-free and regularly sized and the carrots, leeks and potatoes are still caked in soil, but the taste is invariably superb. My guests comment on the exquisite taste and juiciness of the misshapen tomatoes, red all the way through – at home they look good but taste of cotton wool; the size of the huge red, green and yellow peppers; the shine on the deep purple aubergines; the firmness of the courgettes which come frequently with frilly yellow flowers still intact. All go in the basket in preparation for the cooking of *ratatouille*, one of Provence's most frequently served dishes. It really does taste different cooked here. It must be the sun, or the red wine I pour in nonchalantly, or my liberal use of *herbes de Provence*.

The basket used to carry the vegetables home is all-important. When I first arrived, I trotted around with a linen tote proclaiming 'Martha's Vineyard' (purchased on a side trip from Boston). I have fond memories of time spent on this magical island, but the souvenir marked me out as a tourist. Which basket to buy? It's a bit like the tablecloths: every hue and size and shape of basket, heaped up to tempt customers. I didn't rush in. By careful observation of our village's older residents, I came to identify a certain basket with soft sides, leather trim and handles as the authentic market basket, the only one to carry confidently. Mine still looks a bit raw, but a few more shopping trips and it will look the part.

Many of our visitors doze on the car journey to the market and are awakened with groans, but they all acquiesce that the early rise was worth it. Plenty of time in the afternoon to terrace lounge or grab a siesta. Where in Britain can you spend three hours walking round a market and never feel bored? Purchasing takes patience. You ask questions, prod the vegetables and fruits, eye up the fish, and take advice on how to cook it. What will be the ideal herbs to use? The best accompaniments? Then you move on, searching for the best capers, anchovies, olives to complete the dish. Quickly I learned that going to the market with preconceived ideas about what I was going to cook was the wrong approach. You look at what's available, in season; then you concoct your menu. You would only make *ratatouille* in summer, at a pinch in early autumn. The best mushrooms, walnuts, almonds come into season in October, so that's when you cook dishes based on these ingredients. Between November and March, nearby Carpentras becomes a hot-bed of intrigue as vast sums are exchanged furtively for unpromising looking brown lumps – truffles. Lots of nose rubbing, nods, winks, and the transaction is completed. Thanks to the much-maligned Peter Mayle, I know which café to frequent, sipping my thimble of bitter coffee, to witness the dealing. One market stall-holder ostensibly sells baskets of mushrooms and a few duck eggs; however, smelling an interested customer, he whips out a cloth-covered pannier from underneath the counter to reveal – a truffle. Not a very big one, and why is he selling it on the black market? Who knows, but we gave into temptation and the tiny, brown lump was sensational, stored beside the eggs to infuse them with heady perfume, then shaved over the omelette of free-range, organic, bright yellow-yoked eggs.

I love sharing my home in Provence with visitors. Maureen, one of our first guests, I've known since we were twelve and at school together. We have a shared history like no other. Many visitors are friends we have made on our foreign assignments. You find yourself running a country house hotel, complete with baskets of miniature purloined toiletries. Yes, we have the room – even if it means giving up my own precious bed to accommodate the extra guest they've squeezed into the car. "All right that we'll be arriving at Nîmes Airport just before midnight?" "No problem," I reply, wondering how I'll stay awake until that ungodly hour. In the village, most locals go to bed at nine or ten o'clock, and I've adopted this habit myself. "Hello, Graham here. Just got a cheap flight to Nice. We'll be there by lunchtime tomorrow?" "No problem." Only three and a half hours in the car each way to pick up and return. Actually, it isn't a problem. We slow down as soon as we arrive in Provence; we seem to have all the time in the world.

People come to relax, to unwind, and to soak up the sun, and almost all are vacation compatible. They arrive with generous hostess gifts: two bottles of Champagne; a bottle of single malt whisky; the must-read summer blockbuster; the latest magazines; Frank Cooper's Original Oxford marmalade, things you miss from home. On her first visit, my cousin Janie brought with her a Provençal-like quilt: blue and yellow, patchwork, much of it exquisitely hand-sewn and embroidered with the date and our names – a real heirloom of the future. It now hangs over the metalwork in the stairwell and will always remind us of her kindness. Second-home dinner guests also amaze us with their generosity and ingenuity: preserved beetroots, grown in their vegetable garden at home; a framed, hand-worked piece of lace from my German friend, Marianne; Belgian praline chocolates; tins of Danish herrings. I reciprocate by bringing boxes of Scottish shortbread, oatcakes, a simnel cake, home-made lemon curd and marmalade, anything from Marks and Spencer or the Duchy of Cornwall.

Most of our house guests are delightful. They help with the myriad of vegetable chopping; polish the glasses to a shine – "I worked as a dishwasher in a posh restaurant during my Gap year" – carry the huge bags of garbage further down the hill to the communal wheelie bin; and recycle the embarrassing number of wine bottles in the bins behind the post office. Few re-alise that to prepare breakfast, even a continental one, for eight people requires a dawn rise and a brisk trot down the steep hill to the *épicerie* and bread depot for the croissants and baguettes – in short supply, so you've got to be in line when the shutters are raised at seven. Mondays are particularly difficult. Closing day for the hard-working *épicier*, therefore a six kilometre drive to the *boulangerie* in a neighbouring village for the fresh croissants. I grumble a bit to myself, but it's hardly a hardship.

Eight people, three meals a day, appetites sharpened by cycling or hiking up the steep surrounding hills with serious walking poles. All that food, not to mention the drink, has to be humped from the car to the house. French supermarkets are very impressive. Seven different kinds of lettuce; fresh, glistening fish displays to rival Harrods Food Hall; and so many cheeses, too many to taste and choose from. Here, the cheeseboard is a serious affair, summed up by the eighteenth century epicurean Jean Anthelme Brillat-Savarin: "*Un dessert sans fromage est une belle à qui il manqué un oeil!*" A dessert without cheese is a one-eyed beauty. The bread is usually a separate transaction, in an adjacent bakery. So much to feast the eyes upon, and not just bread of every shape and composition: choux puffs sweet and savoury, *fougasse* (a traditional layered, flaky bread, heavy on the fragrant olive oil – delicious) studded with slivers of olive or ham; quiches of four varieties, *croque monsieur*, and the tarts of the day. Who would think of struggling at home to roll out pastry when such delectable treats are available in even the smallest *patisserie* or supermarket? Most of our meals eaten with guests end with a fruit tart – I've never had a bad one.

I love cooking when I'm in Provence, even more than I do at home. I love chopping the market vegetables at my pine table; picking the fresh herbs: rosemary, marjoram, tarragon, parsley, sage and thyme, from outside the kitchen door; splashing liberal quantities of wine into the *Le Creuset* pot. However, vegetarian guests can pose a bit of a challenge. Having run through my vegetarian repertoire of Delia's roasted vegetable lasagne, and Elizabeth David's *melanzane parmigiano*, we venture out to sample the local restaurants. Despite the profundity of vegetables on sale in French markets, restaurants rarely include vegetarian dishes on their menus. Delicious lunches always involve dead animals. "Perhaps an *omelette* for *madame?*" suggests the unsympathetic waiter. Not much imagination there. Occasionally, chefs excel themselves and with prior notice will modify their menu heavy on the dead animals (normally served bloody) to produce such delights as 'a symphony of spring vegetables', but these are the exception. A few vegetarians are coaxed into becoming flexatarians, occasionally falling off the no-meat or fish wagon. Just as you can't eat French food without wine – *pas possible* – a meal without flesh is incomprehensible. At home, I listen to polite protestations: "Don't worry about me; I'll just have the veg." But then there won't be enough for everyone else, and what about the starch, the bulking agent? Not all vegetarians are six stone weaklings. Really, what they are expecting is something separate and different – a steaming plate of fresh pasta cooked *al dente*, at the last minute, by the exhausted hostess. Not to mention the sauces, the supply of freshly grated *Parmigiano Reggiano*. Once, I placed the label from the block of parmesan on a guest's plate. She is from Italy, actually from Reggio Emilia, home of the authentic parmesan, and to her way of thinking everything has to come from the 'right' place, a specific zone. I was chastened to learn that my *balsamico* didn't pass muster; it **was** from Modena, but not from the right estate. The label from the True Parmesan raised a smile and a nod of approval.

Tea and coffee – yet another social minefield. Coffee means different things to different people. Our idea of coffee is thick, strong and black, either made in the espresso machine or what Americans call a French press. Actually, Americans are the problem. When we lived in Boston, we would walk miles to the Italian North End for a decent cup of coffee. Most Americans drink coffee resembling dishwater: weak, pale, dirty brown, with lashings of artificial creamer and sweetener. Then there are the visitors who genuinely want to save you any trouble, "A cup of instant will be fine." We never drink instant coffee. I won't have it in the house. Living in Indonesia, we couldn't understand why some expats would reject the excellent, flavoursome, local Sumatran coffee beans in favour of a super-size jar of Maxwell House, hand-carried from Singapore. Another example of seeking comfort in familiar things from back home? Admittedly, seeing the coffee beans being dried at the side of the road was a little off-putting, especially when a two-ton truck parked nonchalantly on top of them, but it just seemed to add to the flavour. Tea too is beset with hidden problems. My cousin had obviously experienced my feeble attempts at making tea. I don't drink tea, so I have to admit that I don't have much of a clue about the niceties of the tea ceremony. Wisely, she arrived clutching her caddy of Fortnum and Mason's Earl Grey, her preferred tipple, and a tea-strainer. All that was lacking was the tea cosy which we failed to track down in the local market or shops. I suspect that only the British knit outsize woollen hats to keep their teapots warm. A few months later, a friend appeared early in the morning looking for tea to take to his still bed-bound wife. "Um, yes, a cup of Earl Grey would be splendid!" Remember, this is in France, in a village with one *épicerie* which (rightly) stocks only French staples. "No problem, "I was able to reassure him as I retrieved the dusty dregs from the Fortnum and Mason caddy and hunted for the elusive tea-strainer. Other visitors have simpler tastes, but some of them drink an amazing amount of tea. Our niece and nephew in one week went through a large box of Yorkshire Teabags, difficult to replace. The following Christmas, we opened our beautifully wrapped and beribboned gift from these visitors to find – a box of Yorkshire Teabags! It was greatly appreciated. We now keep a full stock: three or four different English teas; a large box of variety herbal and fruit teas; a separate box of Menthe (mint – not included in the variety pack); two jars of hot chocolate, light and regular; still no instant coffee.

I gripe. I don't have many gripes about my visitors. We almost always rub along very well. Most arrive by car and we send them off for the day to explore the amphitheatre at Orange, or the Palais des Papes in Avignon. We load them down with leaflets, maps, guidebooks, from our extensive collection. "Make sure you take the tour, and use the audio-guide – well worth the expense. It should take all day, when you include the two hour, light lunch." This will sustain them until the more substantial, four course dinner *chez-nous*. Or they venture out with a picnic basket to one of the two excellent open-air swimming pools in the vicinity. I remember to tell them that the French have rather a lot of rules: no running; no wearing of flip-flops, sandals or shoes beside the pool; no ball games allowed beside or in the pool; no inflatable toys or air mattresses; no portable music; no eating or drinking in the pool; and, most importantly, male bathers must wear *un slip*, a scanty pair of close-fitting briefs – no baggy surf shorts allowed. Apart from that, you're free to do as you please. While they're away, I have time to freshen the towels, load the washing machine, and prepare a few *hors d'oeuvres*. If I'm lucky, I snatch a siesta, or indulge in a spot of terrace-lounging. How do I hold down a full-time job in London? How do I manage without this essential afternoon nap?

Our guests return in the early evening, just in time to freshen up before *apéritifs* in the courtyard and a three to four hour supper on the terrace, washed down with copious amounts of local wine. We are avid re-cyclers and I cajole guests to take a few empty bottles with them on every trip. The row of wine bottles beside the front door is just too embarrassing when locals come to call. Or perhaps when I catch them staring at the bottles it is in wonder and admiration of our almost French drinking prowess? My guests are generous. Many will stop on the way home from these outings, in Vacqueras, Cairanne, Châteauneuf-du-Pape, or in Gigondas itself, for a tasting and the purchase of a few bottles of wine. I'm handed pungent cheeses that they've picked up from some little stall, or a clutch of bursting, perfumed, striped Cavaillon melons.

The Provençal diet is mainland Europe's healthiest, so we can tuck in guiltlessly to oven-roasted *ratatouille*, *salade niçoise*, wonderfully fresh Mediterranean shell-fish and Mont Ventoux lamb, grazed on wild thyme, rosemary and marjoram. I buy the lamb from a butcher in nearby Carpentras. You can't rush the transaction. How many people will be coming to dinner? Do they have small or large appetites? Then, I'm given the history of the leg of lamb. *Madame* knows which slope of the mountain the lamb will have been grazing on, what it will have been eating during its short but pleasant exis-tence. Perhaps she knew the actual sheep? Then, I watch as the lamb receives a final butchering. It is tied with fine string in four different places and wrapped tenderly in a white, spider-web caul to ensure moist cooking. How am I going to cook the lamb? I assure *madame* that I will take the utmost care of her prized lamb and cook it to perfection. For the French, that means almost gambolling off the plate. I'm a regular customer now, so I think I have just about won her trust.

At first, when I invited neighbours to join us for tea, or come for dinner, they were a little hesitant, a little apprehensive. Afternoon tea doesn't seem to be a big event in Provence – perhaps because of the heat – although there are a few *salons de thé* and the *patisseries* are bursting with delectable cakes, most of them oozing cream. However, after the long siesta, and before the long, late evening meal, a familiar pot of tea can be very welcome. I love sharing with foreigners my traditional British scones, crisp shortbread and Victoria sponges oozing jam and cream. Yes, the scones may be spread with the delicious local honey or nostalgic quince jam, but apart from that they are very British and a real novelty. They are a novelty for us too; not something we have time for every day.

We grew up in Scotland, better known for its deep-fried Mars Bars with a side order of chips than a healthy diet. I married young, in 1970, straight after university, and moved from the cosmopolitan West End of Glasgow to the suburbs. As a new and totally undomesticated wife, to fit in I had to learn quickly the art of baking. Neighbours who visited, even for ten minutes, expected at least a homemade biscuit with the tea or coffee. On a student's straightened budget and busy social life, I'd never been interested in cooking. However, it seemed that acceptance in this new environment would only come if I mastered home baking. I observed my mother-in-law and learned how to make a mean sponge cake. For two years, despite me holding down a full-time job, the cake tins always contained something tasty. I remember being amazed the first time I was invited to coffee after we moved to live in England and was given – a cup of coffee.

But fashions change. We have become much more aware of the inadvisability of too much sugar and fat, so now cakes and scones are only baked for fundraisers or special occasions. Inviting French neighbours for afternoon tea counts as a special occasion.

They were even more hesitant to accept an invitation to lunch or dinner. Britain really does have a reputation as a country with terrible food. Perhaps the French have read about the Scottish penchant for greasy stodge. In July 2005, President Chirac's sneering comments about our inadequate fare may have contributed to Britain winning the sympathy vote to stage the 2012 Olympics. He rated British food with a re-sounding *nul points*. In his opinion, only Finland has poorer food. Fortunately for us, Finland had four votes, and we won the Olympic vote by – four votes. Since then, our French neighbours have been mumbling incessantly about *deux mille douze* (2012). We don't think they'll ever get over the perceived slight. I don't dare ask how they feel about the recent vote in the highly regarded *Restaurant* magazine which rated the British *Fat Duck*, in Bray, the best restaurant in the world. Last year was even worse: *The French Laundry* in Yountville, Napa Valley, California was rated by the same publication the best **French** restaurant in the world!

I rave about French produce and cooking, but many of our own dishes are nothing to apologise for. I **do** use a lot of French recipes, however, I've come to realise that foreigners, after a bit of convincing, will enjoy a good, old-fashioned fish or shepherd's pie, toad-in-the-hole ("Like frogs' legs, *non?*" *Non*!), or an English Sunday roast. Sometimes, they have difficulties with the accompaniments: "Why do you eat jam with your meat?" This perplexed enquiry came after serving redcurrant jelly with the roast leg of Ventoux lamb and Shrewsbury sauce. Apple sauce or mint sauce seem equally bizarre in their eyes, so un-French. Yet, if they can be persuaded to try the 'jam', they become converts. So too with Yorkshire pudding (actually, very similar to the French *clafoutis* batter). English or Scottish desserts have proved particularly popular. The French have wonderful tarts, exquisite, dainty pastries, but they tuck with gusto into school dinner offerings of apple crumble, spotted dick with custard, summer pudding and trifle. The latter has proved to be a real hit. The only adaptation that I have made to my mother-in-law's recipe is to replace the sherry with lashings of the local, sweet *Muscat* from nearby Beaumes de Venise – a distinct improvement. The

French can be rather parochial, and frequently in a restaurant or supermarket you can't get even a wine from a different region, never mind one from Australia, New Zealand or Chile.

Most of all, I enjoy the conversations, the anecdotes told over dinner. An exception would be on one occasion when I was trying to make an Italian guest feel at home. My son was going to live in Italy for a year and I felt it essential that he should know the classic Italian tale from my childhood: *Pinocchio*. I couldn't quite remember the story and asked our native Italian if she could help me out. Very earnestly, she began to outline the plot. Twenty minutes later, she was still intent on telling us every tiny important detail. She couldn't be dissuaded. By the time she had finished, we'd all lost any interest we'd ever had in the wooden puppet who wanted to be a real boy.

Many of our friends we've met on our travels, during our expat assignments in far-flung parts. You seem to make good, long-lasting friendships when you have met in places where you are required to make your own entertainment and to rely on people with whom you're flung together. We keep in touch. We've adopted the American style round robin Christmas letter, excellent as long as you resist the temptation to boast about the exploits of your children. No-one really wants to hear that little Sophia is top of her class yet again, or that James has achieved seven top grade 'A' Levels. Keep the tone light and upbeat and you can't go wrong. Once upon a time I would have cringed at this form of communication, but it's a great way of keeping in touch. Many of these friends are attracted by the romantic notion of Provence. And I don't think they're disappointed. They enjoy the weather, the special clear, golden light, the sunflowers, the olive trees, the lavender, the medieval *villages perchés* – they really do exist and not just on the postcards and in the glossy coffee-table books. The pure southern light bathes and blazes and the resultant primary colours intoxicate. Truly, this is an artist's land-scape. They talk excitedly, about the adventures of their day, shared adventures in far-flung parts, nothing very serious. Few guests read a newspaper or watch television while they are here. We laugh a lot. I wonder what they really think of us? Mad to spend so much of our time here in a small village, so far from London – not as though you can just pop over for the weekend? I wish I had Robert Burns' gift to 'see ourselves as *ithers* see us'.

Celebrations

Recently, we accepted an invitation from neighbours to attend a *soirée* in a nearby village. We've attended many *fêtes des vins* over the years, but always as outsiders, the foreigners on the fringe, observing but not really part of the proceedings. On 7 May, 2005, this changed at the celebration of the seventieth anniversary of a local wine *domaine*. Starting time was billed as 18:30.

"Much too early," tutted our hosts. "We'll arrive about 19:30. Plenty of time."

So, we rolled up at the appointed hour. There were lots of people already there, listening to a rather good jazz band, however, not an *apéritif* in sight. Finally, an hour later, bottles of chilled white and *rosé* were ceremoniously carried to the long, trestle tables, along with welcome trays of tempting *canapés*. We spent a pleasant hour or so getting tucked into these and began to doubt that the promised dinner would ever materialise. Oh ye of little faith!

At one point, a stranger approached and introduced herself as a member of the Raspail family, the founders of the modern wine industry in Gigondas. She had lived in our village for many years and missed it since her move to Serignan, near Orange. Surprisingly, she wanted a chance to speak English. She had spent the previous Christmas in Edinburgh with her daughter who was studying there; she had visited the Cotswolds. A real Anglophile! We'd never come across this before. People we meet are friendly, but the Provençals, on the whole, deny speaking any English at all. Only when we struggle with our gallant attempts to speak French do they helpfully dredge up a few words of English.

We lost sight of our new friend as people surged towards the opening doors of the cave for the long-awaited feast. Nine o'clock already and we hadn't even sat down. However, everything was well-organised. Three long, laden tables fillet the giant hangar-like space full of large vats and wine-making equipment. Beautiful white linen cloths, candelabra, flowers, sparkling wine glasses, multiple settings of cutlery, name cards at each place. What style! The usual *bonjours* and handshakes introduced us to our table companions from nearby Jonquières and Camaret. *Monsieur* sitting opposite told me that he made important decisions at the *nucléaire* plant. What could I say? It reminded me of a party in Singapore where an acquaintance had introduced her husband with: "Hi, this is Ken. He cuts down rain forests." How should you react to that?

Thankfully, we moved on to more mundane topics, such as nationality, home country, size of family, etc., things we're pretty good at talking about in French by now. Everyone was so friendly. On hearing that we were Scottish, there were lots of positive comments about *entente cordiale* and the sixteenth century Auld Alliance between Scotland and France. This was followed by some rather doubtful jokes about our reputed meanness; however, we laughed and refused to take offence. Apparently, of the two hundred and forty people there, we were the only foreigners. The *nucléaire* worker had seen tossing the caber on television. Actually, he described it as 'a man wearing a skirt and underwear throwing a big, fat stick over his shoulder', but we recognised what he was describing. Was this a regular event? Our hosts informed him that it only took place at *fêtes votives écossaises*, Scottish religious fêtes, and the event was followed by girls in national costume dancing strange dances, strange music and strange food. That's a pretty good explanation of a Highland Games gathering and the evening's entertainment was very similar.

The copious wine made up for the dearth of food. It soon became clear that the caterers were struggling to provide two hundred and forty five-course meals, and we finally sat down to the main course at around midnight. It reminded us of a wedding in Spain, except that there we sat down to the first course around midnight and were still eating at five a.m. So, lots of time to chat, to enjoy the entertainment from the brass band, most of all to be amazed by the enthusiastic, gyrating antics of the dancers. The *compère* set the ball rolling by teaching willing participants a new dance – the Madison. Wait, didn't we do that in the 1960's? Sure enough, it seemed very familiar, as did the Twist which followed.

Soon, we came to realise why many of the 'French' songs also seemed so familiar. One definitely bore more than a passing resemblance to 'If I Had a Hammer'. Another just might have been a 1960's Tom Paxton number. A retro evening? Had the songs just hung around and been played ad infinitum since the 1960's? Who knows. Everyone seemed to know all the (French) words – and all the actions – and they joined in lustily. All apart from the old *monsieur* at the next table. He sat morosely, clad in his buttoned-up to the neck, dun-coloured raincoat and black beret despite the heat of the evening, paper serviettes draped over both ears to drown out the noise. That is until the trumpet voluntary heralded the Provençal national anthem. *Monsieur* was helped to his feet and proudly raised his glass to the multi-versed *Coupo Santo*, bawling lustily, the beret and serviettes respectfully removed for the occasion.

It was a highlight for us. The hall reverberated to the passionate patriotism, and even though we couldn't understand a word of it, we felt the emotions expressed. I'm not sure that 'God Save the Queen' is quite so rousing.

As guests wearied of the long wait for food, one table set up a kind of football chant, or so it seemed to us. Monsieur opposite excused this by muttering, "They must be Belgians." Our hostess rushed off to investigate, eager to interact with people from her homeland, but of course they were all French, indulging in a gentle form of football hooligan-like behaviour.

At one o'clock, the lights were dimmed, another fanfare, and a giant strawberry cake was carried in, borne aloft on a spectacular sedan chair, illuminated by giant sparklers. The ensuing photograph opportunity prompted two bottles of the *domaine*'s finest to appear miraculously beside the cake – no opportunity missed for promoting the product. Earlier, long speeches by local dignitaries had been quite open about *la Crise* in the local wine industry. Bumper production had not been followed by bumper sales. We'd heard this complaint before: very few tourists around; Americans are not visiting France since 9/11 and France's adopted position over the Iraqi War. Who knows? For the last few years, the area had seemed a little bereft of tourists. The wine seems rather expensive when compared with the New World wines so readily available and of such high quality. Also, the French themselves are drinking less. Perhaps they are becoming more health conscious, or is it as a consequence of the police enforcing drink-driving regulations more vigorously? In July 2005, the unthinkable happened: the EU pledged one hundred million pounds under the common agricultural policy to turn French and Spanish wine into undrinkable ethanol for use as factory fuel. About twenty six thousand bottles of French wine will go to the distillers. Never before have quality *appellation d'origine contrôlée* (AOC) wines suffered such indignity. No doubt some fine Provençal wines are destined to become factory chemicals. We love the Provençal wine and hope that the crisis will prove temporary. Perhaps a film should be made about the local wine? The promotion of the beautiful scenery alone would I am sure increase sales. Recently the American film *Sideways*, about a road-trip taken by a pair of dysfunctional Californian wine-tasters, won an Oscar. More importantly, the film promoted Pinot Noir and in the nine months since the film was released, there has been a 44% hike in sales. Sales of $95 balloon glasses, promoted in the film as enhancers of Pinot Noir, are up 45%. Oaky Chardonnay is still America's best seller, but the Pinot Noir market is surging ahead. You can now go on a wine trip similar to the one taken by the characters in the movie: through the Santa Ynez Valley in Santa Barbara. Even in Britain, sales of the rather expensive Pinot Noir have increased 20% since the film was released.

Well past the witching hour, we finally called it a day, foregoing the coffee and chocolates. Truly, we had experienced what the wine growers, the *vignerons,* had wished us at the beginning of the evening, *une soirée excellente.*

Over the years, we've come to realise that the French always seem to be celebrating something, or looking forward to a celebration, or organising one. In addition to the numerous saints days, which are holidays from schools and often work, numerous special markets and fêtes are held throughout the year, a veritable cycle of celebrations. Mimosa, asparagus, strawberries, apricots, tilleul (lime blossom – very popular to make tea infusions), melons, lavender, olives – all are celebrated as they come into season.

Another fascinating event to watch out for is the gypsy fête, held in May, in the Camargue, home to cowboys, white horses, pink flamingos and black bulls. According to legend, Mary Magdalene, Martha, Mary Jacobé and Mary Salomé, all followers of Jesus, were exiled from Judea in AD 40. Accompanying them was their servant, Sarah. The boat miraculously arrived at the place which bears their name: Saintes-Maries-de-la-Mer The local church claims to have their bones. Sarah became the saint of gypsies, and once a year around 20,000 of them gather here from all over Europe for their pilgrimage to the sea They sing and dance the flamenco in homage to the servant girl Sarah believed to have come from Egypt, the alleged ancestral home of today's *gitane* race.

The first of May heralds a festival that I'd never heard of until we happened to be staying in Provence at that time. It is *Le Jour de Muguet*, the day of the lily-of-the-valley. For a week beforehand, the florists are full of the plants in little terracotta pots or tied in mini bouquets, wrapped in cellophane and ribbons. By enquiring, we learned that it is customary to offer the bouquet to your family, friends or neighbours, and it brings good luck for the rest of the year. What a good idea! Apparently, not to participate in the giving and receiving would be unthinkable and sixty million sprigs of lily of the valley, *brins de muguet,* are sold in France to celebrate the first of May. I think it's a charming custom, perhaps one that we could adopt. We spent May 1 in London this year and a South African friend, Margie, who had stayed with us in Provence the previous year, presented me with a pot of growing *muguets* which are now planted in our garden. They will remind me of France and the charming custom.

In July, the celebrations really hot up. Every village has its wine fair where the best of the local vintage is displayed, tasted, judged and changes hands. Every village has its distinctive costumes, instruments and dances. Most of the fêtes involve a communal meal, games for the children, stalls selling everything from honey, to dried lavender tied in bunches, *saucissons*, paintings and pottery. Very colourful, and often very noisy, involving the blowing of hunting horns or banging of drums. If you're really lucky, you might have a jazz band or a brass ensemble – every fête is slightly different.

Gigondas, our village, has its *fête votive* at the beginning of September and it goes on for three days. You really can't miss it as it kicks off with an extremely loud singing contest. A week before the event, an elaborate, covered stage and judges' table are erected; bunting is looped over the shady plane trees in the square; fairy lights are strung up between the bunting; children's sideshows jostle for room on the periphery. This fête will have been advertised for miles around. It was one of the first things that we noticed on our arrival in the area. On the edge of each village, posters are erected on a weekly, sometimes daily, basis, heralding an upcoming *vide grenier* (literally empty attic, the car boot equivalent), a book fair, a *thé dansant*, an antique market, painters in the street, a musical ensemble, and of course the village fêtes.

In my naiveté, I imagined half a dozen elderly white-haired entrants for the singing contest. How wrong I was. On the Friday, the preliminary heats are held, and young and old, from miles around: Avignon, Orange, Valreàs, Marseilles and Aix, and little villages in between, arrive for the contest, primped and preened, with supporters in tow. Small, cute children lisp the latest pop tune; teeny-boppers belt out a rendition from flavours of the month; serious opera singers, some clad in full evening dress, trill their arias; Charles Aznavour clones sing their mournful ballads, of which the French seem inordinately fond. Every song seems to fit into one of the specified categories: *enfant, jeune,* variety, original, the list seemed endless. One young boy arrived as Michael Jackson, complete with single glove. He had perfected all the actions and was only hampered by his diminutive size. One little girl proved a great hit with the audience as she twirled around in her pink ra-ra skirt and sparkly top, flashing her almost American white teeth and tossing glossy, black ringlets. Every so often she patted her bottom which seemed to go down very well with the audience who clapped and cheered at each sexy movement. Not very appropriate movements for a nine year old, I was thinking, however, she won her section of the contest, to huge roars of approval.

You cannot escape. Even with the windows tightly shut you can still discern the amplified offerings from the top of the village. The first round takes all day, until after midnight, despite the fact that the contestants are limited to roughly a three-minute rendition of their entry. Of course, there are pauses between numbers to allow the judges to arrive at a decision. These gaps were filled by a rather doubtful *compère* who delighted in telling dirty jokes, many of them definitely non PC. He targeted dogs, gays, the English, the US, the USSR, and most of all, Parisians. The last category seemed to get the best response. Maybe the British are not the only ones to find the Parisians rude and arrogant?

Some contestants drop out at the first hurdle. Mothers (not many fathers around) console tear-stricken children whose hopes have been dashed so quickly. But the twenty five best entries are handed a card and number, an appointment to compete in the Saturday evening finals.

The finale is worth attending, especially as the ticket price includes participation in the communal meal. Long, trestle-tables draped in colourful Provençal table-cloths are set out in the square, under the shady plane trees. To our amusement, many of the places were already reserved when we arrived, bags and wraps taking the place of German beach towels on poolside sun-loungers. After an *apéritif* of the village rosé and the ubiquitous olive spread, *tapenade,* you line up for generous bowls of thick, steaming *pistou*, soup made of beans, a multitude of vegetables, and the all-important, pungent, small-leaved, local basil. It's incredibly sustaining, bursting with flavour, and hardly requires the accompanying grated Gruyère cheese and generous hunks of baguette. The best part of the spectacle is the camaraderie of the villagers and their visitors. Multitudes of kisses, *Bonsoirs*, shaking of hands, back slapping, greetings of recognition, laughter. Despite the language problem, this is a celebration that translates very well.

Every one of the singers receives an accolade and a prize, however, the winner also benefits from a large cash prize and the 'honour'. Perhaps the winner goes on to greater things? The equivalent of Britain's 'Pop Idol'? Riches and fame await?

The Saturday heralds further celebrations as teams of men clad in shorts, singlets, sandals and tattoos congregate from neighbouring villages. Each carries his *boules*, his bowls, two in each hand, ready for the serious competition of the *concours de pétanque*. *Boules* has been played since the days of the Greeks and Romans, but in the nineteenth century Provence updated the game and renamed it *Provencale*, or *Longue* (slightly different rules).

Lots of ribald joking and rivalry; lots of serious drinking in the café. My long-term friend Barbara and I, two solitary women sitting outside the café just before the games commenced, were propositioned: "You want to play? Yes?" This invitation was followed by much laughing. Only once have I seen a woman player at these events; it seems to be very much a male sport, and a working class one at that. I've seen photographs of famous film stars, such as Yves Montand, playing *boules* at St Paul de Vence; of politicians earnestly rolling their balls (the equivalent of baby kissing in Britain?); however, mostly it's the working man, relaxing after a hard day in the fields or factory. Not that it is not regarded as a serious sport: forty three countries are members of the International Federation and there are 460,000 licensed players in France. For the first weekend of July, Borély Park in Marseilles becomes the Wimbledon of *boules*. Perhaps one day it will be recognised as an Olympic sport.

While this is going on, some of the more elderly residents are in the *salle des fêtes* playing *belote*, a traditional card game. And the children are not left out. For them, there is a treasure hunt, *le clown Momo*, coconut shies, candy floss, fishing for ducks, a dance and gym competition. The conclusion is very civilised: *un apéritif musicale*, wine accompanied by pleasant music before the main event of the evening, *le grand bal avec l'orchestre Laurent Comtat*. It really is a grand ball, but more than this, a real extravaganza, similar to the *Folies Bergères* in Paris or a Las Vegas show! The first time that we participated in the spectacle, we were amazed. In this, perceived by us as a rather traditional, straight-laced village, scantily clad showgirls strutted their stuff on the small stage, flashing their thongs, tossing their feathers, singing and dancing most professionally. Many of the songs seemed very 'gay': *Waterloo, Viva España, and YMCA*. Any moment, I expected to see a police officer, an American Indian Chief, a construction worker, a soldier, a cowboy and a biker prance on to the stage. The audience loved every camp offering and joined in lustily with all the words and actions.

In between the numerous costume changes, a television personality kept the audience entertained by telling anecdotes, jokes, singing, recitals on the accordion, the guitar, the key-board. What versatility! The audience was invited to participate, to sing along, perform the actions, to dance in the space cleared in front of the stage. And what dancing. They knew all the steps to the tango, the salsa, what looked uncannily like the St Bernard's Waltz, the Alabama Two-step. How had they learned all these steps? Neighbour danced with neighbour, perhaps cementing good relations for another year.

Pausing for breath, they partook of the gizzard salad (it doesn't translate well), the *taureau camarguais*, the Camargue bull stew (tastier than it sounds), the communal repast of the evening. This rich stew, black with wine and caramelised onions, can impart serious stains and I noticed that those clad in elegant white linen tended to avoid eating this course. They did manage to drink with relish the proffered *kirs,* champagne and Cassis, a black-currant liqueur, wine and non-alcoholic beverages – not many takers for these.

What a spectacle! During all this, small children ran about in gangs, holding aloft balloons, stuffed bears, sticky, pink candy floss, relishing the freedom offered to them as their parents sat engrossed in the show. Others dozed in parents' arms, worn out by the non-stop festivities. We retired to bed about one a.m., leaving most of the audience to participate in the finale, to drink a few more glasses of Gigondas.

The following morning saw the culmination of the celebrations: a *dérailleurs des Dentelles*, a bicycle race through the mountains behind the village. I glanced outside the window at seven o'clock in the morning and the large field behind the post-office, on the edge of the village was already crammed full of cars and bicycles. Again, people had flocked from miles around for the event. Perhaps some were revellers from the night before. Had they returned home after the extravaganza? Could some possibly be accused of being drunk in charge of a bicycle? The race ended several hours later with more feasting, this time on a huge paella. Frequently you see these on market day, cooked fresh, bursting with locally grown saffron and ocean-fresh seafood. People in Provence take their seafood very seriously, so you can be assured that it will be fresh and delicious. They have a passion for their *fruits de la mer* that borders on the obsessive and you can safely eat seafood in an inland Provençal restaurant in the middle of a blistering summer.

Yes, we have numerous village fairs and fêtes in Britain, especially in the warm summer months, and they bear some similarity to the French affairs, but they are rarely on the same scale. Last year, we were in Provence for the *Fête du Patrimonie,* on September 19. This day of culture and traditions is celebrated all over France, however, in Pernes-Les-Fontaines, a fairly large village famous for its numerous fountains, the whole population participates, all of them in traditional costume. Even the babies are clad in bonnets and pinafores from another age, wheeled along in ancient perambulators that have seen a lot of service. The parade of these baby carriages, vintage cars, ambulances, fire trucks, post vans, horses and carts and Camargue gypsies on horseback took twenty five minutes to pass the thronging crowds lining the streets. The whole village had been transformed by the laying down of bundles of straw and the setting up of traditional farming implements and trades, to resemble a village in medieval times. It was extremely well done and climaxed with yet another communal meal, this time a *soupe d'épautre*, a soup of wild wheat, spelt, an ancient crop which is sold widely at the markets and is said to be very nutritious. Pernes-Les Fontaines' other claim to fame is that the last public executioner in France lives there. You can discover his whereabouts by spotting the miniature guillotine in his window.

Autumn brings the wild mushrooms, every variety imaginable, and many, such as the black *trompette de mort*, not seen by us before. They are heaped on market stalls, with signs imploring no touching, please. An unusual request in France where touching and prodding are expected, even encouraged. But these morsels are delicate and expensive and are carefully and lovingly nestled by the vendors in their brown paper bags. A little goes a long way, in a risotto or an omelette. The hiding places of mushrooms are a closely guarded secret. Frequently, we see locals furtively carrying wicker baskets, however, no-one ever offers to share his knowledge of where the wild mushrooms lurk. Even if you can find them, the chances of the mushrooms being poisonous and inedible are high. Each pharmacy displays a brightly coloured warning poster in the window, outlining the dangers. It is very difficult to tell the good from the bad, the *bon* from the *fatal*. The *champignons vénéneux* greatly outnumber the *champignons comestibles*. I keep a copy of this poster in the kitchen as a constant reminder that mushroom picking is a serious undertaking. At the height of my interest in mushrooms, I spotted a specialist mushroom magazine during one of my forays to the épicerie. As I handed it over, Monsieur Claude, the *épicier*, became rather excited. In French he asked me: "Madame, do you go out foraging for mushrooms?" I don't know what made me do it, but I nodded in affirmation. "Here, or back home in England?" "Oh, both," I replied nonchalantly." He beamed and looked at me with a new respect.

Early autumn is also the time of the *vendange*, the grape harvest and a most important time of the year. In nearby Séguret, the vines have been blessed during a fête at the beginning of August. We've been lucky enough to catch it twice. A procession of about fifty villagers, in traditional costume, ambles up the hill. Several are dressed as hunters and carry shotguns, to ward off harmful pests. They walk behind the priest who is protected from the fierce sun by a beribboned canopy as he sprinkles incense and blesses the symbolic vine cuttings outside the church. People crowd in to the ancient church at the top of the hill and pray for favourable conditions for a good wine harvest. Their livelihood depends upon it. At the end of September, each wine producer waits eagerly for the official announcement that the harvest can begin. No rain, or too much rain, a freak storm can devastate the crop at the last minute. Some farmers delay picking, allowing their grapes to a few more weeks on the vine. Sometimes, this proves to be the best strategy of all.

Last year, in September, we were invited by the Séguret post-master, a tennis partner, to a blessing of the forthcoming harvest. We didn't know quite what to expect, but turned up at the allotted hour with Marie and Lars, Danish friends from Gigondas. It was quite different in flavour from the August blessing. This was a more private occasion, with only a few of the villagers and owners of the surrounding *domaines* to witness the ceremony. To the beat of a side drum and the toot of a pipe, the procession appeared: a group of six men and one woman, members of the wine *confrérie*, all clad in medieval-looking long, robes of purple, surmounted by maroon silk cloaks and Wee Willie Winkie style hats. Each sported a large medallion, the leading figure carried a crested banner proclaiming 'Séguret 1685', and another a gnarled vine festooned with red and yellow ribbons (the colours of Vaucluse). The post-master, my husband's regular tennis opponent, was almost unrecognisable in his fancy dress, apart from the fact that he was the only one wearing white tennis shoes. They mounted a stone dais, and several speeches later we were offered trays of grapes, followed by elaborate canapés and some excellent chilled rosé. I can't say that I understood too much of the proceedings, but the Masonic-like pageantry was obviously important to the event and the coming *vendange* and greatly appreciated by the onlookers.

The end of October heralds a truly wondrous event, the Soup Festival, *Le Festival des soupes du pays de*

Vaison-La Romaine. As in Scotland where we grew up, soup in this area of northern Provence is taken very seriously. Every year, twelve villages host the twelve heats of the soup-making contest. At each *soirée*, huge, steaming tureens of soup are ladled by the contestants into tasting cups – *consommés, veloutés, soupe à maçon* (literally builder's soup in which your spoon will stand up of its own accord). And we're not talking boring old tomato: *velouté de potiron aux moules*, cream of pumpkin with mussels; *soupe de courgettes et croûtons au fromage*, courgette soup with cheese croutons; *soupe de pois chiches aux épinards*, chickpea and spinach soup; *potage aux cuisses de grenouilles*, frogs' legs soup; *soupe aux saveurs de Provence*, soup with the flavours of Provence – a virtual symphony of soups. Almost all are delicious, drained to the last drop, welcome sustenance in the cool autumn evenings. "It's a typical cold weather pursuit in village Provence," a friendly participant tells me. "It's very 'peasant'. You won't find such activities in the towns. In my grandfather's day, people regularly ate soup for breakfast. I remember sometimes he added a glass or so of red wine to the soup, dipped his bread into the bowl and fed some to the dog." "That's nothing," his neighbour rejoinders. "My grandfather had a glass of *marc* (a kind of brandy) placed in front of him at eleven thirty every day, just before lunch. He dipped his bread, always day-old bread, in the *marc* and then fed some to his dog." No wonder French dogs look so happy. There's a party atmosphere: the village halls or marquees hosting the event are festooned with bunting; contestants, just as many males as females, ladle nervously as eager imbibers jostle good-naturedly for position; customers chatter excitedly, comparing tastes and textures; in the corner, a small band in Provençal costume plays familiar tunes; a few brave souls dance in the square metre of uncrowded floor; and the official judges, *le jury*, dressed in voluminous white aprons and chef hats, a wooden spoon suspended from their necks, look suitably serious and hope that their carefully considered decision will be popular. At last, there's a drum roll and the winner, *le lauréat*, is announced. Such excitement! Such honour! It's more prestigious than winning *Master Chef*. On the final evening, winners of village heats gather in a huge marquee in Vaison-la-Romaine for the final judging, *La Grande Finale*. On this occasion, the public is *le jury*, and after much supping and deliberation, they complete their *bille de vote*. Their chosen champion soup-maker is presented with a large wooden ladle on a chain, in lieu of a medal, to hang round his neck; a giant framed certificate depicting a soup ladle; and the promise that the winning soup will be on the menu of leading local restaurants the following day. But the 'losers' have their recipes published in *Le Livre des recettes Du Festival des Soupes* – everyone's a winner The eagerly awaited and coveted recipe book sells out quickly; even the quirky, cartoon-like poster advertising the event, depicting the venues, the customers, the soup judging and the entertainment is a collector's item, eagerly snapped up for framing. My ambition is to have Gigondas included as one of the 'soup' villages. Francine, a good friend and permanent resident, has made a tentative approach to the village mayor. She returned quite hopeful but rather concerned. "You know, Shena, there are many people in the village who would also like to enter this competition, and they are very good makers of soup. You may not win." "No problem, Francine, I reassured her. In Britain we're quite used to not winning." So, who knows? Maybe next year, or the year after that, Gigondas will be included as one of the soup villages.

Then comes the truffle season, a serious business in Provence. Between November and March the small market cafes in Carpentras are full of eager buyers and sellers, men trading surreptitiously. Last November, we made a trip to Richerenche, north of Vaison, billed as the world capital of the black truffle, *le diamond noir*, the black diamond. We joined in the communal meal of truffle omelette, prepared to celebrate the beginning of the season – truly memorable. To while away the time before the omelette arrived, we studied our informative paper tablemats: drawings of truffle-hunting dogs, *chiens truffiers*, and the two-pronged fork/ pick used to unearth the delicacies. Several poems dedicated to the truffle, and even ten verses of the truffle growers' song, *Li Rabasso*. From November to March, a truffle market is held here every Saturday, but the big event takes place on the third Sunday in January: the *Masse aux Truffes*. People flock to venerate Saint Antoine, the patron saint of *trufficulteurs* and truffles are donated to the church and later auctioned. Many restaurants offer special truffle menus, each delicious course flavoured with the fragrant fungus. In Provence, people take their food and traditions seriously and the seasons certainly command respect.

Christmas in Provence is celebrated from December 4 to January 6 and the tradition of displaying *santons*, small clay figurines, is probably the best-known. The word is derived from the Provençal for 'little saint' and they became particularly popular during the Revolution when midnight mass and the crib were banned. A Marseilles potter had the idea of creating a series of little terracotta figures that people could display in their homes. Séguret boasts two *santons* makers and we never tire of watching the potter paint the tiny, exquisite figures. There is the shepherd, *lou pastre*, the angel *Boufareau* blowing his trumpet, the incorrigible drunkard *Bartomiou*, the sleepy miller in his nightcap, the *tambourin* player, the baker carrying his *baguette*, the red, white and blue be-ribboned French mayor and the usual farmyard animals with the addition of dogs and cats. Such artistry does not come cheap. At the end of each summer, I visit the workshop, the *atelier,* and buy one tiny *santon*, ready to join the other villagers round my nativity crib in London. This year, it was a brown cat. We've yet to spend a Christmas in Provence. I would love to attend the living Nativity midnight mass and afterwards eat the *gros souper*, the big supper. Traditionally, this ends with thirteen desserts. When I first heard about this, I thought, who can possibly eat so many desserts in one sitting? But, they're not really desserts as we know them. Each family has its own little favourites, but certain things are always included: the *pompe à huile*, a thick, rich, round bread flavoured with olive oil and orange peel; white and black nougat (the locals prefer the black nougat); and the *quatre mendiants* (four beggars) – almonds, dried figs, raisins and walnuts; quince jam; *calissons*, the moreish diamond-shaped almond and melon sweets from Aix; sugar-crusted crystallised fruit, such as plums, apricots, pears, melons, figs or pineapples, for which the area is famous;

and winter fruits such as dates and oranges. Whatever the combination, it is essential to have exactly thirteen desserts on the table to represent Jesus and his twelve disciples. I'd have to include a British Christmas pudding as one of the choices. Christmas wouldn't be Christmas without this once a year treat.

Wherever we have travelled, we have always tried to get back home for Christmas. We haven't always managed it, but we try. We enjoy the ritual of Christmas, our huge artificial tree and four hundred bargain, coloured, non-flashing fairy lights, bought in K. C. Tang's in Singapore, decorated with little mementoes from all over the world: a lobster perched on a crate from Boston; an Indian silk elephant; Chinese New Year red and gold symbols; a red and gold Korean money bag; a *Wayang* puppet from Indonesia; a koala from Australia; a bauble made from blue and yellow Provençal *indienne* material – a little tacky, but they bring back happy memories. I do admire friends' elegant, colour co-ordinated, designer trees, but we're not quite ready to acquire one for ourselves.

Souvenirs retain something of the place. They act as a memory, a reminder of where and what you have been. I think the trick when buying souvenirs is not to get carried away by the atmosphere of the souk, for instance. Sometimes, a look just doesn't travel. In Iran, we'd been tempted in the bazaars to buy brass camel bells, tinny tea trays and numerous metal plates depicting scenes from a Persepolis frieze. They were not a big hit. The gifts of outsize tins of pistachios and bottles of pomegranate syrup were more successful. In Indonesia, I bought traditional wood and leather *wayang klitik* puppets and huge dolls dressed in traditional Javanese costume, correct in the minutest detail. They seemed wonderful at the time; however, they looked pretty tacky in the grey English light of home. I'd found that too with the bright jewelled coloured silk I'd had made up into shirts and dresses in Thailand, India and Singapore. When we'd arrived in India, I'd felt very dull in my English neutrals. Someone once said that pink is India's navy blue, but navy blue is a much more sensible colour for business suits in England. Liven them up with Italian socks. During extensive business trips to Florence, I discovered the delights of Italian sock shops. Unlike the British, Italian men in particular take their socks very seriously. Not for them a dull multi-pack of six pairs of grey or navy woollen socks. They like their socks to make a statement, to be made of the finest silk, best quality cotton or luxurious cashmere. You can find whole shops dedicated to socks, and I don't mean something equating to *Sockshop*. Italian sock boutiques are extremely elegant. Each pair is like a work of art, lined with coloured tissue paper and lovingly pressed. From France or Italy, olive oil makes a very welcome gift, but avoid purchasing the cheeky little red that tasted so good in the little *taverna* or *trattoria*. Most countries produce pottery. I avoid pots announcing, 'Present from . . .' but do buy small bowls with interesting glazes, useful for nuts and olives. You can never have too many bowls. I've found too that old French linen goes down very well, especially those monogrammed, linen hand towels you find in the markets or at the local antique fairs. All these souvenirs add to the general layers of a house, make it a home. I'm a romantic and nostalgic and I like my possessions to remind me of places that I have visited. I treasure still the paper 'weather forecast' placed on my pillow every night in the Florence hotel, in lieu of a chocolate mint; it translates as 'Whatever the weather – clouds, rain or sunshine – may your day be radiant', followed by a cross beside the expected sunshine, clouds, rain or snow.

Living the Dream

In recent years, there has been a glut of television programmes encouraging viewers to live the dream and move abroad. They are tempted by stories about people with no savings, no work in prospect, and few language skills rolling up in a French village or a Spanish Costa. In no time at all, they renovate a ruin and are embraced fully by the locals. The programme fades on a scene of *entente cordiale* as the expats are warmly embraced by the locals whom they have invited to the housewarming.

What the programmes don't show is the life thereafter. Does the dream go on working? Is it all rather boring? Don't they miss the friends and relatives abandoned back home, the job that seemed at the time a bit of a rat race? I read an article recently on a survey from the Office of National Statistics which showed that an all-time high of 190,900 people left the UK in 2003 to 'live the dream'. However, 105,000 of them came back again, having run out of money or overcome by home-sickness. They miss their network of friends and family and perhaps come to realise that, as you get older, it's difficult to adapt to a new way of life. Sometimes they find that the restful village becomes boring, and far from friends, family and things to fill the day, *ennui* sets in. The fact that the Côte d'Azur enjoys Europe's highest rate of Prozac use suggests that indolence in the sun is not all it is cracked up to be.

The heatwave in the summer of 2003 prompted serious soul-searching about France's treatment of the old. According to folklore, the Feast of Assumption, on August 15 heralds a break in the weather. On this day, our French neighbours begin to pack away their summer garden furniture, convinced that winter is on its way. Forecasters confidently predicted that the scorching three month drought would end. However, the day passed uneventfully and the temperature remained in the unbearable 40's. We found it hard enough to bear the constant heat, but the elderly in France fared much worse. It later emerged that over 12,000 old people had died during the heatwave. Of course, all of France closes down in August. And the politicians allegedly did noth-ing to alleviate the distress. Has the mutual support system of the French family become a myth?

I think we **are** living the dream, because our dream was to have a holiday home, a place in the sun, some-where not too far away to escape to when our feet, used to travelling the world, became a bit itchy. It is a country where we knew already that we loved the food, the wine, the people, the traditions, and the fairly slow pace of life. None of these have disappointed. Only once have we had a bad meal and that in a touristy café in Arles, where we were served life-threatening paella of re-heated rice, pink-fleshed chicken and mostly unopened mussels. On every visit, we discover new places to eat, many of them very simple, where a dish of the day, a *plat du jour,* can be had for around eight euros. Others, Michelin standard, but without the London Michelin prices. We never tire of visiting the traditional, colourful markets. The market in mountainous Sault, famous for its high quality lavender, has been held every Wednesday morning since 1515. We visit weekly our favourite Vaison market stalls for the best of the season's vegetables and fruit, the new violet garlic, the fragrant honey, the five-seeded bread bursting with pumpkin seeds, sesame, poppy, caraway, and sunflower; the jam makers selling pots of nostalgia as customers remember long, hot summers and yellow-fruited quince trees, *coings,* growing in their childhood gardens; and the wonderful array of Mediterranean fish fresh from the sea, some of it still wriggling impatiently on ice, some less lively but resplendent with bright eyes, red gills and shiny skin. The fish stall is not for the faint-hearted. It's the one stall my husband says he can't cope with on his own. First the queuing, or rather the lack of it. Diminutive *Madame* standing behind me in the queue enquires anxiously: "Excuse me, are you in line to buy the large Brittany mussels just in?" I reassure her that I am not, but a moment later she appears miraculously in front of me and shouts her order. I feel almost as anxious about the giant tuna, a big draw, which is shrinking as each customer buys a thick *tranche*. The previous week, I'd failed to purchase any of it as, while I was standing patiently in line, Patricia Wells, the American cookery writer who lives for part of the year in Vaison, snaffled the complete fish for her cookery class. At last it's my turn and I ask for the shiny-skinned fillet of tuna perched atop a bed of ice. *Madame* the fishmonger sniffs audibly when I turn down her offer of having it cut expertly into slices. Then follows a long and detailed explanation of how thick each slice is to be cut and the necessity of using a very sharp knife. I listen intently, nodding as I'm told exactly which vegetables I should serve with the fish – only spinach or ratatouille will do. I buy the delicious prepared fish soup and ask the *vendeuse* for some extra fish to add to the broth. "It must be nothing but *rascasse,*" *madame* insists, "and you must add it to the soup for the last three minutes of cooking only." So many instructions. So much to remember. Yes, shopping here takes much longer than the weekly trip to Waitrose; however, it's an enjoyable excursion, the highlight of the week, a time to chat with familiar stall-holders, meet with neighbours, whet the appetite for lunch, dawdle over a *grand crème* on the terrace of the *Salon de Thé*, most of all to people watch.

We always knew that Provence had good wines, perhaps not as highly regarded as a Burgundy or Beaujolais, but very good. It wasn't until we came to know the area really well that we realised just how important wine is to the area. Our village is surrounded on all sides by vineyards. They curl up the steep hills behind us, dug deep into the terraced hillsides where it seems that it will be impossible for a tractor to work the land. For miles in every direction snake vineyards, carefully tended, anxiously watched over. Almost the whole economy depends on the fate of the wine and the weather plays a starring role. We complain when it rains during our holiday, but we are chastised by the wine growers, the *vignerons*, who have waited expectantly for this rain. "It has been a cold but dry winter. The rain is very welcome." Conversely, in the extremely hot summer of 2003 we welcomed the heavy rain at the end of August. However, for the grape-growers it was almost a disaster. Rain at the wrong time, just before picking, can ruin the harvest. "Much will now depend on the skill of the individual winemakers," we were told. "Only the very best will succeed in producing a good vintage." In fact, some of the 2003 Gigondas wine is superb, but it was a worrying time.

The village depends on its wine. Almost every resident is involved in its growing, picking, creating, bottling, promoting and selling. And every village for miles around is the same: Sablet, Beaumes de Venise, Vacqueras, Cairanne, and Rasteau. We have come to realise that there are so many *domaines* where the wine is superb. Recommendations are gleaned from Robert Parker, the American wine critic on whom France's wine trade has come to depend. He visited our village in August 2004. Let's hope he gave the wine growers high scores.

We love the people as much as the wine, although not the *pastis*, the immensely popular aniseed drink. We relish the water, on tap, straight from the *source* at the top of the hill behind the house. You've got a warm climate for about ten months of the year, so we can practically live outside, stroking our adopted, purring cat, dining on the terrace, and never tiring of the glorious, big-sky sunsets. Catherine, our adjacent Parisian neighbour, rarely misses a sunset, and we exchange a few words of mutual admiration of the more often than not spectacular crimson display. We feel completely at home in Provence. We don't seek out other Brits, although sometimes we relish reading an English newspaper or watching a familiar television programme. For several months each year, we immerse ourselves in local Provençal culture and enjoy it to the full. It has lived up to our expectations, the picture portrayed in films such as *Jean de Florette* and *Manon des Sources*, *Le Gloire de Mon Père* and *Le Château de Ma Mère*. We love the bright blue skies that greet us most days, even in winter, the 2,500 hours of almost guaranteed sunshine. We love the villages, our village in particular. Built of local materials and arranged against the contours of the hillside, everything – church, château, hospice, houses, school, shops, café, salon de thé, restaurant, ramparts, *lavanderie* (communal laundry), fountains, Roman arch, squares and the labyrinth of little streets – fits together in a wonderfully integrated whole. Nothing overwhelms anything else. Peter Mayle came to write about Provence as a late-comer. The Romans praised this land of milk and honey. In the fourteenth century, the Italian Renaissance poet Pertrarch, lovesick for the married Laura, immortalised her in his poems and wrote about the wonder of ascending Mont Ventoux. When we first arrived here, we thought that we would live a quiet life of anonymity, but that hasn't happened. The locals have not lived up to their stereotypical reputation of being insular and unfriendly. On the whole, they are unfailingly polite and friendly and welcome our stumbling attempts to master their language, to learn about local traditions. I think that we are patient observers of how people do things and have respect for the place we have come to and the people we are living among. In return, they are eager to hear about our traditions in Britain, how life is lived there. Monsieur Claude, the *épicier*, eagerly imparts the proud news that his son is now working at a restaurant in Liverpool to improve his English. "Just you wait. He will marry an English girl," my husband quips. "Our son went to work in Italy for a year and now he is going to marry an Italian girl." "No problem. I hear that some English girls are quite pretty."

Even the firemen and police called out by an anxious onlooker when we started a small fire on our adjoining land were friendly. Before lighting the bonfire, my husband had scanned the notice board in front of the *mairie* to make sure that there was no piece of official-dom banning fires. At times, the undergrowth is tinder-dry and even hikers are not allowed into the mountains. No, nothing. The officials shook their heads in disbelief. "Don't you know that you cannot light a fire before the second Saturday after September 9, and only then if it has been raining and there is no wind?" How could we not know that? We were given a friendly remonstration and promised never to do it again.

However, Britain will always be our home and to us 'living the dream' is about having the best of both worlds: a base in France to escape from the pressures of our possession-laden life in fast-moving London; a place where our friends and family can visit and enjoy for a few days or weeks the sun, the olives, the wine and the *fêtes*. We drive there at a leisurely pace, avoiding the perils (and my fear) of flying, especially on long-haul flights. Flying is one of the most unnatural environments you can put yourself in. and the food is lousy. Apart from anything else, the food on airlines is consistently overcooked and unappetizing. Why do I live in hope? After being sealed, stored, frozen, transported, thawed out and heated up, the end product is guaranteed to be a long, long way from gourmet. My taste buds are activated by the fanciful description of the organic lamb raised on a picturesque hillside, caressed with jus (never gravy) and garnished with a medley of green beans. But the lamb is more likely to resemble an old piece of shoe-leather sitting in a pool of thick, congealed, unidentifiable brown stuff, garnished with pond weed. Not too much of a problem if you take only the occasional flight, but for frequent flyers the in-flight meal forms a significant part of their diet. Then there's the de-hydration, caused by low oxygen leading to low humidity. You feel constantly thirsty, but you are quite likely to catch an infection from onboard water fountains. If you're lucky enough to fly on a major British airline between London and Singapore, don't expect any sort of service during the hours of darkness. Of course, I should have been pre-warned by the announcement at the beginning of the flight: "We're coming round with the drinks trolley. If you wish a drink with your meal, take it now, as we won't be coming round again." They're not joking either! That must be why the guy sitting across the aisle from me had multiple cans of beer stacked up on his table. Who needs food anyway? More time to worry about developing deep vein thrombosis, despite wearing the agonising, constricting, knee-high socks. Time to worry about the almost certain jet lag and how you're going to cope with a high-powered meeting, or a formal social function, shortly after landing.

Sometimes I get myself really organised and prepare a picnic for the flight. This proved fortuitous on a long journey from Sumatra to Bali, via Jakarta. I'd been pre-warned by seasoned travellers on this route to expect the worst – a heap of cold, cooked rice heaped on a banana leaf was the standard fare. Thus, we went prepared, loaded down with freshly cooked roast beef sandwiches and frozen cartons of apple juice. Things went well until we reached Jakarta. Then the dreaded announcement came over the Tannoy of a three-hour delay before re-boarding the plane for Bali. Boy, did these sandwiches and ice-cold juice taste good! People around us were drooling, stomachs rumbling, as there was nothing to purchase in the waiting area. When we finally re-boarded, the smell of overcooked chicken and rice kept warm for three hours was overpowering. A luxury lunch on that flight, but thankfully we didn't have to eat it.

The only pleasant thing about flying is getting to your destination. Even that can be fraught with difficulties. Will they have mislaid my bag yet again? If you travel from London to Marseilles via Charles de Gaulle Airport, Paris, the odds against you are stacked very high. When I approached the bored looking assistant in the lost baggage office to inform her that my case had not come off the carousel, she gave a Gallic shrug and assured me that it was *normal*! On one occasion, we flew from Houston on Aveatica to Mérida, in the Yucatán area of Mexico. We interpreted the flight attendants stuffing their faces before the flight with food purchased on the ground as a bad omen for the in-flight catering. They were so busy wolfing down their tortillas and enchiladas that they were reluctant to help us with the essential land-ing forms, written totally in Spanish. My Spanish is rusty, but even I could decipher that you had to choose a profes-sion from the following: merchant, farmer, worker. No other options. We all opted for 'worker'. On another memorable flight between Houston and John Wayne Airport in California, the flight attendant's lapel badge announced: "Warning: crap tolerance level is low." I kid you not. You couldn't make it up. My husband swears that his most memorable flight was from London to Saudi Arabia. The flight attendant said her goodbyes as the passengers got ready to disembark, "Goodbye. Thank you for flying with us. I hope you enjoy your stay. I expect I'll be slipping into a little black number this evening."

He must have forgotten about the flight home to Singapore from India. The journey got off to a bad start. A group of about a dozen young Chinese teenagers got on and made their way to the rear of the plane, close to where we were sitting. They looked very fit and were all wearing the same corporate track-suit. Perhaps a football team? A few minutes later, a similarly clad group of young Indians boarded and were seated directly beside the first group. There were a few angry mutterings. Then all Hell erupted. A Kung-fu gang fight in a very restricted space! The passengers watched in horror as the rivals began to beat each other up, using some kind of martial art. One guy was hanging off the overhead storage locker, kick-boxing. The diminutive cabin crew were totally out of their depth and asked for help from the passengers. My husband and our six foot three friend Ray remonstrated with the two main participants, and when that failed my husband placed the kick-boxer in a headlock. Fortunately, the situation quickly defused. One group was moved to another part of the plane, and despite our lingering reservations, the decision was taken to proceed with the flight.

I've become a bit intolerant in my old age. I've made many journeys as the mother of the baby in the bassinet, juggling the one year old sibling on my knee, trying to limit the annoyance to fellow passengers. My children are world travellers and both flew at six weeks old, before they'd travelled by bus or train. They still love travelling, perhaps as a result of flying all over the world from Boarding School to visit us in far-flung places. These days, they're making better inroads into my list of 'fifty places to see before you die' than I am. As are the friends we've made on our travels. While living in Boston, I made friends with Marie, a first generation Italian-American. What seemed strange to me was that Marie spoke no Italian and had never visited Italy. In fact, neither she nor her husband had ever left the US and had no desire to do so. I could almost understand this. America is a vast country, every state different, in some cases almost like different countries. It would take you a long time to do the country justice. However, as trite as it sounds, I believe that you should travel as much as possible, to countries and people unfamiliar. It helps in your understanding of people, of the world, but also of your own country. And do it now. Don't wait for the right moment, the right travelling companion. I think the nineteenth century New England political and social thinker, Henry Thoreau, got it right when he said: "The man who goes alone can start today, but he who travels with another must wait till that other is ready, and it may be a long time before they get off."

Marie listened to my anecdotes about our travels, our sojourns in unfamiliar places and gradually came to realise that perhaps the world out there was worth exploring. In the past ten years, she has visited most of Europe, including visiting us in Provence and London, China, South America, the Galapagos Islands . . . there's no stopping her. She's been to Italy, explored her roots; viewed the works of van Gogh, Cézanne and Michelangelo in situ. If anything, she appreciates Boston, and America, more than she did before, but she has experienced and learned so much.

And we too have learned a great deal from our travels, about the places and about the people, whether indigenous or visiting expats like ourselves. Like Tennyson's Ulysses, 'I am part of all that I have met'. Travel expands the mind and gives you a broader understanding of the world. I've become a stronger person; I have developed inner resources; I have learned that wherever I am in the world I must carve a niche for myself to avoid being defined by my husband's job status. My widely differing experiences, for example, in Sumatra as Vice-President of the Women's International Group, where I had to stand up in front of 150 women and hold their interest for hours at a time, attend international conferences, chair meetings, help to fund-raise, become heavily involved in an extensive social welfare programme, and work to a budget; in Singapore where I taught pupils from many different cultures and participated in monthly SEED seminars (an international network which explores multi-cultural and gender issues and concerns in education); and at Harvard in Boston as a mature student, mixing and competing with much younger students, have increased my confidence and tolerance and given me skills which I could transfer to the workplace. On returning to teaching full-time in the UK, I had no problem holding the attention of 250 pupils when taking morning assembly. I could empathise with pupils struggling to master a new skill or concept, or feeling homesick. I could confidently re-organise the English Department and turn it around to become highly successful, using skills that I had honed during my travels as a mobile wife. I know that I can survive in an alien land far from home, sometimes devoid of facilities that I would have taken for granted if I had never left home. I know that I can make friends and sustain these friendships, even if we meet up infrequently. I am used to being foreign in a foreign country. Perhaps that's why I feel comfortable spending so much time in France? I think that our marriage is stronger and we are closer as a family than we would have been if we had stayed put and never travelled. If you get the opportunity to live in another country, seize the opportunity. Chances are you will love it and gain so much from the experience.

My favourite destination has to be Boston because I feel totally at home there. I like the people and their values, the history and atmosphere of learning, and I revisit frequently. On the other hand, although my husband enjoyed much of what Boston had to offer, his job assignment there was exceedingly stressful and I think he was glad to leave at the end of two years. He was really happy in Adelaide. The men he worked with were laid-back and enjoyed their sport, beer and wine in equal measures. He liked the climate and the wide open spaces; however, he too felt very far away from his family in the UK.

As I said earlier, your habitat is where you feel that you really belong, and for that reason we will always return to England, with its grey skies and high prices, but also its world-class scenery, theatre, museums, art galleries, shops, village cricket, Last Night of the Proms, decent television and music – and inaccurate weather forecasting. And, of course, our family. We will always remain Scottish, although it is in other places that we visit where we feel most Scottish. On nostalgic visits to Scotland, locals mistake me for English, but landscape, language, education and the more marginal things like a sense of humour make you Scottish. The more you travel, the more you see that things are the same: Maori art looks remarkably similar to Celtic art; traditional Breton dances and bagpipe music could pass for Scottish; creatures from Celtic myths turn up in the lore of many different countries.

We travel less now, at least to far-flung destinations. We must be improving our carbon footprint. My husband thrived working abroad. He enjoyed the stimulation of new working and social environments. But frequent business trips can be very tiring and stressful. Living in hotels, no matter how luxurious, soon palls. Eating off unhealthy room service or in a lonely dining room at a table for one is less than glamorous. These days, he has little inclination to travel very far. It is very likely that we will never again live in an incestuous expat community, insulated against an alien outer world.

Recently, I decided to take early retirement. It seems that everyone I meet is doing the same, or downshifting, working less and living more, but leisure can be more stressful than a high-powered job. You can quickly drift into a torpor of inactivity and indecision. The upside is that I have more time to do the things that I really enjoy doing, such as walking; going to the theatre to see plays not on a school syllabus; reading novels and poetry for pure pleasure rather than analysing every little nuance; attending exhibitions; seeing friends; having long, leisurely lunches; writing; day-dreaming. I live life at a slower pace, which gives it more meaning. But, we become defined by work and it is difficult to adjust. Sometimes, I feel guilty reading novels during daylight hours, but I've come to enjoy it, especially if it's a cold, rainy day. Travel is still wonderful, but you don't really feel that you are on holiday if you are not counting the days until you are back at the grindstone. I'm actually pretty busy most of the time; I just do things more slowly and I don't miss the frenetic lifestyle that goes with holding down a full-time job and running a home. We're both learning just to be. We do miss living in exotic situations, in tight-knit, supportive expat communities, where like the characters in the American sitcoms *Cheers*, *Friends*, *Sex and the City* and *Desperate Housewives* you are inextricably involved in each other's daily lives and know each other intimately. Coffee mornings are a daily event for many of the expat wives and gossip the daily exchange. In between, there are games of Bridge, Mahjong, Golf, Tennis, Sewing Bees, parties and involvement in the local community. Friends who visit us in Provence relate tales of wife-swapping and torrid affairs in our far-flung postings, but mostly these passed us by. This expat lifestyle can feel restrictive, claustrophobic. You are always on show; it's like living in the proverbial goldfish bowl. For example, in Sumatra you couldn't do anything without someone knowing about it. Neighbours knew exactly where you were at all times, which parties you'd been invited to (or hadn't been invited to). One day, my friend's driver knocked at the door and asked to buy our jeep. "But how would we get around without it?" "Oh, but you are leaving and will not need the jeep." He was right; he'd overheard a conversation between two bosses while driving them around. Within the week, we had been informed when we would be leaving and given details of our next assignment; we were mobile again. At one of the numerous going-away parties – I told you, any excuse for a party – we were touched to be given by close friends an old, framed map of the island of Sumatra. Every time I pass it, I reminisce, and they are happy memories. Living in close communities also brings multiple benefits: a strong support system, happiness, fulfilment and lasting friendships.

We've got so much out of living abroad as expats. The wide open spaces of New Zealand were glorious. A recent assignment to confining Saudi Arabia was not and made us even more convinced that life (for us) is not a beach. Japan seemed alien, but perhaps we weren't there long enough to get under its skin. While staying in Houston, my husband made frequent trips to Japan, once a 'day trip' to attend a meeting! However, his last assignment involved living for eighteen months in Florence and Paris – hardly hardship posts. We'd been to both cities before, many times, but spending weeks urban trekking in Florence, overdosing on the rich history and culture, I felt very much part of the city. Yes, at certain times of the year it is over-run by tourists, but it's possible to avoid them, to discover just off the beaten-track small streets, bookshops, cafés, gardens, churches and museums. Florence is overflowing with outstanding restaurants, but feeling the need for a tranquil oasis we dined at *Villa San Michele*, a luxurious, old monastery hotel, high on the hill at Fiesole, overlooking the misty splendours of the city. If I ever win the lottery, I will book myself in for a month. I made side trips to Sienna which was getting ready for the *Palio*, the world's most hectic horse race, and Alba, white truffle capital of the world, to visit our son. I was lucky to arrive at the peak of the six week truffle market, but the white 'gold' proved too pricey and I had to make do with dried *porcini*. We made frequent business trips to Massa, on the coast, close to Carrara and its wonderful marble. The resort was off-season and the closed beach with its striped beach huts reminded me of *Death in Venice*. In Paris, I visited and re-visited the *Musée d'Orsay*, home to many of the paintings I'd studied at Harvard in my History of Art class on late nineteenth century Impressionists. It was an unforgettable experience. We were based in Versailles, so again I had the opportunity of visiting a national monument on a daily basis. When we heard that we had been assigned to Singapore, I remember a fellow expat exclaiming, "But you can visit *Raffles* every day if you want to!" Of course, we never did. And when we were staying in Florence and Paris, it was comforting to know that we could visit every day if we wanted to the *Duomo* or the *Uffizi*, *Sacre Coeur* or the *Louvre*. Not forgetting the best ice-cream parlour in the world, *Vivoli*, in Florence (the *River Café* owners share our passion). And our children have been exposed to different cultures and from an early age have been more independent and have a broader outlook than most of their non expatriate peers. They remain close and we remain close as a family, seeing each other frequently, perhaps making up for the years when we were apart.

However, I think that the days of accepting foreign assignments are now over. We've seen the couples who can no longer go back home. They become addicted to the expat way of life, to living overseas with its attendant glamour, travel and affluent lifestyle. Most of the accommodation provided by the Company was cavernous. In Iran, despite being desperate to move out of the hotel where we'd lived for three months with two children under five, we turned down the first seven houses offered to us. What could be wrong with seven different houses?

Much too big. Some had ten bedrooms, five bathrooms, huge gardens – too much to furnish and look after. The house that we finally chose had a manageable four bedrooms and four bathrooms, but the children could ride their two-wheeled bikes (with stabilisers) round and round the cavernous living room, cornering sharply to avoid the numerous marble columns. There were thirty-seven light bulbs in various computations in the living room alone, and some of the bulbs needed replacing on a weekly basis. I would phone the company maintenance team who would promise to attend immediately to the problem. Frustratingly, it wasn't until my husband returned home from work and made a fuss that the team of at least four men and a ladder would arrive with the replacement light bulbs.

When we first arrived in Sumatra, Indonesia, we lived in the aptly named Pioneer Camp, in a trailer, where you had to move the bed if you needed to get something out of the wardrobe. The furnishings were absolutely hideous. I learned later that as soon as a house was vacated, the vultures would descend and 'swap' less desirable pieces of furniture for something more stylish. So, as the latest arrivals, we ended up with the migraine-inducing orange-patterned carpet, the chipped white dining table with the wobbly leg, the plastic 'leather' sofa. Worse was to come. We had no television and, initially, no music system, so evenings were spent quietly reading. Munch, munch, munch. "Did you hear that?" No doubt about it; there were eating noises coming from inside the plasterboard walls. Perhaps mice? Are cock-roaches noisy eaters? By now I was used to opening kitchen cupboard doors on scuttling black cockroaches, or if we set traps finding them belly-up the next morning.

We called in the experts who knew at once what the problem was. "Only termites. Eating the electricity wires. No problem!" But there was a big problem. Years before, in Iran, we'd had to evacuate our house while the fumigators moved in to eradicate the termites. We moved back into the dreaded hotel for a few days while our house was cordoned off and a large board with a picture of skull and crossbones was nailed to the gate. This time, the infestation appeared to have got out of hand. Nothing for it but to move house. So, we moved to the trailer next door, while our original trailer was used to store excess company furniture. A good way to ensure that all receivers of furniture would also receive some unwelcome visitors.

However, the trailer park was next door to the beach; it was surrounded by coconut palms; we had a kaffir lime tree and coconut palm in our garden; an open-air swimming pool across the road; almost no traffic; and there was a close-knit community to provide advice and support. The only minor downside was crossing an ancient burial place to reach the Commissary, where we bought our supplies. It always had a slightly eerie feel, but it wasn't until someone told me that it was a grave-yard – nothing to indicate this – that my imagination began to work overtime, especially when, at dusk, the bats came out and circled around, swooping in and out of the shadowy, rustling trees.

Within a year, we'd moved to the white palaces on the hill, about three miles from the beach. They were pala-tial, but socially divisive. Houses were of two sizes, awarded according to seniority and grade level. Families who had been in Sumatra for ten years and worked themselves up to living in the best houses, surrounded by the best company furniture, suddenly found themselves demoted. It caused a lot of friction, although, in truth, there was very little to choose between the two styles of homes.

The other most memorable accommodation is the penthouse flat we lived in, in Cambridge, Massachusetts. It was magnificent, on two floors, directly overlooking the Charles River, and beyond that Beacon Hill and the golden-domed State House of Boston. It was much more luxurious than we could have afforded to buy, or rent, in London. We enjoyed the luxury, the ever-changing view, the in-house gym, the swimming pool, and twenty-four hour concierge. When we left, the over-large sofas we'd bought in iconic *Crate & Barrel* had to leave the apartment the way they had come in – through the window, twelve floors from the ground. The squad of men in black: black pants, black, high-laced combat boots, and black t-shirts proclaiming them to be *Death Wish Piano Movers* made light work of abseiling the sofas safely to the ground. And the crowd who had gathered with necks craned let out an audible sigh of relief.

Home help is also part of the expat lifestyle and expectations. People who had never as much as employed a cleaner back home suddenly found themselves with a maid, a driver and a gardener. Soon, they came to think that an under-maid would be useful, and a cook. I stuck to the single maid; she was enough to handle; and we took on the partial support of her family too, her daughters, her aged mother, her much-repaired house. We paid our maid the going rate, unlike some who ignored the local economy and paid American wages. Our maid received small gifts brought back from our travels. Before one such trip, she approached me shyly and asked for a watch, with "picture of small American animal." Two weeks later, she was proudly sporting a Mickey Mouse watch with a pink strap. In her eyes, it was much prettier than the copy Rolexes gifted to several of her friends. In Indonesia, expats would return from Singapore with armfuls of copy watches (illegal). Soon, they tired of these, were earning big money, and graduated to the real thing. The rejected copies were passed to the maids, so you had the bizarre sight of barefoot young women clad in sarongs and Rolex watches. Expats like to dress up and there were lots of opportunities to indulge their passion. They decked themselves out in jewels, heels and posh frocks at every opportunity. I don't know how this translated to wheeling the shopping trolley round Sainsbury's or K-Mart. Expat living is a shortcut to upward mobility. It gives many women the chance to re-invent themselves, to have more status than they had in their home country. Salaries are high and facilitate a lifestyle previously only dreamed of.

Expats returning home found themselves with huge shipments of huge furniture, bought to furnish the huge homes lived in on location. The bulky furniture, the huge batik paintings, refused to fit into the compact home-country lifestyle. Some extended their homes; others moved house. We partially solved this problem by off-loading some furniture on to our children who were buying their first homes. And, of course, by purchasing our home in Provence and moving some of the mementoes there. These bring back gloriously happy memories of my time as a mobile wife. Time distorts memory, but our expat experiences were on the whole extremely enjoyable and life-enhancing.

We will continue to enjoy life in Provence, with its big skies and nourishing light, the patchwork vineyards speckled with craggy perched villages, where everything seems to have stayed the same for generations. It has a timeless quality. There we can indulge our hankering for village life, where traditions are maintained and celebrated. It appears to us that the French have worked out how to live well. Recently, I read a quotation by Robert Adams that sums up how we feel about our adopted second home: 'In order fully to comprehend the art of living, it is perhaps necessary to have spent some time among the French.'

Lightning Source UK Ltd.
Milton Keynes UK
03 July 2010

156472UK00001B/2/P

9 781907 211416